HITLER'S BATTLES FOR EUROPE

H N & S Russia 139,140
Nicht abändern 211, 212
Ausradieren ———— 221
H description by
others ————— 242

HITLER'S BATTLES FOR EUROPE

John Strawson

There's no need for you to try to teach me. I've been commanding the German Army in the field for five years, and during that time I've had more practical experience than any 'gentleman' of the General Staff could ever hope to have.

Hitler to Guderian, December 1944

CHARLES SCRIBNER'S SONS *New York*

Library of Congress Catalog
Card Number 70-143944
SBN 684-12379-7

Contents

Illustrations

The author and publishers wish to thank the Imperial War Museum for providing all the illustrations for this book, with the exception of: fig. 2, Heinrich Hoffman, Zeitgeschichtliches Bildarchiv; cover and fig. 14, Suddeutscher Verlag, Munich; figs. 6-9, Ullstein Bilderdienst, Berlin.

Acknowledgments

The literature which deals with Hitler's conduct of war, and which I have consulted, is very extensive, but I must record an exceptional debt to the works of Professor Alan Bullock, Professor H. R. Trevor-Roper, William L. Shirer and Sir John Wheeler-Bennett. The labour we delight in physics pain, and re-studying their books has been to enjoy instruction of a quality to induce veneration. For campaigns involving British arms the Official Histories have as always been agreeable and unimpeachable sources; more particularly Alistair Horne for the Battle of France, Alan Clark for the Eastern Front, and Chester Wilmot for the last year of the war in the West are in a class by themselves; for first-hand accounts of how Hitler exercised command, the recollections of Guderian, Halder, von Manstein Warlimont and Speer, to name only some, are indispensable; most forcibly memorable of all are Hitler's own written and spoken words.

My thanks are due to the following Authors and Publishers for permission to quote from the books mentioned: John W. Wheeler-Bennett, *The Nemesis of Power. The German Army in Politics 1918-1945*, Macmillan & Co. Ltd; Sir Isaiah Berlin, *Mr Churchill in 1940*, John Murray (Houghton Mifflin Co.); Alan Bullock, *Hitler A Study in Tyranny*, Odhams; Arthur Bryant, *The Lion & The Unicorn*, Collins; Winston Churchill, The Second World War, Cassell & Co. Ltd. (Houghton Mifflin Co.); Ciano, *Ciano's Diary*, Chicago Daily News; Alan Clark, *Barbarossa*, Hutchinson & Co. Ltd; David Scott Daniell, *4th*

Hussar, Gale & Polden; L. F. Ellis, *The War in France and Flanders,* Her Majesty's Stationery Office; General Heinz Guderian, *Panzer Leader,* Michael Joseph; Franz Halder, *Hitler as War Lord,* Putnam; Adolf Hitler, *Mein Kampf,* Hurst & Blackett Ltd; Alistair Horne, *To Lose a Battle,* Macmillan & Co. Ltd; A. G. Macdonnell, *Napoleon and his Marshals,* Macmillan & Co. Ltd; Fred Majdalany, *The Monastery,* the Estate of the late Fred Majdalany; Field-Marshal Erich von Manstein, *Lost Victories,* Atheneum Verlagl; Hermann Rauschning, *Hitler Speaks,* Thornton Butterworth Ltd; Erwin Rommel, *The Rommel Papers* (ed. Basil Liddell Hart), Collins; H. R. Trevor-Roper, *Hitler's War Directives 1939–1945,* Sidgwick & Jackson Ltd; H. R. Trevor-Roper, *The Last Days of Hitler,* Macmillan & Co. Ltd; William L. Shirer, *The Rise and Fall of the Third Reich,* Secker & Warburg Ltd; A. J. P. Taylor, *The Origins of the Second World War,* Hamish Hamilton; Raleigh Trevelyan, *The Fortress,* Collins; Vercors, *Put Out The Light,* Jean Bruller; Vercors, *The Battle of Silence,* Collins; Chester Wilmot, *The Struggle for Europe,* Collins.

I am grateful to Colonel Philip Panton, Librarian of the Imperial Defence College, for his tireless assistance in getting books of reference for me; also to Lieut. Colonel R. A. Rickets and his colleagues at the Staff College Camberley, for producing material on the battles for Normandy. I would like to thank my wife for her invaluable help in interpreting books and documents in the original German and for her critical reading of my drafts. I am indebted to Mr Peter Kemmis-Betty for his valuable suggestions for amendments to my final draft. I am responsible for statements of fact or opinion in the book.

Finally I wish to thank Cpl. N. Davis for helping me with the index.

EXTENT OF HITLER'S CONQUESTS, 1942

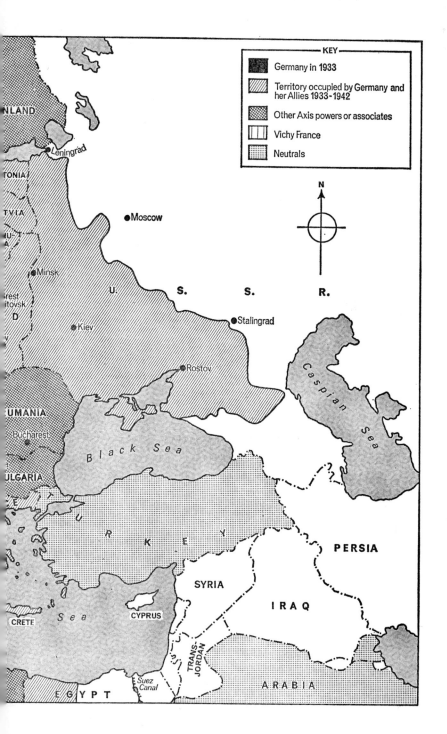

KEY

- Germany in 1933
- Territory occupied by Germany and her Allies 1933-1942
- Other Axis powers or associates
- Vichy France
- Neutrals

N

NLAND

Leningrad

TONIA

TVIA

U
A

Minsk

rest
itovsk

D

V

Kiev

●Moscow

U.   S.   S.   R.

●Stalingrad

Rostov

Caspian Sea

UMANIA

Bucharest

Black   Sea

ULGARIA

E

CRETE

U
R
K
E
Y

Sea

CYPRUS

SYRIA

PERSIA

IRAQ

TRANS-
JORDAN

EGYPT

Suez
Canal

ARABIA

Note on Hitler's Command Organization

In February 1938 Hitler established a new High Command of the Armed Forces, *Oberkommando der Wehrmacht* (*OKW*) to replace the former War Ministry. He was himself already Supreme Commander-in-Chief of the Armed Forces, *Obersterbefehlshaber der Wehrmacht*, and by staffing *OKW* with his own chosen supporters, notably Keitel and Jodl—he made certain that his orders, political and military, were, as Professor Trevor-Roper put it, 'transmitted through the whole war-machine of the Reich without the possibility of legal opposition; and it was through this machinery that he applied and controlled his strategy throughout the war.' In particular he imposed this strategy on the stronghold of the German General Staff, the High Command of the Army, *Oberkommando des Heeres* (*OKH*). Those generals who tried to regain control of operations received either an evasive or a dusty answer. Orders from *OKW* went also to the Air Force High Command, *Oberkommando der Luftwaffe* (*OKL*) and the Navy High Command, *Oberkommando der Kriegsmarine* (*OKM*), but the Commanders-in-Chief of the Navy and Luftwaffe, Göring and Raeder, unlike the Army Commander-in-Chief, were (Raeder's apprehensions about war with England notwithstanding) Hitler's men from the start. By assuming command of the Army as well in December 1941, Hitler completed his absolute mastery over strategic and tactical operations.

The *place* from which Hitler exercised command varied. Sometimes Führer HQ was specially constructed and fortified—*Wolfsschanze* in East Prussia or *Adelshorst* in the Taunus hills; he had other headquarters in France and the Ukraine; often he was in Berlin, at the end in the Bunker. Where Führer HQ was, *OKW* was too; and from *OKW* issued Hitler's Directives for the Conduct of the War. At his HQ the daily military conferences were held, at which after hearing and discussing the situation, Hitler would give his orders. As we shall see, these orders ran from the broadest strategic guidance to the minutest tactical detail. Throughout the war, from the almost realized goal of *Weltmacht*, world power, to the nihilistic alternative—*Niedergang*, ruin—there was no doubt about who was in command.

1

A Jumped-Up Corporal

To delight in war is a merit in the soldier, a dangerous
quality in the captain, and a positive crime in the statesman.
Santayana

On 21 April 1945, the day after his 56th birthday, Adolf Hitler,
Führer of the Third Reich, Commander-in-Chief of the Armed
Forces and of the German Army, Supreme War Lord of a war
that had long been lost, was directing a battle. For the last five
and a half years he had been doing little else but direct battles.
Indeed his whole life, as *Mein Kampf* testifies (and on this
point it received ample, irrefutable corroboration), had been
concerned with fighting battles. War, Hitler had declared twelve
years earlier, was an everyday business, a natural state of affairs.
This last phrase was echoed by von Seeckt, the general who had
built those foundations from which a re-armed Germany rose up.
He had talked of war as the summit of human achievement, a
natural, ultimate stage in man's historical development. Such
expressions found an instant response in Hitler. War, in fact,
was life. Certainly it had become his, and had brought Germany
to the brink of total defeat. By 21 April Marshal Zhukov had
got as far as Berlin's eastern suburbs, while his fellow Marshal
Koniev was nearing Dresden; on the same day General Eisenhower, choosing a natural junction for his armies to link up
with Soviet forces and avoid accidental clashes with them, was
giving orders for his leading formations to halt on the general
line of the Elbe and Mulde.

Yet Hitler was still making or thought he was making, his
last stand in Berlin and giving precise tactical instructions to
General Koller, a Luftwaffe officer and Göring's Chief of Staff
who had stayed behind with Hitler in the bunker when Göring

left the day before. In spite of the hopelessness of further resistance, Koller was not the man to stand up to Hitler. Few were. Elderly, scrupulous and a fusspot, much given to hand-wringing and soul-searching, he would endure the Führer's raving, screamed insults and threats—'the entire Luftwaffe staff should be hanged!'—with a tremble, but without a protest. Hitler's orders on this occasion, indeed as on most occasions since his assumption of the Supreme Army Command, were couched in the greatest detail. These troops here would be withdrawn from the north of the city to counter-attack the Russians in the southern suburbs; those Luftwaffe ground units there would take part; every tank that could be mustered, every aircraft the Luftwaffe could put into the skies, every man of every battalion —for Hitler, *supreme* commander though he was, dealt in battalions, not corps and armies—everything and everybody would make an all-out, final, desperate attempt to throw back the enemy. An SS general, Obergruppenführer Steiner, would command the attack. Hitler's orders were accompanied by customary threats. Commanding officers who did not thrust home would find their lives forfeit. Koller's own head would guarantee the vigilance and totality of the effort to be made.

All was in vain. Hitler had long since, in the phrase used by Marmont about Napoleon, been making pictures, had long been living in a military world created by his own imagination, his own refusal to acknowledge unpalatable fact. Will-power had done much in the past. It could do nothing now. Battalions which did not exist could not influence a crisis which did. The attack never came off at all, never even got under way, withdrawal of units from the north merely allowed the Russians to surge through that part of the front and occupy the centre of Berlin with their armoured forces. If it were possible for the military position to worsen, it was just such cold comfort that Hitler was obliged to stomach.

He did not stomach it lightly. When at the military conference next day he discovered that it was so, he once more lost control of himself. The last of the shrieking, shouting matches —matches wholly one-sided—with the generals and the staff was duly played out. Three hours of denunciation followed. He had been deserted; the Army had failed him; all was treason,

lies, deceit, cowardly incompetence; it was the end; his great
mission and the Third Reich itself had failed; nothing was left
but for him to stay in Berlin and die. If the conference left his
staff bewildered, exhausted, distraught, the final effect on Hitler
himself was very different. Decision calmed him. He seemed
able now to face the, albeit limited, future serenely. Yet at the
very moment of resigning himself to failure and death, he took
the unwarranted and unforgivable step of resigning too from
that great position which he had so long coveted and enjoyed—
command of the Army. He would not delegate. He gave no
orders to his principal military assistants, General Keitel and
General Jodl, respectively Chief and Operations Chief of OKW.
He simply abdicated all responsibility. From the former position of directing the entire war machine, personally, continuously and arbitrarily, he swung fully about and would have
nothing more to do with it. Jodl described it thus to Koller:

> Hitler declared that he had decided to stay in Berlin, lead its
> defence, and then at the last moment shoot himself. For physical
> reasons he was unable to take part in the fighting personally, nor
> did he wish to, for he could not run the risk of falling into enemy
> hands. We all attempted to bring him over from this decision
> and even offered to move troops from the west to fight in the
> east. His answer was that everything was falling to pieces any-
> way, and that he could do no more: that should be left to the
> Reichsmarshal [Göring]. When someone remarked that no soldier
> would fight for the Reichsmarshal, Hitler retorted: 'What do you
> mean, fight? There's precious little more fighting to be done and,
> if it comes to negotiating, the Reichsmarshal can do better than
> I can.' The latest development of the situation had made the
> deepest impression on him, he spoke all the time of treachery
> and failure, of corruption in the leadership and in the ranks.
> Even the SS now told him lies.

There were eight days still to pass before Hitler fulfilled his
declaration and shot himself. Having killed untold millions of
human beings, he killed one more. The last enemy was conquered. During the previous five and a half years Hitler had
destroyed many other enemies, and in the end he destroyed the
instrument with which he did it all, the German Army itself. It
is likely long to be a source of puzzle that the former lance-
corporal of the Reichswehr had been able to do it, to wage war

for so long, on such a scale, with such varied fortunes and remarkable results. In his ever readable and more than ever exciting record of Hitler's Last Days, Professor Trevor-Roper puts the case this way. 'No one, I think, can have read this account of life in a monkey-house without asking at least two questions to which he may expect an answer: firstly, how did such monkeys succeed in seizing and retaining power; and secondly, how did they so nearly win the war?'

The answer (Professor Trevor-Roper's own one apart) has, of course, been the subject of many former studies. Of them all the most notable is still perhaps Alan Bullock's great work and the most voluminously annotated William Shirer's *Rise and Fall of the Third Reich*. Sir John Wheeler-Bennett has shown what Nemesis awaited those soldiers who misused power, while Chester Wilmot, seeing for himself how campaigns were managed and battles fought, has left behind a piece of military history whose place on the shelves of students of war is assured. Hitler's generals, political colleagues and administrators have all had their say. The Führer's own spoken words—and there were not a few of them—live on in print and celluloid. Statesmen, historians and men at arms the world over have dissected, analysed, pronounced. Yet for the student of military history fascination with this gigantic and single-handed exercise of power persists. How great a commander was Hitler, we still ask ourselves, and in what fashion did he conduct his battles? The purpose of this volume is to examine some of the battles which Hitler directly influenced, either in concept or execution, and to see how this influence contributed to success or failure. It will be necessary to tell the story principally from the German point of view, while lending proper emphasis to the 'enemy' whether Polish, French, Russian, American, British or any other nation. There will be less to say about the war at sea and in the air as books dealing specifically with the struggles here (e.g., The Battle of Britain, of the Atlantic, of the Mediterranean, the Bomber Offensive) have already appeared, and because Hitler was much more interested in and influential over operations on land.

It is important at the outset to understand how complete and comprehensive Hitler's direction of the war was. The various

1 Hitler in the Odeonplatz, Munich, August 1914

2 Hitler (seated on right) as a soldier in the First World War

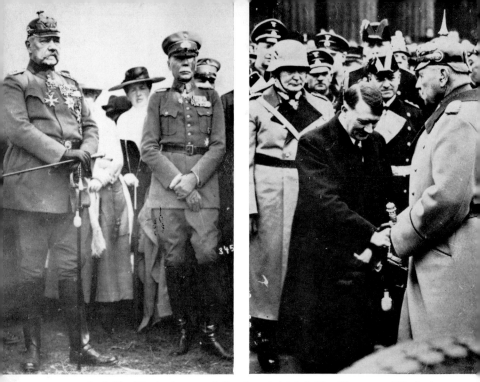

3 (left) Hindenburg and Seeckt   4 (right) President von Hindenburg and Hitler on his appointment as Chancellor; standing behind Hitler, Göring and Raeder

5   Hitler speaking at Hindenburg's funeral

campaigns which he conceived and launched would invariably find expression in one of his War Directives, which were sometimes as hypnotic as their author's voice, eyes and physical presence. Rommel once declared that if you were going to make war on the whole world you had to think in continents. Hitler's Directives make clear that this is just what he did. A look at some of them, therefore, will enable us to view the strategic stage before going on to see how the Führer began to control the tactical conduct of war as well. According to Albert Speer, Hitler's astonishingly successful Minister of Armament and War Production, his master regarded military leadership as a matter of intellect, tenacity and nerves of iron. Will-power was all. Audacity in attack, stubbornness in defence—these were the supreme virtues, and with them alone battles could be won. In spite of Hitler's total ignorance of how battles were in fact conducted, his interference, intuition and will-power were often decisive in winning victories; equally this ignorance led at other times to catastrophic failure. We shall therefore do well to see how this inexorable grip of the Wehrmacht's armies told on what happened in the front line, one way or the other. Moreover, what did happen there, that is the outcome of Hitler's battles, nearly always had its effect on his future conduct of the war.

But before we look at his career as War Lord, it is necessary to understand the means by which Hitler set about gaining absolute control over the most formidable military instrument that the world had yet seen. His progress to political power was successively either thwarted or assisted by the Army. Sometimes in spite of, sometimes because of the one supposedly stable and incorruptible influence in the state, the post-Versailles 100,000-strong Reichswehr, Hitler became Chancellor of the German Reich. Throughout his struggle for power he was obsessed with the idea of expanding, controlling and using the armed forces. *Mein Kampf* is full of references to how on coming to power he would employ military might to erase the humiliation of Versailles, unite all German peoples, and give them the *Lebensraum*, the living space, they needed and deserved. Hitler's career is thus bound up with, goes hand in hand with the creation of a new, revolutionary Wehrmacht.

What this Army was like and the steps which led to his personal ascendancy over it are indispensable preliminaries to the question of how he exploited his control of it. And as he did control it, we must look too at his predilection for and grasp of military affairs, and in particular his intuitive vision of how the Second World War would be fought. In this way it will be possible to show how successful was the appearance, if not the reality, of Hitler's strategy whilst he retained the initiative, and how disastrous for Germany were the consequences when he lost it. Hitler's war thus divides itself into the battles of conquest from 1939 to 1942, and those of resistance from 1942 to 1945, when the final act of Götterdämmerung in 'a world in flames' put an end to the nightmare of National Socialism.

From the very start Hitler had no twinge of conscience. Vercors, in a moving passage of *Put Out The Light*,* portrays the sympathetic German officer, Werner von Ebrennac, hoping that France will cure the canker in his own nation, and regretting the malign influence of Darlan. But the Frenchman to whom von Ebrennac addresses his remarks can, when the German speaks of secret murders sticking on his hands, think only of the tyrant at the head of the German Reich. Von Ebrennac is the greater realist. If there were anything which stuck on Hitler's hands, it was not murder.

Murder has three ingredients—motive, means, opportunity —and Hitler's murder of Europe was no exception. The first of these ingredients, motive, unlike the other two which had to be created, was readily to hand and found its origins in Hitler's own experiences as a soldier. These experiences were a theme to which he would constantly refer in his speeches and talk and writings both during his rise to power and his exercise of it. He was tirelessly fond of reminding his audiences that his origins were humble, that he had sprung from the great mass of the people. Less than four months after becoming Chancellor he told the Congress of German Workers in Berlin that Providence either capriciously or designedly had set him amongst the masses. As one of the common people he had earned his bread as an ordinary labourer. And again as an ordinary soldier he took his place for a second time amongst

* *Le Silence de la Mer.*

the masses. During his bullying of Czechoslovakia before Munich, in a speech at the Berlin Sportpalast on 26 September 1938, Hitler offered Benes a choice of peace or war, and invited the world to take note that throughout his life, whether as a politician or his four and a half years as a soldier, he had never been a coward. Now he stood before his people as their first soldier, and behind him marched a nation wholly different from that of 1918. On the very day of his attack on Poland, the day his war began, he pointed out in a repetition of this favourite phrase that he was no more than the German Reich's first soldier. He had donned once more the uniform which was so sacred to him, and would not put it off again, no matter what hardships he himself had to share with the German people, until victory was theirs. What then were Hitler's experiences as a soldier which prompted this endless iteration?

They had not been distinguished by holding high rank, or leading men into desperate fights, or enjoying great responsibility. Hitler was a battalion runner, *Meldegänger*, in the List Regiment. As such his job was to carry messages from Company to Regimental Headquarters and back again, dangerous enough employment even if not that of the fighting infantryman in the actual trenches. He was, according to one of his comrades 'a peculiar fellow'. Not sharing a soldier's normal interests, not caring about leave or pleasure haunts, not even receiving letters or parcels from home, he was an odd man out. But he did his duty as a soldier, bravely and conscientiously. Twice he was decorated for bravery, firstly in December 1914 with the Iron Cross, Second Class, and then again in August 1918, for exactly what action is not clear, with the Iron Cross, First Class. Whatever the occasion, however, it was a most uncommon distinction for a mere lance-corporal, and Hitler was proud of it. He invariably wore the medal with his uniform when he was Chancellor.

Yet it was not duty and danger that left their lasting impression on him. It was rather the fact of being a soldier at such a time and in such circumstances. He later wrote that the war had come as a deliverance from the distress of his youth. Carried away by nationalistic enthusiasm, by the idea of participating with the masses in a moment of 'historical greatness', of leaving resentful frustration behind him, of joining a community which would offer comradeship and discipline, above all, purpose, he unashamedly went down on his knees to thank Heaven for living at such a time. Sentiments of this sort he no doubt shared with a million others. But for Hitler there was more to it than mere patriotism, the excitement of taking part in stirring events, of being identified with and protected by a great and growing organization. He identified himself with war itself and took upon himself, unasked indeed but not insignificant, responsibility for the military issues of the day, advance and withdrawal, success and failure, victory and defeat. He delighted in war—a merit, as Santayana tells us, in the soldier. His exultation is to be seen by a curious chance at the very moments of war's declaration amongst the crowd photographed in the Odeons Platz on 1 August 1914. When Hitler, the Austrian down-and-out, became Hitler, the German soldier, and donned the cherished uniform of his adopted country, uniform he was not to doff again for nearly six years, he was at home. His years as a soldier then were immensely important in moulding his character and his creed.

If Hitler's identification with the German Army, the German Reich, the German people, with the justice of their cause, the invincibility of their armed forces, with the certainty that they would prevail, was so complete, so absolute, what must have been the effect on him when all these hopes and certainties suddenly, totally collapsed, without warning, without expectation, and with catastrophic results? We may perhaps leave aside the motive for exaggeration which manipulated the wording of *Mein Kampf* without doubting that Germany's surrender did profoundly shock Hitler, was a deeply felt experience which influenced the path and goal he now set himself:

> Everything went black before my eyes as I staggered back to my ward and buried my aching head between the blankets and pillow . . . The following days were terrible to bear and the nights still worse . . . During these nights my hatred increased, hatred for the originators of this dastardly crime.

It was not only the collapse of all he believed in which dealt Hitler so devastating a blow. It was also the emergence of the despised Social Democrats at the head of a democratic Republic that lent a spur to his decision to 'take up political work.' During his years in Vienna and Munich Hitler had developed his own wholly unoriginal political philosophy. It was a philosophy of hatred. He hated the Jews, the Hapsburgs, the leaders of religion, and even the working men who belonged to those despicable organs of equality and organization, the trades unions and the Social Democratic Party. In spite of his subsequent proud reiteration that he himself had sprung from the masses, in spite also of his quick understanding that a man who manipulated the masses inherited power, in spite even of his own uncanny gift for doing it and thus his reliance, as it were, on them, it was the masses themselves for whom Hitler felt a special contempt. According to Karl Kraus a demagogue's secret lay in making himself as stupid as his audience thereby inducing the belief that they were as clever as he. Whether or not Hitler was familiar with this sentiment, it was almost echoed by his own contention that 'everybody who properly estimates the political intelligence of the masses can easily see that this is not sufficiently developed to enable them to form general political judgements on their own account'. So that when Hitler found the masses disparaging all that he believed in—the nation, the Fatherland, above all authority—and asked himself whether such men 'were worthy to belong to a great people', he was able to put the blame for such systematic poisoning of the masses on others: on the leaders of the Social Democratic Party, who exploited the workers for their own cynical purposes, and on the Jews with their 'Marxist' doctrine which 'repudiates the aristocratic principle of nature and substitutes for it and the eternal privilege of force and energy, numerical mass and its dead weight'. The worth of personality, the significance of nationhood and race—these, to Hitler, were the foundations of existence and civilization. Nietzsche had not taught the *Übermenschen* for nothing, and Hitler was in no doubt that he belonged to the *Herrenmensch*, the master race.

If Hitler's disdain for Social Democracy began when he observed its Austrian party in Vienna, it was to be confirmed and reinforced by the behaviour of the German Social Democrats after they had formed a government on 9 November 1918. As so much of his subsequent propaganda was founded on what Alan Bullock has called 'a fraudulent lie', we should perhaps remind ourselves here and now that those who were repeatedly charged with betraying the nation, the so-called November criminals, did what they did in a general honest thought and common good to all. The supreme irony of it was that in doing so they were aided and abetted by those others whom they were later accused of stabbing in the back—the Army. When Gröner, Ludendorff's successor as First Quarter-master-General, and Ebert, the Majority Socialist leader and first Chancellor of the German Republic, allied themselves to save each other from the extremes of revolution, a bargain was struck. The Army would prevent anarchy and see to it that order was maintained. The Government would provision the Army and help the Officer Corps both to suppress Bol-shevism and preserve discipline. Thus two parties, each facing the collapse of all they stood for, made a pact. But to Gröner, whilst he respected the constitutional authority which Ebert represented, two things were clear. On the one hand responsi-bility as ultimate guarantor of the State would remain, as it had done traditionally, with the Officer Corps; on the other, responsibility for the Armistice would rest firmly in the lap of the civilian government. Gröner succeeded brilliantly in having it both ways. Within six months of the German Army's being in a position of collapse, it had done all that Gröner promised, and more. It had prevented civil war, preserved the country's unity, and, most important of all for its own leaders, restored its reputation and influence to the point where once more the Army was a force which politically could not be ignored.

Nor was there any doubt where responsibility for making peace lay, and the Allied terms were harsher than the most pessimistic German had ever contemplated. Unbearable was how the Government itself described them. Yet it had to bear not only the terms, but the odium which accompanied their imposition, odium slow to disappear. Four years later we find Hitler in a typical denunciation of the government harping on the same old theme:

We want to call to account the November Criminals of 1918. It cannot be that two million Germans should have fallen in vain and that afterwards one should sit down as friends at the same table with traitors. No, we do not pardon, we demand—vengeance! The dishonouring of the nation must cease. For betrayers of the Fatherland and informers, the gallows is the proper place.

Indeed it is difficult to imagine what Hitler would have done without the treaty of Versailles, so often did he make use of it in furthering his own passage to power. The message of *Mein Kampf* was 'the destruction of Versailles' and as such commanded support from almost every shade of German opinion. If we are seeking a motive for Hitler's murder of Europe, we have only to look at the shape in which Versailles fashioned this self-same Europe. 'The first war,' observes A. J. P. Taylor, 'explains the second and, in fact, caused it, in so far as one event causes another.' Hitler himself constantly repeated his belief that the second war grew naturally out of what happened in the first. 'When I returned from the war,' he adds, 'I brought back home with me my experiences at the front; out of them I built my National Socialist community of the people at home. Today [November 1941] the National Socialist community of the people takes its place at the front.' Motives, like metaphors, may be mixed. Hitler's underlying motive for everything was simple and unmixed—power, power primarily for himself to wield, but at the same time on behalf of his adopted nation. The opportunities for both realizing this power and making use of it were inextricably woven with the means by which power most nakedly expresses itself—force of arms—and it is this fabric which we must now scrutinize.

Hitler's actual rise to power has been so indelibly drawn by Alan Bullock that we need not retrace it here. What does concern us are his dealings with the armed forces, those features of his programme which commended his leadership to them, and the nature of this leadership.

In trying to understand Hitler's relations with the armed forces both before and after he became Chancellor, we must go back a bit and remember that they did not merely represent means without which he would be unable to enjoy the exercise of power inside and outside Germany. They constituted a political force and had done so throughout the Weimar Republic. During these years the Army's leaders were not just concerned in politics. They were obsessed with them. Hans von Seeckt, who became Commander-in-Chief of the Reichswehr in March 1920, was the very model of a political general, and aimed as high as the presidency. This is not to say that Seeckt's Reichswehr had anything to do with party. It was above party. 'The Army serves the State.' In Seeckt's eyes the Army's self-identification with the State was absolute, almost, one might say, as complete as Cathy Earnshaw's with Heathcliff—it *was* the State. What satisfaction Seeckt must have known when during the period of passive resistance to Allied occupation of the Ruhr in 1923, Ebert appealed to him and asked if the Army would stick to the Republic. *'Die Reichswehr,'* he replied, *'steht hinter mir.'* 'The Army will stick to me.' It was in this sense, as the final protector of the Reich, ready to do whatever was necessary for the Reich, that the Army was non-political. But this did not alter the reality of its independence. It had become in a phrase immortalized by Seeckt himself 'a state within the state'.

Seeckt's successors, Gröner and von Schleicher, continued both his policies and his protestations. It was all very well for Gröner, who became Defence Minister in 1928, and was later to describe Hitler as 'a modest, decent fellow who wants the best', to stress the non-political character of the Reichswehr during a talk to the Infantry School at Dresden in 1930. What he meant was that dabbling in politics must not be allowed to curtail the Reichswehr's real political asset—power. This must be unassailable. 'Enormous strength of the Wehrmacht,' his notes for the talk read, 'if united from top to bottom, firm internally, forming an instrument of state which no one can push aside.' Such philosophies were not confined to soldiers. Admiral Raeder, later to find notoriety as Hitler's Naval Commander-in-Chief, had spoken two years earlier of the Wehrmacht as the 'firmest and most reliable support of our German fatherland, the German Reich, the German Republic and its constitution and we are proud of it'. We cannot help but note how many Germanies it was supporting. Had it remained loyal to the republic, how different might have been history's course, never leading to the menacing unity of *Ein Volk, Ein Reich, Ein Führer.*

Raeder went on to explain how reliable an instrument of power the army and navy were 'in the hands of its leaders and of the president of the Reich himself'. Who held this instrument in his hands, therefore, possessed the power of the state. Never must it be exercised by any but constitutional authority—not even the political parties. 'The Wehrmacht must be entirely non-political, composed only of soldiers who decline to take part in any political activity.' Raeder believed that soldiers would not take part in politics. Gröner maintained that no one could push aside this instrument of state. Neither reckoned with Hitler. Indeed much of Gröner's thinking, even as late as 1932, showed how optimistic his estimate was as to the Wehrmacht's position *vis-à-vis* the government. The Reichswehr, he claimed, did not have a position, a stance; it would simply do what it was ordered to do. No doubt this might have been so had Gröner's own pre-condition of the Wehrmacht's being united from top to bottom still prevailed. But in 1932 it did not. Hitler's appeal of nationalism and his repudiation of Versailles had seen to it that there were 'politicians' not only at the head of the armed services, but throughout its ranks. The generals might hold back; some of the younger officers thought that Hitler alone could save Germany.

During Gröner's years as Minister of Defence there stood behind him another soldier, General von Schleicher, who as Under Secretary of State was his political adviser, and later became Defence Minister himself in von Papen's government. Schleicher was frequently writing papers about the Reichswehr's attitude towards the state. In one of them he made it clear that this attitude could not be one of indifference or hostility, but that it should rather act as a counterbalance to extremes. They should be prepared 'if the government's pendulum swings too strongly towards the right or left, to put the weight of the Reichswehr quite imperceptibly on the opposite side'. If this was not providing the armed forces with a political character, there is perhaps little that would do so. Schleicher was also fond of explaining how he would 'tame' Hitler by giving the National Socialists a voice in government. In the event, not only did Hitler oust Schleicher as Chancellor, but effectively tamed *him* by having him shot during the Röhm purges of 1934. The final touch to this phase of the political or non-political controversy was provided by Hitler's first Minister of Defence, General von Blomberg, when in June 1933, speaking in far more realistic terms, he proclaimed that the business of 'being non-political is finished'. There remained only one thing for the Army to do—'serve the National Socialist movement with complete devotion'. The fears of General Heye, like Seeckt a former Commander-in-Chief of the Army, that one day because of rapid political changes military influence would fall into the wrong hands, had come to pass. If Seeckt too had cause to apprehend the uses to which his legacy might be put, there was little wrong with the legacy itself.

If, while he was mounting the first rungs of his political ladder in Munich, Hitler had not been tolerated and to some extent supported by the Army, it is doubtful whether he would have made any progress at all. For the protection which was thus afforded to his career of violent agitation, he was principally indebted to one man, a man who later figured even more dramatically in Hitler's deal with the Army. This was Ernst Röhm, like Hitler a member of the German Workers' Party, unlike Hitler a member of the Officer Corps. Any organization which seemed likely to further Röhm's dream of re-establishing a powerful united Fatherland commanded his allegiance, and Röhm, differing here from most other members of the Officer Corps, saw that this dream was unrealizable without capturing support from the masses. He was also realistic enough to dispense with the idea that the Army should remain aloof from politics. As he viewed it the very contrary was needed. If the sort of state in which the Army could thrive and enjoy all its former privileges were to come about then the Army must play an active political role in order to secure just this circumstance. He, like Hitler, wanted in short to do away with Versailles. The two men had much in common as far as methods went, and even as far as the creation of a revolutionary, nationalistic state was concerned. It was in the use to which the state would thereafter be put that their paths diverged. In the early stage of their partnership Röhm did more than act as a powerful liaison officer between the Army in Bavaria and the builder of the German Workers' Party. He helped build up the Party himself, and took steps which led to the creation of the Party's own army—the SA (Sturmabteilung) or strong-arm squads, and so enabled Hitler to proceed with his methods of intimidation.

Yet these advantages, solid though they were, did little to aid Hitler at the time of his first real confrontation with the Army in 1923. This year seemed to be one full of opportunity. Given that National Socialism could only prosper under conditions of economic distress and internal insecurity, the year 1923 was peculiarly propitious. The catastrophic collapse of the Deutschmark, which brought ruin and misery to millions, touched off, or at least accelerated as it was, by the French and Belgian occupation of the Ruhr, lent weight to Hitler's reiterated denunciation of the Republic. He was able to condemn once more the 'November criminals' in terms which everyone understood. Acceptance of the Versailles treaty had brought personal affliction into context with national humiliation. Hitler's dilemma was how to turn the opportunities presented by general discontent and unrest to his own advantage. At this time in his career, as he confirmed in 1936, Hitler was thinking of 'nothing else than a *coup d'état*', that is the overthrow of the Republic, and aimed first to unite those Bavarian groups hostile to it, and second (provided always that he then had sufficient power at his disposal) to march on Berlin. It was at about this same time that Seeckt had observed that he, Seeckt, was the only man in Germany who could make a putsch, by which he meant a successful one, and that he assuredly would never do so. In November 1922 Hitler had excitedly shouted to Schweyer, Bavarian Minister of the Interior, who had warned him against incitement, that he too would never so long as he lived make a putsch. Shortly afterwards he set about making one.

In January 1923 Hitler addressed his Stormtroopers at Munich. He made it plain in his speech that his attitude to French occupation of the Ruhr was not that the Reich should present a united front in successfully resisting the French, but that this further instance of 'betrayal' and 'crime' should pro-

vide a lever for unseating the guilty men. In extolling
enthusiasm for the glory of the Fatherland, he proclaimed:

> Whoever wants this fire to consume every single German must
> realize that first of all the arch-enemies of German freedom,
> namely the betrayers of the German Fatherland, must be done
> away with. . . . Down with the perpetrators of the November
> crime. And here the great mission of our movement begins.

In other words nationalism—but only as a means to revolution, which was a synonym for power, his own and the Party's.
This above all must come first. Dealing with France was
secondary and could wait. It was this essential contrast in
attitudes which underlined the difference between Hitler and
Röhm as to the purpose of the SA. To Röhm, every inch a
soldier, the SA was yet one more clandestine army, like the
Freikorps and the Defence Leagues, just one more disciplined
and trained body of military men, one more reserve, which, if
a point of open or guerrilla war with France were reached,
would swell the ranks of that small 100,000 Reichswehr allowed
by the terms of Versailles. Thus for Röhm the SA's military
efficiency was paramount. To Hitler the situation appeared in
a very different light. Wars of revenge against France there
might one day be. But it was not for the SA to fight them. Its
rôle was far more important, far more historic, far more likely
to lead in the end to a reversal of Versailles' harsh humiliation
—it was to hoist him, Hitler, into power. The SA troopers were
political soldiers and were to be employed to gain political
ends. Once these ends had been achieved, once the political
power of the state was in his hands, then he could turn to other
objectives—building up the state's military strength, avenging
Versailles and making Germany once more great, once more
feared in Europe. Priorities were then crystal clear. Party came
first. The Army, indispensable though it might be, had to be
harnessed to Party. But in order to put Party first he had to
have his own soldiers. Too great a dependence on the Reichswehr would not do. It is no surprise to find the character of
these personal, political troops lucidly spelled out in *Mein
Kampf*: 'The SA must not be either a military defence organization or a secret society. . . . Its training must not be organized

from the military standpoint, but from the standpoint of what is most practical for Party purposes.' Nonetheless Hitler's great dilemma in 1923 was how to carry out a *coup d'état* which could only hope to succeed with the Army's tacit, if not explicit, support, yet which must not be so wholly dependent on the Army that its fruits might be denied him.

It was in the same year, 1923, that the two men who had abjured any idea of making a putsch, von Seeckt and Hitler, met. The meeting was not a marriage of true minds. After listening to Hitler's violent condemnation of the French and of the German Republic, and his demand for action against them, General von Seeckt, a man with all the precision of the soldier and the *savoir-faire* of the enlightened, asked a question as to his visitor's views concerning the soldier's oath of allegience. The answer was so unsatisfactory that in bringing the interview to an end, he coldly remarked: 'You and I, Herr Hitler, have nothing more to say to each other.'

Hitler soon had cause to find further fault with the soldier's oath. On 1 May 1923, having succeeded in arming the SA for the purpose of breaking up the socialists' and trade-unionists' May Day parades in Munich, he was obliged under humiliating circumstances to hand back the arms and abandon the whole project. 20,000 of the SA were there to know the reason why. But Hitler gave way. His bluff had failed. Over-reliance on the Army's neutrality had forced him to capitulate. Yet six months later Hitler was to capture the limelight as never before, and although he was to suffer another defeat as far as force of arms went, it was a defeat perilously close to political victory. The events leading to this next attempt began with the Stresemann government's decision to finish with the Ruhr passive resistance policy. However wise a move this was, it quickly provoked vituperation from the Nationalists. Hitler spoke of subservience, sacrifice of national dignity, cowardice, ready acceptance of every human humiliation. As was to become customary with him, his actions spoke as loudly as his words.

He first alerted 15,000 of the SA and declared that 14 mass meetings would forthwith be held in Munich. The Bavarian Government, understandably alarmed, made the right-wing Gustav von Kahr State Commissioner with suitably sweeping powers. Kahr at once banned the meetings, unmoved by Hitler's threats and ravings of revolution. These ravings were not futile. They led to the putsch of 8-9 November. That it failed was not remarkable. What was remarkable was that it took place at all. Given the situation as it was, Hitler calling for a new German régime, and the central government, whilst alive to the dangers of civil war, being in the fortunate position of having the unreserved support of von Seeckt so that an attempted coup by Hitler would be opposed by all the strength at his Reichswehr's disposal, the outcome could not be in doubt. Indeed it was only because Hitler found unexpected support in Bavaria itself that things went as far as they did. The two incidents which most command our interest are Hitler's 'formation' of a new German government and his march on the HQ of GOC, Bavaria, General von Lossow. The first of these, arising as it did from a combination of bluff and oratory, had enabled him to announce amongst other things: 'I propose that, until accounts have been finally settled with the November criminals, the direction of policy in the National Government be taken over by me.' In this brazen effrontery Kahr, Ludendorff and von Lossow had all acquiesced. This was no mean achievement for a former lance-corporal, however short-lived the adherence of Kahr and von Lossow.

The second incident displayed Hitler in less heroic a light. A few shots from a police detachment had crumpled the overwhelmingly stronger SA column at whose head Hitler marched. He himself had ignominiously made his escape whilst Ludendorff brushed through the line of police carbines. But the point which Hitler emphasized in explanation—that the use of force had never been intended, that there was no question of fighting it out with the Army, that 'we never thought to carry through a revolt against the Army; it was *with it* that we believed we should succeed'—this point was valid. He appealed to the Army again at his trial. 'Never was Hitler's political ability more clearly shown,' writes Alan Bullock, 'than in the way he recovered from this set-back. For the man who, on 9 November 1923, appeared to be broken and finished as a political leader—and had himself believed this—succeeded by April 1924 in making himself one of the most-talked-of figures in

Germany, and turned his trial into a political triumph.' Perhaps most important was his renewed plan for alliance with the Army. In recording his satisfaction that it had been the police, not the Army, who had fired on them and that the Reichswehr was thus untarnished, he predicted an hour when this same Reichswehr would stand at his side. In his closing address to the court he made it clear that another court, the eternal one of history, would judge him and his fellows

> as Germans who wanted only the good of their own people and Fatherland; who wanted to fight and die. You may pronounce us guilty a thousand times over, but the goddess of the eternal court of history will smile and tear to tatters the brief of the State Prosecutor and the sentence of this court. For she acquits us.

During the nine years which passed between Hitler's offer to the Army and their acceptance of it, the game between them went on. The key to relations between the Nazi Party and the Army lay in Hitler's insistence that he meant to come to power legally. A speech at Munich in March 1929 stressed the need for the Army not to stand aside from politics in the Seeckt tradition, not to continue to 'go along with the Social Democrats', a course which could end only in the Army's own dissolution, above all not to oppose the very Party which would, as Hitler so often promised, expand the Army and so give back both to it and the nation their former greatness. In September 1929 Hitler had another opportunity to appeal to the generals, and by this time the generals were prepared to listen for that month's elections had made Hitler leader of the second most powerful party in Germany. The Nazis had polled nearly $6\frac{1}{2}$ million votes and had 107 members in the Reichstag. So that when Hitler gave evidence during the trial of three officers accused of spreading Nazi propaganda in the Army, the generals took note. He did much to reassure them, first by brushing aside any idea that the SA was there to fight against or replace the Army, second by dismissing the notion that he contemplated any disintegration of the Army itself. On the contrary, 'when we have come to power, out of the present Reichswehr a great German People's Army shall arise'. As for legality Hitler insisted on his basic principle that any Party regulation in conflict with the law would not be carried out. The German National Revolution was to be considered only in a political sense. It was an uprising of oppressed peoples, but the uprising would tolerate no illegal means, no use of force. 'But when we do possess constitutional rights, then we will form the State in the manner which we consider to be the right one.' What menace this simple statement contained, plain though it was, had yet to be comprehended.

Yet there was something else wholly at odds with all this talk of legality. If the movement were to shed its revolutionary appeal, how many would wish to belong to it? The balance was a delicate one, and since it was the SA which most personified the Nazi Party's revolutionary character, control of the SA was paramount. In October 1930 Hitler succeeded in getting Röhm, who had resigned in 1925, to return and re-organize it. His success can be measured in numbers alone. A year later its numbers had trebled to a total of 300,000, which was also three times the size of the Reichswehr. Himmler's SS (Schutzstaffel—the élite black-shirted troops who swore personal allegience to the Führer) also came under Röhm. Hitler's dilemma with regard to the SA was contained in the declaration by Wagner, a Nazi deputy, that the Party would never leave the people in peace until power was theirs. And the way in which the people would not be left alone was by means of ceaseless propaganda, backed by force either actual or threatened, the force of the SA. They were, as Professor Bullock puts it, to be 'the shock troops of a revolution that was never to be made'. How far to use the SA to trick and bully his way into power and at the same time avoid a clash with the Reichswehr—this was the problem.

Hitler was greatly assisted in the resolution of this problem, albeit unwittingly, by General von Schleicher, who was head of the Ministeramt in Gröner's Defence Ministry. Schleicher, like Gröner and Hindenburg, was opposed to suppressing the Nazi movement by force. Rather he wanted to harness them to the machinery of government. Whereas Schleicher's intention was to 'tame' the Nazis by participation in government, to Hitler such participation might offer the very means to power, which the other paths—force, which he had rejected, and an

6 Von Runstedt

7 Jodl

8 Halder

9 Guderian

10   Panzers in Russia

11   Stukas: Ju. 87s over North Africa

elected majority, which eluded him still—did not. Hitler was quick to see the possibilities which Germany's present method of government, decrees by President Hindenburg made necessary by Brüning's failure to command a parliamentary majority, might be turned to his own advantage. If Hindenburg could rule by decree, why not Hitler? Thus, if he could gain the co-operation of those men who closely surrounded the President, von Schleicher, Hindenburg's son, Oskar, Brüning, the present Chancellor (or his successor, von Papen), might not he become Chancellor himself, and like those before him make use of the President's emergency powers to govern by decree? However unlikely such an arrangement might have seemed, negotiations between this group of men on the one side and Hitler with his principal advisers on the other began in the autumn of 1931.

Hitler's first meetings with Brüning and Hindenburg were not auspicious. Yet it was the latter's reluctance to continue, unless his term of office could be extended without resort to re-election, which obliged the former to seek Hitler's support in securing that extension. Hitler's rejection of this offer resulted in the extraordinary step of challenging Hindenburg for the Presidency itself in the elections of March and April 1932. Hindenburg won, and Brüning remained Chancellor, but not for long. The machinations of von Schleicher made first von Papen Chancellor, then Schleicher himself. Each of these Chancellorships was short-lived. During them Hitler had survived one of his most serious reverses. His demand, at the time of negotiating with Schleicher and Papen in August 1932, for the Chancellorship on the grounds of leading the largest party in the Reichstag was refused. In offering him the Vice Chancellorship, Hindenburg coldly made it clear that Hitler and his party were only acceptable as part of a coalition. He was, in short, not 'good enough' to be Chancellor. In refusing to compromise and in restraining Party pressure to abandon the discredited policy of legality and to attempt seizure of power by force, Hitler faced great difficulties. Yet he stuck to his guns and waited. In December 1932 Schleicher replaced Papen as Chancellor, drawing heavily in the process on his great authority as Minister of Defence and spokesman for the Army. He made it clear that the Army could no longer support

Papen at the risk of civil war. Once more the Army had shown its hand as king maker. But Schleicher, the arch-intriguer, for once intrigued too deeply. He both overestimated the popularity of his own programme and underestimated the power of the opposition to it. He went so far as to boast that Hitler's movement was of no danger to him; the Nazi problem was 'a thing of the past'. While it is true that Hitler's fortunes—particularly those concerned with Party finances—were at a low ebb, a change of tide and luck was at hand. This time the principal intriguer, apart from Hitler himself, was Papen. The issue was unchanged—how to achieve government by parliamentary majority and put an end to rule by emergency decrees. Hindenburg agreed to allow Papen to negotiate with Hitler with a view to forming a new government. On the understanding that he had the Chancellorship himself, Hitler was prepared this time to compromise on such things as allowing certain Ministries—Foreign, Defence, Finance—to be filled by Hindenburg's men, and to seek a coalition which would command a parliamentary majority.

Once again the Army held the key to success, but it was a key wielded by Hindenburg himself, and Hindenburg had by now accepted Hitler as Chancellor, and chose General von Blomberg as Minister of Defence. Blomberg accepted. Hitler could therefore count on the Army's support. Later that year, in September 1933, he recorded his debt and declared how important it was to remember 'the part played by our Army, for we all know well that if, in the days of our revolution, the Army had not stood on our side, then we should not be standing here today'.

But he was standing there as Chancellor of the German Reich. Whatever else might be said about 'the corporal' he had indisputably jumped up. Opportunism had paid its dividend. Now he would have the opportunity for putting his *Weltanschauung* to the test. This conception of life was really a very simple one. His mission was to ensure that the Nazi racist ideology of the élite would save Europe from the Jewish-Bolshevik ideology of the masses. The struggle would be so 'historical', so gigantic, and at the same time so inflexible that it would mean *Weltmacht oder Niedergang*, world power or ruin. World power! If, like his historical hero, Frederick the Great, he was to decide for war, actually embark on a *Griff nach der Weltmacht*, would the means to do so be at hand?

2

Revolutionary Wehrmacht

It was this very quality—a fanatical will to move forward—
which the strange and terrible creed of National Socialism
was instilling into the new Wehrmacht as a whole.
Alistair Horne

The essence of combat does not change. Its elements have been,
and are still, fire power, movement and signalling. A combat-
ant's need to move about, control and apply agents of violence
in order to dismay or dismember his adversary persists. What
does change is method. 'The next war,' declared Hitler in 1932,
'will be quite different from the last world war. Infantry attacks
and mass formations are obsolete. Interlocked frontal struggles
lasting for years on petrified fronts will not return. I guarantee
that. . . . We shall regain the superiority of free operations.'
that Hitler was as good as his word owes much to the achievements of von Seeckt.

Seeckt retired from his command seven years before Hitler
became Chancellor, but in the preceding six years as Commander-in-Chief he gave the 100,000 strong Reichswehr two
priceless qualities which not all the millions belonging to the
Russian and French armies possessed. Each, of course, concerned the winning of battles; the first was leadership, the
second tactical doctrine. Many generals and even emperors
have indulged boasts that their armies were composed of leaders.
Perhaps the most memorable was Bonaparte's—to the effect
that all his soldiers carried the baton of a marshal in their
cartridge-pouches. Nor was the boast an idle one. Several of
Napoleon's marshals began their soldiering in the ranks. But
this was a matter of chance, not of deliberate policy. Seeckt on
the other hand set out to make such an army. *Nicht ein
Söldnerheer, sondern ein Führerheer*—an army, not of mer-

cenaries, but of leaders. This was how Seeckt put it. He trained his majors and colonels so that they could command divisions, his lieutenants and captains so that they could command battalions and regiments. Each sergeant and corporal was ready to become an officer, each private and trooper an NCO. Moreover, out of the total of 100,000, at one time nearly half were NCOs. In short Seeckt retained the kernel for a greatly expanded Army within the nutshell of a tiny restricted one. He outflanked and evaded the Allied purpose of destroying the German General Staff.

When Seeckt had the military training pamphlets rewritten, he did so not only so that they would be appropriate for a completely rearmed and mighty German Reich, but also in accordance with a principle—such was Seeckt's vision—which turned out to be fundamental to successful operations throughout the Second World War. This principle laid down that all the important fighting arms must be closely integrated. Here was the seed which later gave birth to the mixed panzer groups and teamwork so indispensable to mobile warfare and which proved so invincible in action. There was nothing really new in it. Co-operation of horse, foot and guns had long been a principle of tactics. At Marengo in 1800 the timely, point-blank discharge of cannon by Marmont at the Austrian grenadiers, coming almost simultaneously with Desaix's advance with the reserve infantry and Kellerman's flank charge with a handful of heavy dragoons, had turned defeat into victory. Yet the lesson had been forgotten or submerged in the mud of Flanders. In spite of piecemeal tank, infantry and artillery co-operation in the 1914-18 war, the need for this process to be a continuous one had been neglected. Seeckt restored this battle technique to its rightful place, and insisted that mechanized cavalry, infantry and artillery should not merely work as one, but should enjoy the intimate support of new weapons such as anti-tank guns and aircraft as well.

This system of mixed groups, of highly trained teams, which brought together the three elements of combat, fire, movement and signalling, in the most effective and most rapidly exploitable way, was to be a consistent thread in the creation of a new Wehrmacht, and was to pay high dividends. It was in fact to form the basis of all Hitler's great battles of conquest, and was to prolong his capacity for resistance far beyond what a simple comparison of numbers might have been expected to produce.

Seeckt's vision was based partly on his own experience in the 1914-18 war, partly on influences from abroad and from within his own Reichswehr. Indeed the development of his ideas by some of his subordinates was such that they themselves were later to lead the *Panzergruppen* to their most spectacular successes. In the first place Seeckt believed ardently in mobility, in rapid movements, in the need to restore the superiority of the attack by grand, sweeping operations which would engulf, paralyse and annihilate the defending forces. He had good reason, having planned the great 1915 breakthrough of von Mackenson's Army at Gorlice-Tarnov which so decisively swept Galicia clear of Russians. In 1921 he was writing that what would matter in future warfare was the use of relatively small, but highly skilled mobile armies in co-operation with aircraft. The fertility of his ideas was not wasted in barren soil. Amongst the officers who took up Seeckt's ideas and studied them further was the man who later became a Panzer Leader of the first water—Guderian. Unlike some great tactical commanders he was generous in acknowledging the source of his principal designs. This acknowledgment may have been rendered more painless in that the source did not spring from his own military contemporaries, nor even his own country-men. He paid tribute to the writings of Fuller, Martel and Liddell Hart in which the notion of the tank as an essentially offensive weapon, the tank as a battle winner to be supported by other arms rather than be in support of them, the tank as restorer of mobility in the tactical handling of armies, received so great a stimulus.

More particularly, Guderian recorded, it was 'Liddell Hart who emphasized the use of armoured forces for long-range strokes, operations against the opposing army's communica-tions, and also proposed a type of division containing panzer and panzer-infantry units'. It was just such divisions which Guderian had in mind and later created. When we remember how often soldiers are accused of fighting the last war, or even the one before that, it is astonishing how accurately Guderian foretold what would happen in the war to come. Both in the breakthrough and its exploitation he hit upon the very formula that was to cripple every European army unfortunate enough to be subjected to it. To get the most out of tanks you had to use them in mass and move them so fast that they reached the enemy's main defence zone before the guns there could effectively intervene; in the same way the enemy's tanks, attempting to counter this penetration, must be stopped, either by overwhelming them with superior armoured forces or by using tactical air forces, which, Guderian insisted, must be employed in close co-operation with the tanks. Then, when the breakthrough was complete, tank and infantry teams could mop up the gun areas and static defences. The secret of the whole operation lay in expanding initial depth on a relatively narrow front to *a combination of depth and width* thus disrupting the entire enemy defensive zone. Guderian summed up the essentials of decisive Panzer attack as being 'suitable terrain, surprise and mass deployment in the necessary width and depth'. How completely justified Guderian was is evident from the blitzkrieg successes which waited on the Wehrmacht from 1940 to 1942. Nor was this all. When the tables were turned and it was the British and Americans who were trying out these tactics, time and time again they were frustrated by the Germans' managing to bring about exactly those conditions of rapid counter-penetration that Guderian had predicted would be fatal to the attacking force.

Guderian's theories were, in short, revolutionary. Nothing could have suited Hitler better, and just as revolution in the structure of the State took place *after* his assumption of power, so did revolution in the structure of the armed forces. But long before Hitler saw Guderian's tank prototypes and heard him expound his tactical theories, he had been pronouncing his own ideas of warfare. 'I shall never start a war without the certainty that a demoralized enemy will succumb to the first stroke of a single gigantic attack.' What was war after all except deception, surprise, attack? Here Hitler closely echoed Hobbes' point that force and fraud were the two things which mattered in war. Yet Hitler went further. Not only would he hurl himself upon the enemy 'like a flash of lightning' but both the force and the fraud would be on unprecedented scales. In the air they would be supreme. A single blow would do the business, overwhelming attacks on every weak point, stupendous in their effect, a 'gigantic all-destroying blow'. These were the tactics of the eagle—swift in flight, sudden in decision, ruthless in deed. The eagle adorning each member of the Wehrmacht's uniform was, therefore, a fitting symbol.* With the enemy already demoralized from within, his will broken before the battle started, who would be able to resist? Besides he himself would be the one who would make war, not the generals. He too would decide the time and place for attack. He would shrink from nothing. It might be that the war would be the most inhuman that the world had ever seen because it would be total, yet at the same time its very brevity would make it the most humane. Hitler concluded this particular glimpse at his programme as a future war lord with a promise: 'I want war. To me all means will be right. My motto is not: "Don't whatever you do annoy the enemy!"† My motto is: "Destroy him by all and any means!" I am the one who will wage the war.'

With such sentiments firmly embedded in his head, it was small wonder that when as Chancellor in 1933 he witnessed Guderian's progress in evolving the methods of blitzkrieg he was almost beside himself with enthusiasm. 'That's what I need,' he exclaimed as he saw the first tanks manoeuvring, 'that's what I want to have.' Here were the weapons which would exactly fit his designs on Europe. Hitler had previously made many references to weapons and equipment and rearmament in *Mein Kampf*. Without weapons he would never be able to carry through his programme of abolishing the Treaty of Versailles. But more than this, the very shame of Versailles would so brand itself in the hearts and minds of 60 million Germans that 'a torrent of fire bursts forth as from a furnace, and a will of steel is formed from it, with the common cry: *Wir wollen wieder Waffen!*—We will have arms again!' The abolition of Versailles by itself, although it constituted a ready-

* Hitler's HQ in the Taunus hills at Bad Nauheim which he used for directing the Ardennes offensive was called *Adlershorst*, Eagle's nest.
† This was precisely the motto of the French during the 'Phoney' war.

made programme conveniently pursuable step by step, was not enough. Two further conditions must be fulfilled. The Reich's frontiers must be extended to include *all* Germans who were now outside them—not only therefore those of the Polish corridor, but those too of Austria and Czechoslovakia. This was the first condition. Lloyd George warned better than he knew, when during the Peace Conference he had issued a memorandum predicting that if the Treaty's terms induced in Germany a conviction that she had been unjustly dealt with, sooner or later she would exact retribution. Any injustice or arrogance triumphantly displayed by the victors would never be forgiven. It was for this reason, Lloyd George went on, that he strongly opposed any idea of transferring Germans from German rule. 'The proposal of the Polish Commission that we should place 2,100,000 Germans under the control of a people of a different religion and which has never proved its capacity for self-government throughout its history, must, in my judgement, lead sooner or later to a new war in the East of Europe.' And here were the germs of the second condition. Not merely to get back what was 'rightfully' hers, but more, much more; in other words a deliberate programme of expansion—this was Hitler's foreign policy for Germany, and the goal, in the end, was Russia. *Mein Kampf* is once again explicit:

And so we National Socialists . . . take up where we broke off 600 years ago. We stop the endless German movement to the south and west, and turn our gaze towards the land of the East. If we speak of new territory in Europe today, we can primarily have in mind only Russia and her vassal border states. . . . This colossal empire in the East is ripe for dissolution.

But to do any of these things, east or west, and Hitler was not forgetting the west—*Mein Kampf* called also for a final reckoning, a last decisive struggle with France—Germany had to be rearmed. Furthermore the new expanded Wehrmacht would have to be subordinate to his will—a will which proved to be so powerful and implacable that not one of the Wehrmacht's generals was ever able to get the better of it.

If a charismatic leader is one who believes himself to enjoy divine inspiration, to be intended by Providence to lead his people to the accomplishment of some great mission, then Hitler, in his own view and that of many others, was such a leader. 'I go the way that Providence dictates,' he declared, 'with the assurance of a sleepwalker.' But there was much more to the devastating effect of his leadership than this. His un-canny calculation of the odds, his cynical disregard for both 'expert' advice and western 'solidarity', the intuition as to what his adversaries would think and do, above all his *absolute* power—when such a man believed, as he did, that force, or its threat, would solve any problem, he was not likely to hold back in the further creation of this very force which was so indispensable to the realization of his aims.

Within a year of coming to power Hitler gave orders that by October 1934 the Army was to have trebled its strength to 300,000. Before this target had been achieved, two great mile-stones in Hitler's relations with the General Staff had been reached and passed. If he were to go on enjoying the support of the Army, it was not enough that he should fulfil his pledge to expand it. He would be required also to give substance to his promise that the Reichswehr would be the sole bearer of arms in the State, and as he himself had spoken of the generals and the soldiers, 'we see in them the bearers of the tradition of our glorious old Army, and with all our heart and all our powers we will support the spirit of this Army'. But what about Hitler's other army, the political army, the SA? This did not suit Röhm at all. He saw the SA as the means by which the Army would be expanded; he saw it being incorporated into the Army and thus inheriting all the power and privilege accompanying such a move.

Yet this was not his sole motive. Röhm believed that the basis of the new Army must be revolutionary, that it must be his own SA. He refused to countenance the idea that Prussian generals—'the same old clods who will certainly lose the next war'—and National Socialism were compatible. He failed to see how totally Hitler and his programme would intoxicate the younger officers—even though they came from the tradi-tional caste—who had joined the Army only under Hitler. Sooner or later, therefore, the Führer would have to make a choice, a choice between the old Army and the new, the military one and the political one. In making it he was to be greatly influenced by the question of who was to succeed the ailing Hindenburg, who as President was also Commander-in-Chief of the Armed Forces, and as such enjoyed the soldiers' oath of allegience to himself. When the time came, Hitler was determined that this oath of allegience must be his, and his alone. Within the intricacies of these two issues, the future of the SA and the succession to Commander-in-Chief, lay the foundation of a deal between Hitler and the generals.

In April 1934 whilst watching naval manoeuvres Hitler was accompanied in the cruiser *Deutschland* by von Blomberg, Minister of Defence, von Fritsch, Commander-in-Chief of the Army, and Raeder, Commander-in-Chief of the Navy. Here was an opportunity for bargaining and agreement. It was straightforward enough. On the one hand all Röhm's nonsense about the future of the SA was to be extinguished so that the Army's and Navy's position as the State's only armed forces would be inviolate; on the other Adolf Hitler was to be the next Commander-in-Chief of the Armed Forces in succession to Hindenburg. The two events followed hot upon each other. On trumped-up grounds of a plot against the State, the blood purge of 30 June took place. Röhm, von Schleicher, his friend, von Bredow, Gregor Strasser, Hitler's old enemy, von Kahr, were amongst the many—exactly how many has never been conclusively established—but perhaps 1,000 in all—who were eliminated. On 2 July Hindenburg thanked Hitler for his 'determined action and gallant personal intervention which have nipped treason in the bud and rescued the German people from great danger'. It was one of his last acts. A month later he was dead. The time had come for sealing the second half of the bargain, and about this half, like the first, there were to be no inconclusive measures.

Within an hour or so of Hindenburg's death on 2 August came an announcement that the offices of President and Chancellor had been merged, and that Hitler would become head of state. He would also from that day be Supreme Commander-in-Chief of the Armed Forces of the Reich, and on that very day the whole German Army, officers and soldiers, took a new oath of allegience to their new Commander-in-Chief *personally*. 'I swear by God this holy oath: I will render unconditional obedience to the Führer of the German Reich and People, Adolf Hitler, the Supreme Commander of the Armed Forces, and will be ready, as a brave soldier, to stake my life at any time for this oath.' Hitler had it all now, or almost all, and that he had played foully for it was never in doubt. He was dictator of Germany, a position which the German people themselves confirmed by plebiscite on 19 August, Führer, Chancellor, Commander-in-Chief of the Armed Forces. And the armed forces were beginning to be worth being Commander-in-Chief of.

In October the promised trebling of the Army was well under way. Twenty-one infantry divisions were formed and a Panzer Brigade. One year later the Panzer Brigade had become three Panzer Divisions, one of which was commanded by Guderian. These divisions contained a panzer brigade of 561 tanks, supported by a panzer grenadier (motorized infantry) brigade together with motorized reconnaissance, artillery, engineers, signals and anti-tank units. The Panzer Division was designed essentially for bold, thrusting, offensive operations. Seeckt's idea of mixed groups had come into being. It was to survive until the death of the German Army itself. 1935 did not see only the birth of panzer divisions. In March of that year Hitler had announced that a new German Army, based on compulsory service and totalling 36 divisions in peacetime, would be created. Nor was this all. In March also Hitler had revealed to the world that by possessing a Luftwaffe, consisting already of 1,000 operational aircraft, he had gone some way to fulfilling his prediction of three years earlier, before even he had achieved power, that 'in the air we shall of course be supreme'.

The Luftwaffe, built up principally by Göring, was an indispensable part of the whole blitzkrieg concept, that is to say, far from being a strategic force of long-range bombers for striking at a distant enemy and of fighters to win the air battle, in defence or attack, it was designed to support the Army in the field in purely offensive, fast-moving and short-lived campaigns. Göring's policy was to concentrate on a few types of aircraft and raise terrible numbers of them. Since these two features of his policy went hand in hand, rapid expansion was made easy. To start with, the Luftwaffe had four main types of aircraft—the bomber, He-111 and Ju-88; the fighter, Me-109; the transport, Ju-52; and the dive-bomber, Ju-87, the notorious Stuka, an abbreviation of *Sturtzkampfflugzeug* or dive-attack aeroplane. Just as Guderian was the father of the panzer, so Ernst Udet was responsible for developing the tactics and technology of the Stuka, which combined at once the facility for accurate attack with machine guns or 1,000-lb. bombs on men and material with a comparably effective attack on mind and morale by means of its diving, screeching howl. It had one further critical characteristic. It could produce precise fire power quickly, over great distances, and wherever it was needed, thus filling a gap—until self-propelled artillery did the trick—so fundamental to Guderian's doctrine of self-sufficient, all-arms teams. Panzer and Stuka—each in its own right was formidable enough. But together they stood up peerless.

Here then were two revolutionary pieces of equipment in the Wehrmacht, sustained and later manipulated by a revolutionary tactical doctrine; what about its spirit? In September 1935 when Hitler addressed the Nuremberg Party rally among those in the parading troops were units of the new German Army. The Führer took this opportunity to make much of the Reich's great military tradition. In time of war it represented the nation's defiance; in time of peace it was 'the splendid school of our people'. This last point complemented a former observation of Hitler's to the effect that the aim of all education was to produce a German who could readily be converted into a soldier. 'It is the Army,' he went on at Nuremberg, 'which has made men of us all, and when we looked upon the Army our faith in the future of our people was always reinforced. This old glorious Army is not dead; it only slept, and now it has arisen again in you.'

But it was, of course, a very different Army which had now arisen. The very nature of the Nuremberg rallies was such that all the Germans who attended them were inspired by an indescribably powerful ardour, at once nationalistic and revolutionary. To no group of the nation was the appeal of these masterpieces of mass psychology greater than to its youth; and it was the nation's youth which was filling and would go on filling the new Wehrmacht. 'To see the films of the Nuremberg rallies even today,' observes Alan Bullock, 'is to be recaptured by the hypnotic effect of thousands of men marching in perfect order, the music of the massed bands, the forest of standards and flags, the vast perspectives of the stadium, the smoking torches, the dome of searchlights. The sense of power, of force and unity was irresistible, and all converged with a mounting crescendo of excitement on the supreme moment—when the Führer made his entry. Paradoxically, the man who was most affected by such spectacles was the originator, Hitler himself. . . .' If there was no shortage of self-intoxication, it was equally true that he intoxicated the nation. In his brilliant record of how the French Army lost a battle to the Wehrmacht in 1940, Alistair Horne reminds us of Nietzsche's analysis of his own people's readiness to be intoxicated by a leader who held before them the prospects of splendid victories and conquests. It was no surprise, therefore, that General von Witzleben was obliged to admit in 1939 that the young officers were 'drunk' with Hitler. Not only were they prone to it, but the process of intoxication to which they were subjected had been so continuous and so thorough.

It was this point that Röhm had missed when he poured scorn on what he imagined to be Hitler's intention to make a revolutionary army out of the old Prussian NCOs. Instead he wanted to draft his own SA officers and NCOs into the Army direct. He insisted that the *basis* must be revolutionary. Whilst he may have been right in doubting whether the 'Prussian' generals and NCOs would become ardent National Socialists (although it is surprising how many of them did) he failed to appreciate that in a Nazi state the entire male population from the age of six onwards was to be trained to acquire those very qualities most necessary for their becoming ideal members of a revolutionary Wehrmacht—discipline, hardness, marksmanship, parachuting, teamwork, leadership, and absolute devotion to the person of Adolf Hitler. The whole programme from the time these young boys joined the *Jungvolk* and went on to be members of the Hitler Youth (which was itself closely co-ordinated with the Wehrmacht) until they actually became soldiers was uninterrupted indoctrination. It fulfilled Hitler's contention that education should be designed to produce potential soldiers.

It did more than this. It produced an unending flow of active soldiers who were fired with the belief not only that the time would soon come when Germany would re-inherit her great-ness—a belief strongly reinforced by the bloodless victories of 1935-39—but that all of it was the result of the Führer's resolution, his skill, his genius. The fact was that as early as 1935 the revolutionary Wehrmacht had not just been born; it was receiving the nourishment, material and ideological, to make it frighteningly powerful in peace and even more so in war. Nor was it only the Army which was garnering its power.

Another development, unforeseen by Röhm and the Army leaders themselves, was that the suppression of the SA would lead amongst other things to Himmler's SS coming directly under Hitler. Thus, in spite of all his claptrap about the Army as sole bearer of arms, possession of the SS gave Hitler his own political army after all, an army moreover whose leader, Himmler, also controlled all Germany's police forces. Throughout all these forces of the State, Nazism had its own effect on character. Vercors in his autobiography chillingly recalls an encounter with two frontier officials during his first visit to Germany in 1938:

I heard a voice behind me rap out: *'Pässe, bitte!'* I turned round, and had to restrain a shudder. In the open door stood two men in black uniform. One tall and slender, the other just as tall but stockier. Both of them were handsome and fair-haired. The tall slender one was smiling, the stocky one, cold and close-mouthed, kept his face expressionless except for an affected, disdainful indifference. But both kept fixed upon me and my companions the inhuman stare of four blue eyes, as freezing as icicles. The first took our passports, the second stamped them, the momentary lowering of his eyelids making his baby-face look only more cruel. The first took our passports again and handed them to us, still with that smile on his lips under those bird-of-prey eyes. It was a terrifying smile. It seemed to me that if, instead of handing back our passports, the two had been told: 'Shoot those men!' they would have done so on the spot, still with the same smile.

Meanwhile the number of men who were being trained to shoot with a smile was growing. Hitler's decree of March 1935, establishing universal military service and a peacetime army of 12 corps, which so delighted some generals and dismayed others, meant that Germany would be able to muster half-a-million men under arms. By 1937 the number of divisions was in fact 39, three more than originally planned, but potentially it was far greater as the expansion to over 100 divisions on mobilization in August 1939 showed. Yet for the time being all Hitler's talk was of peace.

The timing of one of his 'peace' speeches to the Reichstag was wholly in keeping with his nature. On 21 May 1935 Hitler had reorganized the command structure of the armed forces. The Reichswehr ceased to be called the Reichswehr. It became, and there was menace in the very change, the Wehrmacht. What better instrument could there be to achieve the ever present aim of Weltmacht—itself always part of Hitler's *Weltanschauung*—than the Wehrmacht. By doing this he created a new command, a headquarters, his own headquarters, superior to the Army. He himself was Supreme Commander of the Wehrmacht, whilst Blomberg was both Minister of Defence and Commander-in-Chief of the Armed Forces. Keitel, who always agreed with Hitler's views and actions, was at this time Blomberg's Chief of Staff. Each of the three services, *Heer, Marine* and *Luftwaffe*, had its own Commander-in-Chief. Beck became Chief of the General Staff. As we shall see this was but one step in the game which ultimately gave Hitler absolute control over every branch of the Wehrmacht. Having seen to this reorganization, later in this same day, 21 May, Hitler made his speech. There was no sabre rattling; quite the contrary:

> The blood shed on the European continent in the course of the last 300 years bears no proportion to the national result of the events. In the end France has remained France, Germany Germany, Poland Poland and Italy Italy. What dynastic egoism, political passion and patriotic blindness have attained in the way of apparently far-reaching political changes by shedding rivers

of blood has, as regards national feeling, done no more than touched the skin of the nations. It has not substantially altered their fundamental characters. If these states had applied merely a fraction of their sacrifices to wiser purposes the success would certainly have been greater and more permanent.

There was no question of Germany wanting to conquer other nations. War which subjected an alien people resulted merely in weakening the conqueror and contributing to his defeat. Hitler hardly knew how prophetically he spoke. National Socialist Germany wanted peace and needed peace. He went on to explain his proposals for achieving peace. While collective security—'this damned system of alliances' as von Jagow, German Foreign Minister before the 1914-18 war had called it—tended to spread conflicts, Germany was willing to enter into bilateral non-aggression pacts with her neighbours. In spite of rearmament, Germany 'respected' the non-military clauses of the Versailles Treaty. Hitler, in short, was being 'reasonable':

> Germany has solemnly recognized and guaranteed France her frontiers as determined after the Saar plebiscite. . . . We thereby finally renounce all claims to Alsace-Lorraine. . . . Germany has concluded a non-aggression pact with Poland. . . . We shall adhere to it unconditionally. . . . Germany neither intends nor wishes to interfere in the internal affairs of Austria, to annex Austria, or to conclude an Anschluss.

This was the sort of language the Western democracies wanted to hear, and *The Times* expressed the hope that the speech would everywhere be taken as 'a sincere and well-considered utterance meaning precisely what it says'. *Qui desiderat pacem, praeparet bellum*—this was the sound advice of Vegetius. 'Let him who desires peace, prepare for war.' And let him who wishes to indulge in war make others prepare for peace, we might add as Hitler's tactics at this stage in the diplomatic game. Peace talks were all part of the game, and as long as peace lasted, it was a game at which he excelled. So often did he make monkeys of the cautious General Staff, that when it came to war experience took him by the hand and led him down paths strewn with danger. Then too, when the General

Staff counselled caution and sound military planning, it was swept aside by the 'greatest strategic genius of all time'. All Hitler's talk of peace, therefore, was no more than a ruse to disguise when he would first indulge in warlike acts. As François-Poncet put it six months after this great peace offering—he was referring to reoccupation of the Rhineland—'Hitler's sole hesitancy is now concerned with the appropriate moment to act'. Yet Hitler's 'respect' for the Versailles Treaty specifically comprehended de-militarization of this very area.

To reoccupy the Rhineland? Would not this, in spite of Britain's and France's supine reaction to Hitler's rearmament programme, in spite of Hitler's guarantee of France's frontiers which the Saar's handing over to the Reich had made easier, in spite of Germany's renunciation of Alsace Lorraine, in spite of all Hitler's fair words—would it not be the last straw for France and precipitate the very crisis with the Allies which the German generals so feared and wished to avoid until the Wehrmacht was able to live up to its name and be really powerful? Here was the voice of caution and reason. Such a voice was not Hitler's, and he was already convinced that he knew far better than the generals. Why did he think so?

The truth was that Hitler, however much he might need them, had never thought much of the *Grosse Generalstab*, the great General Staff. Even though he had referred to them in *Mein Kampf* as the 'mightiest thing the world has ever seen', according to General Franz Halder who was Chief of the General Staff in 1938-42, 'Hitler, with the fervour of a revolutionary, hated the older type of officer as representative of an upper class which he regarded as rotten and incompetent'. His experience in fighting political battles had led him to the same conclusion. In the days of indecision leading up to the Röhm purge, von Papen and the Army leaders may have thought that the real power in Germany lay with them. How sharply they were disillusioned when Hitler in a single night of long knives removed threats from right *and* left. His contempt for this 'reactionary crowd' was clearly expressed in conversation with Rauschning:

They're all mistaken. They underrate me because I have risen

from below; because I haven't had an education, because I haven't
the manners that their sparrow brains think right. But I don't need
them to assure me of my historical greatness. . . . The people don't
want a Hohenzollern monarchy. Only I could induce them to
accept it. Only I could make them believe that a monarchy is
necessary. But I *will not* do it. They're at their wits' end, these
miserable busybodies, these second-rate clerks . . . What I have
lost in the trial of the SA I shall regain by the verdict on these
feudal gamblers and professional card-sharpers, the Schleichers
and company.

The verdict on his assuming complete control of the state was
decisive. Nearly 90 per cent of the nation said 'Yes!'. But it
was not merely in matters of manipulating the powers of the
state in which Hitler thought himself so superior to the generals.
It was at their own game as well—the art of strategy and
making war.

Although the generals might at times refer to Hitler as a
'facile amateur' he was, so far as an understanding of military
history and weapon technology went, better educated and
equipped than most of them. The campaigns and writings of
Frederick the Great, Clausewitz's *On War*, the theories and
practices of more recently successful Commanders-in-Chief,
Molkte, Schlieffen, Seeckt—he had studied them all voraciously
and went on doing so during his own war. Frederick's capacity,
endurance and resolution were sources of unending admiration. If Frederick could triumph over 'the greatest superiority
of power and the utmost spite of fortune', particularly as this
triumph was facilitated by the intervention of Providence,
what might he himself not do? It was a theme to which he
constantly returned, and in the death of Roosevelt, at a time
when his own cause was irredeemably lost, he was to see a
parallel with the death of the Czarina Elizabeth which had
saved Frederick from a comparably hopeless predicament.
Hand in hand with Hitler's knowledge of history went his
belief in himself as a maker of history—'a man who has no
sense of history is like a man who has no ears or eyes'—as one
of historical greatness with the mission of rescuing Europe
from 'Jewish-Bolshevik' ideology and replacing it with that of
the Nazi master race. Embedded in this *Weltanschauung* was,

of course, the virtue of struggle. Nature's work was a struggle
between strength and weakness, and thus victory of the strong
over the weak. Force and power were the factors which determined history. 'Only force rules!'

Hitler's acquaintance with history, however much it concentrated on that part of history concerned with power, war and
conquest, was matched—and aided by a remarkable memory
for detail—by his grasp of the technical aspect of war. As
Speer recalled: 'On matters of Army equipment his knowledge
was far superior to that of his military staff. He was better
informed than they about the characteristics of specific weapons
and tanks, types of ammunition and armament innovations.
Actually he knew more than was good for a man in his exalted
position.'* Another advantage Hitler enjoyed was that his very
ignorance of the tactical handling of armies in operations, his
very lack of a formal military education, meant that his ideas
were untrammelled by convention or experience.

'The generals,' Hitler told Hess, 'are sterile, only able to
imagine the future in terms of their own petty experience.' They
were imprisoned by their own professional training and knowledge, incapable of grasping the new, the unusual, the
unorthodox. A creative genius, on the other hand, was outside
the enclosure of expertise. Above all 'I have the gift of reduc-
ing all problems to their simplest foundation'. It was not
simply Hitler's unorthodoxy, however, which so influenced his
strategic thinking. It was also his insistence on the value of
surprise. Surprise was all part of the technique of blitzkrieg,
a major factor in winning the psychological battle which made
winning the actual battle so much easier. A France longing
to be left alone, with little confidence in her political or military
leaders, these latter men concerned only with the defensive,
indeed as General, then Captain, Diego Brosset put it to
Vercors 'they hide their heads in the sand like that doddering
old fool of a field-marshal who usurped his fame in the first
place'—a France like this would be as easy to defeat in the
first sort of battle as it would in the second.

As if these advantages of Hitler's were not enough in his

---

* There may have been some British generals who would have endorsed
this last point with regard to Churchill.

dealings with the generals, the fact was that few of them were able to stand up to him. General Halder, who held no brief for the Führer, conceded that he was the dynamo of the war effort, that with his overpowering will 'he dominated the entire field of war leadership—political to military'. Dönitz kept away from Hitler when he could because exposure to his power and personality always seemed to rob him of his own freedom of thought. Göring admitted that when confronted by Hitler his heart would sink into his boots. 'Generals who arrived at his headquarters,' writes Alan Bullock, 'determined to insist on the hopelessness of the situation not only failed to make any protest when they stood face to face with the Führer, but returned shaken in their judgment and half convinced that he was right after all.' In all this it is ironical to reflect that the Army had its own example to blame, for it was from the Army —an Army of leaders—that he took and then applied the *Führerprinzip*, the leadership principle. *Ein Volk, ein Reich, ein Führer*. The lawyer Dr Hans Frank described Nazi Germany's constitution as the will of the Führer, and the extraordinary power of this will never diminished.

Right until the end this uncanny gift of convincing others that he could make fortune change sides persisted. When Field-Marshal Ritter von Greim spoke from the Berlin Bunker to General Koller at General Staff HQ in Fürstenberg on 27 April 1945 when the end was but days, hours even, away, Hitler somehow or other had cast his customary spell. There was no need for despair, von Greim assured the incredulous Koller. Victory was inevitable. 'Everything will be well! The presence of the Führer and his confidence have completely inspired me!' No wonder that Jodl had claimed in November 1943 that the force of Hitler's will-power and the 'creative riches of his thought' were what held together and animated the Wehrmacht as a whole. Even the disillusioned Speer, determined to frustrate the Führer's designs for a scorched earth policy, determined at one point to go to the lengths of assassinating his master, was astonished to discover during a visit to the front as late as 1945 that the ordinary German soldier still believed in Hitler as the only man who could save Germany.

But all this was well in the future. It took Hitler many years to achieve this position, and just as he had shown infinite patience in waiting until he could grasp not a portion, but the lion's share, of political power for himself, so in his pursuit of absolute ascendancy over the Third Reich's military machine, he advanced slowly and methodically. It was not until December 1941 that he received from the Reichstag the title and reality of *Oberster Feldherr*, Supreme War Lord. Amongst the multitudinous moves in the game perhaps the most dangerous, the most reckless, was the first one involving the use of troops. Yet it turned out to be the first of many victories in which the shedding of blood played no part at all.

3

Bloodless Victories

Germany's problems could only be solved by force and this was never without attendant risk.

Hitler, November 1937

So oder so—in this way or in that—it was with this favourite expression of his that Hitler summed up the opportunistic strategy which he would employ to achieve his aims. If one way to a solution seemed profitless, then he would try another. But, consistent as the aim itself, one feature was common to every method—force, or threat of force, had to be present. The principal choice therefore was between peace and war. As is customary in history it was the soldiers who were anxious to avoid war. To Hitler an army's purpose was uncompromisingly clear. It was to prepare for battle. Without this purpose it would be impossible to build an army which possessed the right sort of spirit or dedication. There was no such thing as an army required to prepare for or guarantee peace. Armies were solely for 'triumphant exertion in war'.

The Generals thought otherwise. A large army, the power that went with it, privilege, position, a strong, respected, honoured Reich, yes; even quick, limited military successes; but on the whole they counselled caution. Hitler was at first surprised and later contemptuous of what he regarded as their pusillanimity. In the summer of 1941 during the first victories in Russia, with all the other triumphs behind him, Hitler bitterly upbraided the General Staff for always obstructing his every design. He likened them to a mastiff, which before becoming Chancellor he had imagined to be straining upon the start, threatening everyone in sight, only too eager to move worlds. Not at all! It was he who time after time had to goad the mastiff into action. In ordering reoccupation of the Rhineland, a move which gravely disturbed the mastiff's peace of mind, Hitler pulled off one of the most colossal pieces of bluff in history. Never was Hobbes' recipe of force and fraud peacefully concocted to better advantage. Yet the fraud was palpable and the force negligible.

One of Hitler's most notable and successful techniques was to disguise each of his aggressive moves as one designed essentially for the defence and security of the Reich. Thus withdrawal from the League of Nations and their Disarmament Conference in October 1933 was presented as a reluctant response to Allied recalcitrance in limiting armaments. Peaceloving Germany, saddened by the failure of her efforts to promote international disarmament, was obliged to quit Geneva. The continued level of Allied military strength together with France's prolongation of compulsory service were what had made German rearmament necessary, purely to underwrite her *Wehrhoheit*, her defence sovereignty, to restore her equality of rights, to end an intolerable humiliation. The fact that he had long before decided on an aggressive course and waited only for the opportune moment to press it home did not deter him from using soft words. This 'language of the League', as Hitler called it (adding that when he spoke of 'peace, disarmament and mutual security' his party comrades would not fail to understand what he really meant) was no more than a sop to those Western statesmen only too anxious to take Hitler's pacific protestations at their face value. If only they could have heard him talking to Rauschning!

I am willing to sign anything. I will do anything to facilitate the success of my policy. I am prepared to guarantee all frontiers and to make non-aggression pacts and friendly alliances with anybody. It would be sheer stupidity to refuse to make use of such measures merely because one might possibly be driven into a position where a solemn promise would have to be broken. There has never been a sworn treaty which has not sooner or later been broken or become untenable. There is no such thing as an everlasting treaty. Anyone whose conscience is so tender that he will not sign a treaty unless he can feel sure he can keep it in all and any circumstances is a fool. Why should one not please others and facilitate matters for oneself by signing pacts if the others believe that something is thereby accomplished or regulated? Why should I not make an agreement in good faith today and unhesitatingly break it tomorrow if the future of the German people demands it?

Hitler, in short, was all for keeping his options open, and it was in this spirit that he treated the Locarno Pact. In his speech of 21 May 1935, whose conciliatory content we have already examined, Hitler not only pledged that Germany would 'uphold and fulfil all obligations arising out of the Locarno Treaty'. He specifically promised that the Rhineland would remain demilitarized. His technique—of inventing or seizing upon pretexts to justify aggressive acts on which he had already decided and the details of which, precise timing excepted, had already been worked out—could hardly be better illustrated than by the fact that almost three weeks *before* this speech von Blomberg, on Hitler's orders, had issued to the Armed Services the first directive for planning the Rhineland's reoccupation.

An excuse for tearing up Locarno was not hard to find. On 27 February 1936 the French Chamber of Deputies ratified their country's treaty with the Soviet Union, an arrangement which Hitler had already condemned as incompatible with the spirit and obligations of Locarno. Here were grounds relative enough. Only two days later he resolved the one detail that was missing—timing. His orders were not received with enthusiasm by the Generals. Beck, Chief of the General Staff, tried to make Hitler agree to a declaration that there would be no fortification west of the Rhine; von Blomberg wanted to make some sort of bargain with the French which would lead to removing troops of both countries from the border areas. Hitler dismissed such weak-kneed notions with contumely. He was sure of his ground. On 7 March one division of troops occupied the Rhineland; a mere three battalions moved across the river to Trier, Saarbrücken and Aachen.

While the German Foreign Minister, von Neurath, informed the French, British and Italian ambassadors of what had happened, Hitler was explaining to an exultant Reichstag how this first act of real military aggression was but one more move in Germany's search for a peaceful solution to Europe's problems. The French Ambassador acidly commented that as Hitler struck his adversary in the face, he made fresh overtures for peace. William Shirer recalls the effect of Hitler's announcement that Locarno was invalidated and that German troops were actually re-entering the Rhineland on the assembled Reichstag members:

> All the militarism in their German blood surges to their heads. They spring, yelling and crying, to their feet.... Their hands are raised in slavish salute, their faces now contorted with hysteria, their mouths wide open, shouting, shouting, their eyes, burning with fanaticism, glued on the new god, the Messiah.

The Messiah is worth listening to. He is making two vows—one never to allow force to prevent restoration of the German people's honour (a vow which may be believed), second, to strive as never before for a European understanding, especially with Germany's western neighbours. Not only had Germany no territorial demands to make in Europe, but she would never break the peace.

Shirer remembers too that the cheering went on for a long time. But the Minister of Defence, von Blomberg, was not one of those swelling the volume of cheers. Ashen-faced, cheeks twitching, it was clear as he left the Kroll Opera House* that his nerve was cracking. He and many of his fellow generals simply could not believe that the French with their overwhelmingly more powerful forces would not march. Yet they did not. Hitler's diagnosis of what Western diplomats and soldiers would do, or rather not do, had been vindicated absolutely. His triumph was not just over these latter dignitaries. It was over his own timid generals, and was therefore of great moment for his future programme. Sir John Wheeler-Bennett admirably sums up their dilemma: 'Thereafter, though they did not cease to express their professional forebodings against the wild ebullitions of the Führer's "intuitions", they made their protest with an increased lack of assurance and with the growing and sickening fear that he was right and they were wrong.'

The generals might lose their nerve. But Hitler's own nerve,

---

* After the Reichstag fire in February 1933, it convened in the Kroll Opera House.

as usual, was of iron. Even so he subsequently admitted to his interpreter, Paul Schmidt, that the 48 hours following the reoccupation were the most nerve-racking in his life. Had the French moved, he conceded, the German forces would have had no choice but to withdraw again, with unforeseeably disastrous results for himself. But his foresight, his *Vorhersehung* (another favourite word) prevailed. He recalled the incident seven years later.

> What would have happened if anybody other than myself had been at the head of the Reich! Anyone you care to mention would have lost his nerve. I was obliged to lie and what saved me was my unshakable obstinacy and my amazing aplomb. I threatened, unless the situation eased, to send six extra divisions into the Rhineland. The truth was I only had four brigades.

France, however, did nothing except reinforce the Maginot Line—a wholly defensive and ineffectual gesture. Moreover this very move underlines a major strategic advantage which Hitler gained by reoccupying the Rhineland. Throughout the war Hitler's principal strategic puzzle was how to combine comfortable security at one point of the compass with violent activity at another; how to conquer in the East whilst guarding the West; how to overrun the West whilst holding in the East; then again how to smash the Eastern threat whilst preserving Western integrity; until in the end he was to turn desperately from East to West and back again in a vain effort to stave off invincibly superior resources and numbers. This dichotomy of purpose was ever present, and possession of the Rhineland in military terms was a first step to its resolution.

Churchill with his sure grasp of strategy was quick to see it. In the House of Commons in April 1936 he foretold the creation of the Siegfried Line, and with it not just the ability which the Germans would enjoy to economize forces there in the event of war or to strike strongly through Belgium and Holland, but more imminently dangerous, if less directly so to the west, German security in the west augured ill for the Baltic States, Poland, Czechoslovakia, Yugoslavia, Rumania and Austria. In short the whole strategic balance in middle Europe would be changed. The most telling support for

Churchill's argument came from the French Army itself. It was thinking in wholly defensive terms. It had become a prisoner of its own Maginot Line and was no more capable of mounting successful offensives than it had been in 1870. France in fact was helping to provide the very security which Hitler sought.

Thus if Hitler's strategy of *so oder so*, whether peaceful or warlike, were to be in essence a ringing of the changes between East and West, and if furthermore he was already of the opinion that a decadent, peace-hungry West would stand idly by and watch him eat up *Lebensraum* in the East without lifting a finger, then his first military adventure had confirmed the soundness of his strategy and left him in a strong position for taking the next steps. Yet he was in no hurry to take them. More immediately he obtained an overwhelming endorsement of his policy by inviting the German people to pass judgment on it by plebiscite. Nearly 99 per cent approved. It was perhaps relatively easy for the Germans to adjust themselves to the changing balance of power in Europe. The process was less agreeable for Germany's neighbours, but having observed both the facility with which Hitler had removed one more, indeed the last, guarantee against both a resurgence of German aggression and France's evident helplessness to stop him, these neighbours had little choice but to begin hedging their own bets in such new circumstances of the race for power.

Meanwhile in January 1937, at the end of his first four years as Chancellor, Hitler was able to indulge in a self-adulatory address to the Reichstag during which he thanked Providence for assisting him, once an unknown soldier in the war, successfully to restore to Germany her honour and her rights. It was not only to this enhanced standing amongst the nations of the world, however that he could point. The economic miracle was a model which no other country had equalled. But the motive force of this recovery was not a healthy economy for its own sake. It was as Dr Schacht, who largely brought it about, recorded, so that the strongest and most effective Wehrmacht could be established as fast as possible. 'The accomplishment of the armament programme with speed and in quantity is *the* problem of German politics, and everything else should be subordinated to this purpose, as long as the main purpose is not imperilled by neglecting all other questions.' In all discussion as to whether or not Hitler was bent on war, this fact—that in the Wehrmacht he would have an instrument indispensable to a policy of expansion— must figure large.

There was already in 1937 much evidence of a different sort. Panzer and Stuka, the peerless pair, were fighting in the Spanish Civil War, and although the former, because of being used in small numbers and over unsuitable country, did not greatly influence affairs*, the effect of the latter in the Condor Air Legion's hands was shattering. Moreover the Luftwaffe perfected in practice one of the basic blitzkrieg tactics which Guderian had outlined so eloquently in theory. They taught themselves how to keep up with the forward troops by developing the mobility inherent in their own transport aircraft. This lesson, unlearned by any other army, was to pay big dividends later. Then, apart from these practical demonstrations, plans for theoretical wars were being entertained and refined. A directive which, on Hitler's orders, von Blomberg issued to the three Commanders-in-Chief in July 1937 was specific about employing a Panzer Army to 'eliminate' Austria or Czechoslovakia. 'The politically fluid world situation . . . demands constant preparedness for war on the part of the German armed forces . . . to make possible the military exploitation of politically favourable opportunities should they occur.' There were two express plans for general hostilities. One assumed a French attack on Germany, and that, in a war on two fronts, Germany's main effort would be in the west. This was *Fall Rot*—Case, or Operation, Red. The second, *Fall Grün*, Case Green (of which we shall hear more) supposed that the war, again on two fronts, would begin 'with a surprise German operation against Czechoslovakia in order to parry the imminent attack of a superior

---

* In the sense that the panzers' effect on the tactical battle was small, this was true. But inversely proportionate to this was the incalculable influence on Allied tactical thinking. Gamelin, French Chief of Staff, said no hope of tank break-throughs; they were not independent enough; anti-tank guns would always stop them. Deverell, the CIGS, dismissed German tanks as fit only for the scrap-heap.

enemy coalition. The necessary conditions to justify such an action politically and in the eyes of international law must be created *beforehand*.' It is not difficult to detect the Führer's touch here. Another special case envisaged armed intervention in Austria—*Fall Otto*. This sort of planning stood in sharp contrast to that which had been going on in England where the starting point had long been an assumption that there would be no major war in Europe for 10 years!

Austria and Czechoslovakia represented the first 'condition' of Hitler's foreign policy on which he had so long before determined, the incorporation into the Reich of *all* Germans. These two countries' neighbours must of course be mollified, but this should not prove to be too hard. Consolidation of the Berlin-Rome axis would help to remove an obstacle to the first of these prizes, and negotiations with Poland, which Hitler so assiduously pursued, in particular his reassurances that *Danzig ist mit Poland verbunden* (Danzig is tied up with Poland)—did much to convince the Polish Foreign Minister, Colonel Beck, of Germany's friendly intentions, and thus smooth the way to Polish neutrality in eastern Europe.

With military plans thus in course of preparation and the acquiescence of those most immediately able to intervene in course of realization, Hitler felt free to embark on his famous discourse as to the future direction of his policy. To most of the small audience—apart from his adjutant, Colonel Hossbach, only five men were there, von Blomberg, the three Commanders-in-Chief, von Fritsch, Raeder, Göring, and von Neurath, the Foreign Minister—his proposals came as a profound shock. They were a blueprint for achieving the *Lebensraum* that Hitler had so often and so vehemently spoken of. German policy, he explained, must be to secure, preserve and enlarge the racial community. Given, therefore, that it was a question of space, space moreover in the heart of Europe, 'in immediate proximity to the Reich', the complementary question was where to carve out the largest gain at the smallest cost. Some cost there would be, for apart from Russia, Germany would be confronted by two 'hate-inspired antagonists', Britain and France, and despite their weaknesses they were antagonists to be reckoned with. Thus only force could solve Germany's problem and use of force was never without risk. If force were to be employed, when and how to employ it were the next things to be considered. Hitler outlined three 'cases'. The first one concerned timing, in that Germany would reach the peak of her military power between 1943 and 1945. 'If he was still living, it was his unalterable resolve to solve Germany's problem of space at the latest by 1943-45.' We cannot deny that he did so, but hardly in the way that his *Vorhersehung* would have wished to contemplate.

The latest possible date would not, of course, necessarily be the actual one. There were earlier times to consider. The second and third cases envisaged an incapacitated France, arising either from internal difficulties or from being engaged in hostilities with another country. Whichever case materialized, Hitler was resolved to seize the advantage thus presented, if need be even as early as 1938. The principal and most urgent objectives would be the overthrow of Austria and Czechoslovakia. These two countries were not just milestones on the road to a Greater German Reich, but furnished critical strategic advantages in denying the West opportunities to threaten Germany from her southern flank, to say nothing of Austria's 12 divisions or Czechoslovakia's economic and armament resources.

Certain questions persisted as to the risk. What would the great powers, Russia, France, Britain, Italy, do? At great length—and throughout the meeting there was only one man who spoke at any length at all—Hitler persuaded himself that they would do nothing. Italy would be embroiled with France and Great Britain. Russia was nervous of Japan. Concerted action was unlikely. Besides the will was lacking. All the same, Austria and Czechoslovakia must be acquired *blitzartig schnell*, at lightning speed.

There has been much controversy about this meeting of 5 November 1937, about Hitler's real intentions in calling it at all, and about the true significance of his pronouncements. Interpretation varies widely. From being an irreversible decision to go to war it becomes a mere manoeuvre in domestic affairs. In fact there was something of each in it. The great momentum of the Nazi movement which fostered rearmament and guaranteed full employment had to be maintained. Objections to the pace of rearmament on economic, not moral, grounds must be allayed so that this pace could be kept up, even accelerated. Hitler's review of policy would help to do so. Yet any idea that he was at this time charting a precise course based on hypotheses must be dismissed. He was far too skilful a politician for that. His whole political strategy was one of opportunism with no fixed time-table, one of profiting by others' mistakes, even letting others do his work for him (an exercise at which Chamberlain proved so apt a pupil), getting all he wanted without resort to war. So that while rearmament was relevant to the meeting, there was really nothing new in what Hitler was proposing. It was all in *Mein Kampf*. In reiterating his intention to use force—the only formula for solving Germany's problem, albeit not without risk—Hitler was moving from the caution of his first four years as Chancellor to a second stage, when confident of the power he disposed and the success he boasted, he was ready to raise the stakes of violence, gamble more, threaten more, and rely more on the last resort of force, simply because more of it was at his command. This was the only change.

That he should have called such a meeting at such a time solely to convince men like Blomberg, Fritsch and Neurath about the rearmament programme, when formerly he had not hesitated to lay down an intensely overtaxing expansion of the Army without even consulting them, and when within three months he was to get rid of all three men, simply does not ring true. To go to such lengths was not Hitler's style at all. Göring and Blomberg, both of whom rapidly swallowed any misgivings they might have harboured about the Führer's plans for aggression, reassured Raeder by telling him that the whole thing had been designed to 'ginger up Fritsch and the traditional reactionaries into an acceleration of the tempo of rearmament'. There was no question, they said, of taking what the Führer had forecast seriously. Raeder's apprehensions about the dangers of a naval conflict with England were thus dispelled.

But the truth is that Hitler's mind was made up. The broad issues were clear. Timing, exact circumstances, details of method—these were left open. Just how things would be done

12 Nuremberg Rally, 1938

13 Munich, October 1938: (1. to r.) Chamberlain, Daladier, Hitler, Mussolini, Ciano

14 Hitler and Rommel in Poland, 1939

did not at this point matter; *so oder so*; but that they would be done, that the new task of expanding the *Lebensraum* of the German people would be set in motion—this was not in doubt. Professor Trevor-Roper takes a similar view. Hitler's programme, he maintains, however adaptable as to exact timings and priorities, was clearly devised. First detach eastern Europe from the West; then neutralize or crush the West; finally launch war on Russia, not later than 1943. If a programme of this sort, drawn up in 1937, was to be realized, it might be necessary to make war on the West as early as 1938. A great deal has been made of the 'priceless' year gained in 1938 by Britain at the price of humiliation at Munich. Yet it was in the end not so much a year gained by the West; it was a year lost to Hitler.

Before Hitler took the first steps in putting his blueprint to the proof, he further tightened his grip on both the economic and strategic management of the Reich. Schacht, in charge of Economics and War Economy, resigned in protest at Göring's roughshod interference in economic affairs. Hitler, whilst reluctant to lose so skilful a manipulator of trade agreements, was determined to gear the German economy to war, and left it in Göring's hands to do so. Schacht was one matter. The 'dead wood', Hindenburg's legacies of Blomberg, Fritsch and Neurath, was another thing altogether. Means of removing them varied in detail, but not in character. All were shabby. Blomberg, by marrying a 'woman with a past', had dishonoured the Officer Corps and had to go. Trumped-up and wholly false charges of disgraceful conduct against Fritsch, who refused to defend himself, sufficed to ensure his suspension. Neurath was simply replaced by the pliant, subservient, vain and egregriously blundering Ribbentrop. It was not merely the removal of Blomberg and Fritsch which signified, however. It was the arrangement that followed. Hitler did not replace Blomberg—who, it will be remembered, combined the office of Minister of Defence with Commander-in-Chief of the Armed Forces—by another. He assumed the office himself. It is true that von Brauchitsch (who as a lieutenant-colonel in 1923-24 had helped Guderian conduct joint tank-aircraft exercises) became Commander-in-Chief of the Army, an appointment acceptable to its reactionary members, but Hitler had outflanked the Army. His announcement of 4 February 1938 dissolved one more of the checks and balances:

> From henceforth I exercise personally the immediate command over the whole armed forces. The former Wehrmacht Office in the War Ministry becomes the High Command of the Armed Forces [Oberkommando der Wehrmacht or OKW] and comes immediately under my command as my military staff. At the head of the Staff of the High Command stands the former chief of the Wehrmacht Office [Keitel]. He is accorded the rank equivalent to that of Reich Minister. The High Command of the Armed Forces also takes over the functions of the War Ministry, and the Chief of the High Command exercises, as my deputy, the powers hitherto held by the Reich War Minister.

Thus, with compliant generals like Keitel staffing it, Hitler had established a new command structure, so that his own orders, whether concerned with military or other matters, would be transmitted, as Trevor-Roper puts it, 'through the whole war-machine of the Reich without the possibility of legal opposition; and it was through this machinery that he applied and controlled his strategy throughout the war'. The Army could no longer be 'a state within the state'. It had become an instrument of the Führer's will. Fritsch's subsequent comment was that Hitler was Germany's destiny for good and evil. 'If he now goes over the abyss'—and Fritsch believed that he would—'he will drag us all down with him. There is nothing we can do.'

On the very same day as the Führer's decree about leadership in the Armed Forces, the first step towards the abyss was taken. The stories of the *Anschluss* and Czechoslovakia's destruction are too well known to require detailed elaboration here. What do concern us, however, are the features of these upheavals which had direct bearing on Hitler's conduct of military affairs, the effect on the Army and its leaders, and Hitler's reaction to success.

On that same evening of 4 February one of the pawns in the game, von Papen, Hitler's special representative in Vienna, was informed by telephone from Berlin that his mission was over and that he was recalled. Papen had long been aware that Schuschnigg, Federal Austrian Chancellor, would not be averse to a meeting with Hitler in order to clarify German-Austrian relations. He therefore saw Hitler at Berchtesgaden next day and proposed such a meeting to him. The Führer enthusiastically embraced the idea—probably as he at once saw it as a means both to exert more pressure in the Austrian problem and to distract attention from the Fritsch-Schacht dismissals—and Papen returned to Vienna to arrange it. On 12 February the two men met. Hitler's systematic bullying of Schuschnigg, with generals scurrying about at his beck and call, produced the results he wanted. His excessive demands were accepted: Nazi Ministers of the Interior (Seyss-Inquart), War and Finance; no ban on the Nazi party plus an amnesty for those imprisoned; the Austrian economy to be harnessed to Germany's. Any hesitation by Schuschnigg was shouted down:

> The whole history of Austria is just one uninterrupted act of high treason.... The German Reich is one of the Great Powers, and nobody will raise his voice if it settles its border problems.... I have achieved everything that I set out to do, and have thus become perhaps the greatest German in history.... You don't seriously believe that you can stop me, or even delay me for half an hour, do you?

His patience was exhausted—how often this exhaustion was to recur! Unless Schuschnigg agreed *now* to his demands, force would settle the matter. He did not believe in bluffing. All his past proved it. 'You will either sign as it is and fulfil my demands within three days, or I will order the march into Austria.' When Schuschnigg still demurred, Hitler shouted for General Keitel. The Austrian Foreign Minister, Schmidt, expected to be arrested at any moment. Then Hitler, with a manoeuvre he was to repeat on other comparable occasions, conceded three more days for the agreement to be put into effect. Schuschnigg signed.

There was almost exactly a month between this meeting and the day Austria ceased to exist. Hitler hoped all along for a 'non-revolutionary' outcome to the Austrian question. He told the leading Austrian Nazis on 26 February that 'he did not now desire a solution by violent means, if it could at all be avoided, since the danger for us in the field of foreign policy became less each year and our military power greater'. In other words force was going to be used all right, but not yet, not until it was overwhelmingly superior to anyone else's. Hitler also predicted that the Austrian problem would automatically be solved if the far-reaching protocol signed by Schuschnigg were fully carried out. So much was this prediction coming true, so independently of the Government were Seyss-Inquart and his Nazi colleagues conducting affairs, that Schuschnigg felt the reins of authority slipping from his fingers. But he had not yet had the last word. He resolved on 8 March to hold a plebiscite five days later, at which the Austrian people would be invited to declare whether they were in favour of a 'free, independent, social, Christian and united Austria—*Ja oder Nein?*' As soon as he heard about this new move, Hitler acted, and military plans were drafted. The former *Fall Otto* (designed to prevent Otto of Hapsburg, pretender to the Austrian throne, from successfully reclaiming it) was the only plan in existence for armed intervention in Austria. It was rapidly revised, and on 11 March Hitler issued Directive No 1 for Operation Otto. It gave a foretaste of many directives to come:

1. If other measures prove unsuccessful, I intend to invade Austria with armed forces in order to establish constitutional conditions and to prevent further outrages against the pro-German population.
2. The whole operation will be directed by myself....
3. The forces of the Army and Air Force detailed for this operation must be ready for invasion on March 12, 1938, at the latest by 1200 hours....
4. The behaviour of the troops must give the impression that we do not want to wage war against our Austrian brothers.... Therefore any provocation is to be avoided. If, however, resistance is offered it must be broken ruthlessly by force of arms....

In the end Hitler had it both ways—a 'peaceful' solution and the occupation of Austria by his armies. But before this came about, two men had to be reassured and one further bullied into subjection. Mussolini received a long letter which drew a definite boundary between Italy and Germany at the Brenner Pass, and so relieved him of the fear that southern Tyrol was also to be incorporated in the Greater Reich. The second man to be reassured was Dr Mastny, Czech Minister in Berlin. Göring told him that Austria was purely a family affair, and 'I give you my word of honour that Czechoslovakia has nothing to fear from the Reich'. Mastny was only too ready to be duped, and had probably not heard of Touchstone's knight who, swearing by his honour that the pancakes were good and the mustard naught, could not be forsworn even if the contrary were true for he never had any honour, or, if he had, had long since sworn it away. What mattered was that the Czechs undertook not to mobilize their army. The bullying of Miklas, Austrian President, to nominate Seyss-Inquart as Federal Chancellor, was more protracted but not less successful.

Whilst Seyss-Inquart was being jockeyed into the Chancellorship, Göring obtained his agreement—a faked telegram was the method—that in order to maintain order and avoid bloodshed the provisional Austrian Government requested the German Government to send troops as soon as possible. In this way was 'legality' preserved. Early on the morning of 12 March Seyss-Inquart asked General Muff, German Military Attaché in Vienna, to telephone Berlin and call off the occupation. But Hitler was not to be deflected now. The troops would march. The Führer was going to liberate Austria and put his fellow Germans out of their distress. Next day Seyss-Inquart was able to tell Hitler that Austria was a province of the German Reich, and on 14 March the Führer entered Vienna—not in the best of tempers, for the renowned panzer units had performed with less speed and reliability than had been expected of them.

There was a saying in the British cavalry during Hitler's war that an armoured division, a British one, that is, only really advanced and went on advancing when there was no opposition. At the same time, no matter what the level of command, whether squadron, brigade or corps, there prevailed a fierce pride in keeping all tanks and armoured cars in good running order, on the road in fact. For the occupation of Vienna Guderian's XVI Army Corps, containing the 2nd Armoured Division and the Waffen-SS Division, SS Leibstandarte Adolf Hitler, met no opposition, yet the panzers did not advance without difficulty. Jodl maintained that 70 per cent of the armoured vehicles broke down on the road from Salzburg and Passau to Vienna. Although Guderian denied that the percentage was as high, two things are clear. First Hitler was furious at this poor showing of his military machine; second some useful lessons were learned. The main ones, according to Guderian, were about tank maintenance, fuel supply and road discipline. Whatever the fury and whatever the lessons, the fact remains that the two divisions had motored between 400 and 600 miles in two days— no mean achievement for troops and staffs unpractised in such long route marches. But any achievements in the military sphere were dwarfed by those in the political. The Austrian plebiscite —for Hitler decided that after all Austria should have a plebiscite, only the issue was changed and became an appeal for four more years of power in which the whole of the new Grossdeutschland would participate—confirmed Germany's and Austria's approval of the *Anschluss* and Hitler's policies. 99 per cent said Yes.

Amongst the 1 per cent, in spirit if not in name, were some of the generals. 'Before 1938-39,' declared von Blomberg in 1945, 'the German Generals were not opposed to Hitler. There was no reason to oppose him since he produced the results which they desired. After this time some generals began to condemn his methods and lost confidence in the power of his judgement.' They must have been far-seeing indeed, must have had a greater share of the *Vorhersehung*, which Hitler regarded as peculiarly his own, than they have so far been credited with. Yet there was much in the way that the *Anschluss* had been conducted which marked a departure from his former tactics. This was no reversal of the humiliation of Versailles. It had nothing to do with the nation's rights. It was naked aggression. The myth, the mask of injured morality was down, all pretence of legality put aside. But the place vacated was not left empty; it was taken by the reality of the jackboot. This was the beginning of the murder of Europe. Motive, means, opportunity— all were now to hand.

Force had done it, and force was a very serious thing. On 14 March Churchill told the House of Commons:

The gravity of the event of March 12 cannot be exaggerated. Europe is confronted with a programme of aggression, nicely calculated and timed, unfolding stage by stage, and there is only one choice open, not only to us but to other countries, either to submit like Austria, or else take effective measures while time remains to ward off the danger, and if it cannot be warded off to cope with it.... A long stretch of the Danube is now in German hands. This mastery of Vienna gives to Nazi Germany military and economic control of the whole of the communications of South eastern Europe, by road, by river, and by rail. What is the effect of this on the structure of Europe? What is the effect of it upon what is called the balance of power....

Czechoslovakia is at this moment isolated, both in the economic and in the military sense.... How many potential allies shall we see go one by one down the grisly gulf? How many times will bluff succeed until behind bluff ever-gathering forces have accumulated reality? Where are we going to be two years hence, for instance, when the German Army will certainly be much larger than the French Army?

The German Army was not yet as large as the French Army, but it was growing. At the time of the *Anschluss* 28 divisions were formed and operational; six months later the number had been doubled. Also during 1938 the Pzkw* III and IV came into service—the famous Mark IIIs and IVs which, when the shooting started, won golden opinions from all sorts of people. What is more Hitler created the post of Commander of Mobile Troops and appointed Guderian to it. Guderian, with all his imagination, dedication and energy plus direct access to the Führer in matters concerned with the training and organization of new panzer units, had little trouble in removing any doubt there might have been in the Wehrmacht that the concept of blitzkrieg was there to stay.

The Army was gaining in power, but it was power of a different sort. Its role was clear. Essentially subordinate to Hitler's will, the Army would supply the force, whether actual or threatened, to further policy. And policy Hitler alone would decide. It was not long before the generals had some more military planning to do. On 21 March, little more than a week since he had 'given thanks to Him who let me return to my homeland in order that I might now lead it into my German Reich', Hitler sent for Keitel, Chief of Staff, OKW, to set in train further consideration of *Fall Grün*, codename for a surprise German operation against Czechoslovakia.

Hitler murdered Czechoslovakia with two blows. The first

* Pzkw: abbreviation for *Panzerkampfwagen*, armoured fighting vehicle.

illustrated his uncanny skill at manipulating a supposed political grievance in such a way that in the end others did his work for him; the second demonstrated the terrifying thoroughness with which the Wehrmacht, after its former *Anschluss* shortcomings, was being trained to operate. The relationship between the two was expressed by Hitler himself whilst instructing Keitel that in planning the destruction of Czech defensive positions, nothing must be left to chance. All must be prepared in minute detail, for 'the first four days of military action are, politically speaking, decisive. In the absence of outstanding military successes, a European crisis is certain to rise. *Faits accomplis* must convince foreign powers of the hopelessness of military intervention.' This would be the purpose and this the prize of military action which was *blitzartig schnell*.

During the crisis over Czechoslovakia which led to Munich, Western leaders, notably Chamberlain and Daladier, seemed to be convinced that all Hitler was after was the return of the Sudeten Germans to the Fatherland. They failed to understand that what Hitler really intended was to 'smash the Czechs', to destroy the whole state and simply absorb it into the Reich. It was this inability to comprehend what Hitler was up to, what the pattern of Nazi aggression was all about which was perhaps one of the two most significant features of the various manoeuvrings that followed, for the Führer saw these leaders of Britain and France at work, and pronounced them to be—'little worms'. The second feature was the ill-managed and wholly frustrated doubts and waverings of the Generals.

The first draft of Operation Green, prepared by Keitel on Hitler's instructions, was ready on 20 May. It began: 'It is not my intention to smash Czechoslovakia by military action in the immediate future without provocation, unless an unavoidable development of political conditions inside Czechoslovakia forces the issue, or political events in Europe create a particularly favourable opportunity which may never recur.' The directive went on to outline how operations might be launched and made provision for intervention by Hungary and Poland against Czechoslovakia. Since the French would not fight only small forces need be left in the west, and the bulk of the Army and Luftwaffe could concentrate on their primary task—'to smash the Czechoslovak Army and to occupy Bohemia and Moravia as quickly as possible'. What is more—and here too the pattern was set in a way that was to become familiar to the world—the war was to be total. Propaganda and economic warfare would play their parts in undermining the enemy's resistance and hastening his collapse.

But somehow the cat got out of the bag. The Czechs, alarmed by reports of German troop concentrations, ordered partial mobilization. The French and British Governments gave grave warnings of the danger of war. The French went further and with Russian support reiterated their promise of aid to the Czechs. All these suddenly erected obstacles to his plans did not please the Führer. But he bided his time while allowing his temper to worsen. Reassurances were given whilst the directive for Operation Green was once more revised, and reissued on 30 May. There were two important changes. The opening sentence now read: 'It is my unalterable decision to smash Czechoslovakia by military action in the near future.' This was the first change. The second one explained what was meant by 'near future' for Keitel's covering letter laid down that the operation must be executed by 1 October 1938 at the latest. In setting himself a time limit, Hitler once more brought to a head the soldiers' apprehension and opposition. General Beck, Chief of the General Staff, convinced as he was that Hitler's expansionist policies would lead to war with France, Britain and Russia, with the United States as the arsenal for the democracies, and that because of her limited military and economic resources alone Germany would be bound to lose such a war, was disinclined to place much faith in the Führer's 'intuition' and was principal spokesman for the soldiers.

But the conditions necessary for a successful revolt by the generals simply did not exist. There was neither the resolution nor solidarity by the Western powers which could reinforce their own predictions of disaster if the attack on Czechoslovakia were actually made; nor was there proper leadership or pluck among the generals themselves; nor finally any likelihood of popular support from the masses. The outcome of Beck's stand was his own resignation and replacement by Halder. Not that all voices were silenced, however; when Hitler—and this was the only time he did so—invited discussion from an audience of generals after subjecting them in August to a three-hour lecture on his politico-military theories (British generals have much to be grateful for!) and one of them pointed out that if the bulk of German forces were engaged in Czechoslovakia, the West Wall could not be held for more than three weeks, he completely lost his temper with such defeatist talk. 'The position,' he screamed, 'will be held not only for three weeks, but for three months and three years.' The generals, he went on, were faint-hearted, with no morale, no vision, worst of all no belief in his 'genius'. However determined and skilful they might have been at fighting battles, they were certainly no match for Hitler's wrath. Jodl, in recording his depression at this rift between the General Staff and the Führer, compared his master with Charles XII. There were at least two points of resemblance. Hitler too was to march on Moscow and his too was a name at which the world grew pale.

The generals soon had further opportunities for turning pale themselves. On 3 September Hitler went over the final plans of Army deployment for invading Czechoslovakia and laid down that X day would be fixed by noon on 27 September; then on 9 September, on hearing their proposals for the actual attack, he again accused them of faint-heartedness—he plumping for the bold, concentrated breakthrough which alone would bring decisive victory, they cautious, conservative, pointing only to the dangers and difficulties. So apprehensive were some of them that there was even a conspiracy to seize Hitler's person between his giving the order to attack Czechoslovakia and its actual launching.

Yet all their fears and conspiracies went for nothing when, after three months of keeping the world waiting, three months in which the West and Russia continued to demonstrate their lack of resolution or solidarity, Hitler's venomous attack on Czechoslovakia during his speech of 12 September at the Nuremberg Rally and his demand for justice for the Sudeten Germans, had such immediate and drastic results. The world grew pale again, notably the world of Paris. Daladier appealed to Chamberlain to make the best bargain he could with Hitler.

At his first meeting with the Führer at Berchtesgaden on 15

September Chamberlain conceded a point of principle from which the rest of the surrender sprang—'he could state personally that he recognized the principle of the detachment of the Sudeten areas.... He wished to return to England to report to the Government and secure their approval of his personal attitude'. The subsequent moves in the game followed inexorably: Chamberlain's presenting Hitler at Bad Godesberg on 22 September with the joint British, French and Czech agreement to transfer the Sudetenland to Germany; Hitler's upping the stakes by rejecting his offer; his insistence that the Sudetenland must be *occupied* by German troops forthwith; the two men's argument as to which country had mobilized first; Hitler's 'concession' to delay the Czech evacuation and German occupation of the area until 1 October, the original X day and thus no concession at all; then his flat terms that the Czechs must accept 'by 2 pm on 28 September' the Godesberg proposal for German occupation not later than 1 October; his raving speech, crammed with invective, at the Berlin Sportspalast on 26 September and his shouting next day to Sir Horace Wilson, one of Chamberlain's advisers, that he would 'destroy' Czechoslovakia. Finally, all these moves culminated in Hitler's letter to Chamberlain which arrived on the evening of 27 September (less than twelve hours before his own ultimatum expired) and in which he expressed his willingness to guarantee the remainder of Czechoslovakia and to negotiate details with the Czechs. Such moderation could not fail to find its target. Chamberlain took up the cudgels once more to seek 'peace with honour'. Peace with honour started off with a telegram to the Führer, assuring him that 'you can get all essentials without war and without delay'. He suggested a meeting at which Italy, France and Czechoslovakia would also be represented. A telegram to Mussolini asked him to urge Hitler to accept.

The comings and goings of 28 September—Black Wednesday —resulted in Hitler's agreeing to Mussolini's consequent proposals, and just before his ultimatum expired, invitations were sent out to the heads of the Italian, French and British governments to meet the Führer in Munich at noon the next day. These invitations were accepted, and any hopes that Halder and the generals might have had about bringing off a *coup d'état* faded absolutely away. Hitler had won. At Munich he got even more than he had demanded at Bad Godesberg—the Sudetenland with its formidable fortifications, substantial gains in economic resources, control of the country's communications. The Czech nation, from which Poland and Hungary also carved themselves slices of territory, was disrupted. Strategically and industrially Czechoslovakia was broken, and at the mercy—a quality in which he was singularly deficient—of the Führer. And then the military side of it, the actual occupation of the Sudetenland, had gone so smoothly. Everything had been thought of—the Czech positions in the greatest detail, topography, roads and bridges, in short a complete estimate of all factors affecting each unit's part in the operation. Yet even this illustration of Teutonic mastery of particulars paled beside the strategic achievement. Jodl summed up the triumph:

> The Pact of Munich is signed. Czechoslovakia as a power is out.... The genius of the Führer and his determination not to shun even a world war have again won victory without the use of force. The hope remains that the incredulous, the weak and the doubtful have been converted and will remain that way.

Jodl hoped in vain, for there were still plenty of doubts in OKH, the Army High Command, but the fact remained that Hitler had got Austria and the Sudetenland as he had said he would. He had insisted against all military advice that France and England would not go to war over Czechoslovakia. Not only had they not done so; they had positively helped him to his victories. In five years Germany had become the most powerful nation in Europe. There had been no war. 'Legality' plus the ever-present threat of force had once more paid off. Hitler's policies were signally vindicated. Churchill considered the Munich settlement to be a disastrous defeat and warned that it was only the beginning.

Indeed Hitler himself was far from satisfied. He felt that he had been cheated, robbed of his role as military conqueror. He still longed to 'smash' Czechoslovakia and ride in triumph through Bohemia. On 21 October he issued a further directive to his military leaders:

> The future tasks for the armed forces and the preparation for the

conduct of war resulting from these tasks will be laid down by me in a later directive.

Until this directive comes into force the armed forces must be prepared at all times for the following eventualities:

1. The securing of the frontiers of Germany.
2. The liquidation of the remainder of Czechoslovakia.
3. The occupation of the Memel district.

There are two points here. One is that the Wehrmacht was now required to prepare for the conduct of war; secondly the smashing of Czechoslovakia was a high priority still, and Czechoslovakia would be the first of non-Germanic lands to be seized as *Lebensraum* for the German people. In peace, as in war, Hitler's directives to the armed forces were the surest means of holding a looking-glass up to his mind, and there were two more of them before 1938 was out. All these directives were to be realized. In November a further eventuality was to be considered—the occupation of Danzig—while in December the Army was to re-plan the occupation of Czechoslovakia on the basis of there being no resistance worth the name.

Three months later, on 15 March 1939, this last directive was carried out. But before Hitler was able to bring about the conditions of no resistance, he and Göring subjected President Hacha to such a bullying that the poor old man fainted and had to be revived by the sinister Dr Morell, who later was to administer so dangerously to Hitler himself. Hitler gave Hacha no chance for anything but capitulation. That the German Army would invade his country was not in question. The only question was whether there would be a fight, in which case the Czech Army would cease to exist, or whether German troops would enter peaceably. Then the Führer could be generous. Perhaps Hacha's visit might facilitate this. In a few hours time the troops would march. 'He felt almost ashamed to say that for every Czech battalion a German division would come.' Göring even threatened to destroy Prague with his bombers. Hacha was unable to withstand such treatment and signed the paper which so effectively sentenced his country to death. The wording of it would have disarmed Mars himself:

The Czechoslovak President declared that, in order to serve

this object [the safeguarding of calm, order and peace in this part of Central Europe] and to achieve ultimate pacification, he confidently placed the fate of the Czech people and country in the hands of the Führer of the German Reich.

Diplomatic protests were thus answered before they were even made.

At 6 o'clock on 15 March the German Army poured through Bohemia and Moravia. All went well. Like the former occupation of the Sudetenland, preparations had been thorough. No detail was neglected. The military conqueror need have no qualms about the efficiency of his machine as he reviewed it in Prague. What is more OKH, nest of the reactionary, faint-hearted, visionless generals, had been out-manoeuvred, not even consulted as to the operation's execution. OKW had given orders direct to those commanders who actually carried it out.

Yet in spite of all these triumphs, something was changing, something which for the time being Hitler almost discounted, but which in the end would prove as great a stumbling block as any he encountered—British foreign policy. It was not that this policy had suddenly switched from one of appeasement to one of resistance, from one of peace to one of war. Negotiation was not thrown out of the window; it persisted as an instrument of policy right up until the outbreak of war. But the British had moved from one gear into another. Chamberlain's Government 'guaranteed' Poland, and recognizing that such guarantees were worthless unless backed by some sort of force set about, however belatedly, putting Britain's armed forces into better condition. Hitler's days of bluff, or rather winning great tracts of Europe for the Reich without resorting to force of arms, were over. He had achieved the two objectives, Austria and Czechoslovakia, which he had set himself when he talked to the generals in November 1937. But any idea that this was the end of the programme, indeed that he was bound to any such notion, was to misunderstand his own programme' which, as Allan Bullock puts it, was 'power, first his own power in Germany, and then the expansion of German power in Europe. The rest was window-dressing. This had been his programme before Prague, as it remained his programme afterwards. The only question was whether the other Powers would let him achieve the German domination of Europe without taking effective action to stop him.'

When Hitler held a meeting in May 1939, comparable with that of November 1937, he was in little doubt that war was inevitable. *Lebensraum* was still the problem. Expansion eastwards was the solution:

> We are left with the decision: To attack Poland at the first suitable opportunity. We cannot expect a repetition of the Czech affair. There will be war. Our task is to isolate Poland. The success of this isolation will be decisive.... There must be no simultaneous conflict with the Western Powers. If it is not certain that German-Polish conflict will not lead to war in the west, the fight must be primarily against England and France.

Hitler went on to outline how England, which he saw as his most dangerous enemy, might best be attacked. It was no longer necessary to invade England in order to conquer her. Cut off her supplies and capitulation must follow. The Army must therefore take those positions from which the Navy and Luftwaffe would strangle England's life-line. This in turn meant occupying Belgium and Holland, as well as defeating France. In this way conditions to fight a successful war against England would be created. If the 14 generals and admirals who were listening looked back on this meeting a year later, they would have been obliged to concede that Hitler's strategic survey was astonishingly prescient. So too was his argument that, had the German Army conducted a wheeling movement towards the Channel ports in 1914 and not aimed to encircle Paris, the result would have been decisive. A year later precisely this strategic decision was his.

To predict with such uncanny accuracy the course that a future war will take speaks of no common strategic gift. Hitler warned also that a conflict with England might be a long one. What his *Vorhersehung* did not tell him was that it would be so long that the incalculable might of the United States and Russia would interfere with his designs upon England. Herein lay the fallacy of blitzkrieg.

4

Blitzkrieg

The only way to predict the future is to have power to shape the future. Those in possession of absolute power can not only prophesy and make their prophecies come true, but they can also lie and make their lies come true.

Hoffer

In September 1922 von Seeckt wrote a memorandum on the need for German-Russian *rapprochement*. One passage refers to Poland as the core of the Eastern problem. Poland's existence he declared to be intolerable, incompatible with Germany's own vital interests. Therefore, Poland must 'disappear and will do so through her own inner weakness and through Russia—with our help'. He could scarcely have forecast Hitler's policy more concisely. And Hitler, unlike Seeckt, had power to shape the future.

He did not waste much time in using this power. Long before swallowing up the remainder of Czechoslovakia, he had turned his attention to Poland. Before we do the same we may perhaps ask ourselves whether, had Hitler stopped his 'programme' after absorbing Austria and Czechoslovakia, jettisoned his search for *Lebensraum*, and consolidated the Greater Reich, he would have gone down in history, as he himself had it, as the greatest German. It is to be doubted, for just as a soldier may only be called really great if he acquits himself with equal skill in adversity and victory, so those rulers whose greatness is indelibly stamped on history have usually triumphed over both fortune's favour and spite. It is at best an idle speculation for it was not in Hitler's nature to call a halt. No military conqueror has ever known when to stop. This ceaseless manipulation of the initiative ends always in its loss, and once Hitler interfered with Poland under the circumstances in which he did, he had, as it

15 Himmler and Hitler watch
Wehrmacht manoeuvres

16 Hitler's 'victory jig' at Compiegne

17   German troops land in Norway, April 1940

18   U–boat patrol in the Atlantic

were, committed himself to a programme which he could not stop, even had he wished to, until, or rather unless, all his enemies were first overcome.

In November 1938 Hitler's demands on Poland—they were fairly modest at this stage, for sticking to his opportunistic formula, *so oder so*, he was still in two minds as to whether with the help of a strong Poland, *Lebensraum* should be carved from Russia or with Russian aid Poland should once more be partitioned—Danzig's return to the Reich and extra-territorial communications with East Prussia, had been rejected by Beck, Polish Foreign Minister. Although Hitler at once amended his directive to the armed forces to include the operation for occupying Danzig which has already been mentioned, he still did not close his mind to an understanding with the Poles. Two events hardened his resolve—Poland's further answer to his demands and the attitude of Great Britain. Immediately after his last bloodless coup in March 1939—the annexation of Memelland, that province of Lithuania to the north of East Prussia—Hitler was in Berlin. While talking to the Army Commander-in-Chief, von Brauchitsch, the Führer made it clear that although Danzig was not to be the lever with which to destroy Poland, indeed that he wished to avoid driving Poland into the arms of Great Britain, nevertheless a satisfactory answer to his two requirements, Danzig and communications with East Prussia, would have to be forthcoming. But Poland's reply was essentially unchanged; moreover Beck told the German Ambassador in Warsaw that an attempt by Germany or the Danzig senate to upset Danzig's position as a Free City would be regarded by Poland as an act of aggression. Three days later Mr Chamberlain announced in the Commons that if Poland were attacked and her armed forces obliged to resist, the British and French Governments would lend Poland all support in their power. At this Hitler lost his temper, promising to 'cook them a stew that they'll choke on', and more practically issued on 3 April a new directive, *Fall Weiss*, for war with Poland. However much there might still be room for compromise on Poland's part, there was little of it in the wording of Operation White, whose language echoed that of Operation Green:

The aim will be to destroy Polish military strength and create in the East a situation which satisfies the requirements of national defence.... The political leaders consider it their task in this case to isolate Poland if possible, that is to say, to limit the war to Poland only.... The great objectives in the building up of the German armed forces will continue to be determined by the antagonism of the Western democracies.... The isolation of Poland will be all the more easily maintained, even after the outbreak of hostilities, if we succeed in starting the war with sudden, heavy blows and in gaining rapid successes.... The task of the Wehrmacht is to destroy the Polish armed forces. To this end a surprise attack is to be aimed at and prepared.

Hitler added three points to this directive: first that everything must be prepared in such a way that the operation could be carried out at any time from 1 September onward; second that OKW was to draw up a precise timetable co-ordinating activities of the three services; third that detailed plans must be submitted to OKW by 1 May.

Once again Hitler had set himself, long in advance, a precise date for military action. Once again he stuck to it. Much was to happen during the five months between issuing *Fall Weiss* and putting it into practice, but in the end what it amounted to was fulfilling the task which Hitler's directive assigned to the 'political leaders'—isolating and limiting the war to Poland. In one sense he was wholly successful in doing both, and the condition underlying his ability to do so was plucked straight from von Seeckt's memorandum of 17 years earlier which had promised that the obliteration of Poland, a fundamental principle of German policy, was to be attained with Russia's help. Before bringing off the Soviet-German Pact, Hitler had consolidated his alliance with Italy by the Pact of Steel, signed on 21 May. Article III contained the critical undertaking: 'If, contrary to the wishes and hopes of the contracting parties, it should happen that one of them is involved with another Power or Powers, the other contracting party will come immediately to its side as ally and support it with military forces on land, sea and in the air.' When Ciano returned to Rome after signing, King Victor Emmanuel told him: 'As long as the Germans have need of us they will be courteous ... but at the first opportunity they will reveal themselves as the great rascals they really are.' 1939 was a good year for predicting the future whether one had the power to shape it or not.

The Pact of Steel was followed almost at once by Hitler's conference of 23 May, which we have already touched on, and at which he announced both his intention to attack Poland at the first suitable opportunity, and, since this would mean war, the decisive need for Poland's isolation. If, in the worst case, Britain and France were to succeed in establishing an alliance with Russia, then he would be obliged to attend to them 'with a few annihilating blows', but such a turn of events was unlikely. Indeed 'it is not impossible that Russia will show herself to be disinterested in the destruction of Poland'. *So oder so*; now that it was becoming clearer that Poland was to be no willing tool of Germany's to Russia's disadvantage, the reverse of the coin began to shine more brightly. OKW's military plans, in which Hitler himself, as we shall later see, had a hand, were complete by late June. Only the date of the attack was left out of the final draft, and that Hitler had already decided.

Yet he had first to give substance to his half-promise that Russia would not ally herself with the Western Powers. The Soviet-German Pact was from the very start a bargain between enemies. Hitler had always realized that the achievement of his final aims—extension of the German empire in the east— would mean war with Russia. 'We cannot in any way evade the final battle between German race ideals and pan-Slav mass ideals', he told Rauschning in 1934.

> Here yawns the eternal abyss which no political interest can bridge.... We alone can conquer the great continental space, and it will be done by us singly and alone, not through a pact with Moscow. We shall take this struggle upon us. It will open to us the door to permanent mastery of the world. That does not mean that I will refuse to walk part of the road together with the Russians, if that will help us. But it will be only to return the more swiftly to our true aims.

To this true aim Hitler returned again and again, but he could not afford the luxury of war with Russia whilst devouring Poland. Stalin's motives were not dissimilarly mixed. He was as anxious as Hitler to postpone war, or even avoid it altogether, but he was not averse to buying those priceless strategic commodities, time and space, at Poland's expense. Who could now say that, strategically, he was in the wrong? When Litvinov, chief advocate of collective security with the West, had been replaced by Molotov as Foreign Minister in May 1939, the path to an understanding was made smoother. If Hitler were to stick to his timetable, there would not be all that time to lose.

The last ten days of August were eventful ones. On 22 August Ribbentrop flew to Moscow for the final negotiation of the Nazi-Soviet Pact of Non-Aggression; Ciano recorded in his diary that by signing this pact Germany had struck 'a master blow—the European situation is upset'; at the Berghof in Obersalzberg Hitler delivered another lecture to his senior commanders. 'There will probably never again be a man with such authority [and here it is to be hoped he was right] or who has the confidence of the whole German people as I have. My existence is therefore a factor of great value. But I can be eliminated at any moment by a criminal or a lunatic. There is no time to lose. War must come in my lifetime.' Before switching to the need for iron resolution, Hitler made a curious admission—'our economic situation is such that we cannot hold out for more than a few years'. Although the argument was deployed to justify action now, it was in fact a truth whose overriding importance was to shape Hitler's strategy as long as he held the initiative. He had thus underlined the intrinsic weakness of blitzkrieg, a military philosophy which only held water if all enemies could be defeated quickly. 'I shall give a propagandist reason for starting the war,' Hitler went on, 'no matter whether it is plausible or not. The victor will not be asked afterwards whether he told the truth or not.' It was in this way that Hitler proposed to make his lies come true. As for iron resolution he made it clear that like Richard III tear-dropping pity dwelt not in his eye. 'Close your hearts to pity. Act brutally. 80 million people must obtain what is their right. Their existence must be made secure. The strongest man is right.' His talk ended with a definite and earlier date for Operation White— 26 August, only four days away.

Hitler also maintained that the chances of intervention by Britain and France were negligible. Yet next day Chamberlain's letter to the Führer left no doubt that there would be no second Munich, that England was not bluffing. On 24 August the Nazi-Soviet Pact was signed, but still to Hitler's astonishment Britain and France took no backward step. It was instead he himself who did so. On 25 August, only 12 hours before H-hour and only just in time (for many units were on the move and were halted literally on the border) he postponed the invasion of Poland.

Yet he did not depart from his doctrine of *so oder so*—either Britain and France would persuade the Poles, as they had the Czechs, to give way; or the Allies would simply abandon them altogether; or he would be obliged to attack Poland and risk war, but it would be a war in which speed of smashing resistance in the east would neutralize hostility in the west. This reservation as to which course was to be followed did not deter him from setting a new zero hour for Operation White. 'Attack starts September 1', General Halder, Chief of the General Staff, noted in his diary on the afternoon of 26 August, 'Führer will let us know at once if we are not to strike.' Subsequent diplomatic activity, and there was much of it, in Berlin, Rome, Paris and London was not such that the Führer did let him know. Only capitulation by the Poles would have done so. On 31 August, by which time all was ready—the frontier incidents (Hitler's propaganda reason for starting the war), the broadcast of Poland's rejection of all German offers, and, most important of all, the military preparations themselves—Hitler signed Directive No 1 for the Conduct of the War:

1. Since the situation on Germany's Eastern frontier has become intolerable and all political possibilities of peaceful settlement have been exhausted, I have decided upon a *solution by force*.
2. *The attack on Poland* will be undertaken in accordance with the preparations made for Case White, with such variations as may be necessitated by the build-up of the Army which is now virtually complete.

Date of attack 1 September 1939
Time of attack 4.45 am.
This time also applies to operations at Gdynia, in the Bay of Danzig, and at the Dirschau bridge.
3. In the *West* it is important to leave the responsibility for opening hostilities unmistakably to England and France....

4. *Should England and France open hostilities* against Germany,
it will be the duty of the Armed Forces operating in the West ...
to maintain conditions for the successful conclusion of operations
against Poland....

Thus from the very outset Hitler's conduct of war—and this
pattern was to persist as long as he was able to initiate and
control its conduct—was characterized by a holding operation
on one front and a blitzkrieg on another. The blitzkrieg started
on time, on the very day which his directive of April had
selected; on the other front hostilities had not yet been formalized. But Hitler was ready with his threats. After declaring to
the Reichstag on 1 September that henceforth his life would
more than ever be devoted to his people and that he was now
'just the first soldier of the German Reich', he returned to the
Chancellory and indulged in another fit of sound and fury
against England. Dahlerus, the mediator from Sweden, reported
the scene:

> He grew more and more excited, and began to wave his arms as
> he shouted in my face: 'If England wants to fight for a year, I
> shall fight for a year; if England wants to fight two years, I shall
> fight two years....' He paused and then yelled, his voice rising
> to a shrill scream and his arms milling wildly: 'If England wants
> to fight for three years, I shall fight for three years....' The move-
> ments of his body now began to follow those of his arms, and
> when he finally bellowed; *'Und wenn es erforderlich ist, will ich
> zehn Jahre kämpfen',** he brandished his fist and bent down so
> that it nearly touched the floor.

This scene is reminiscent of Napoleon shouting at Metternich
that 'a man such as I am does not concern himself much about
the lives of a million of men',† and flinging his hat into a corner
of the room. *'C'est un homme perdu'*, murmured Metternich to
Berthier as he left the Emperor. Napoleon had reminded Metternich before this outburst that unlike himself, brought up in the
field, the Austrian Chancellor had no idea what went on in the
mind of a soldier. But Metternich did know that what went on

* 'And, if necessary, I will fight for ten years.'
† In December 1939 Hitler estimated that the campaign in the west
would cost him a million men—'but it would cost the enemy that too,
and the enemy cannot stand it'.

were unending thoughts of further victories. All his arguments for peace were in vain. 'Misfortune, like success,' he observed despairingly to Napoleon, 'hurries you to war.'

Ciano must have felt a comparable despair when a few weeks before Hitler's raving to Dahlerus, he had attempted to dissuade the Führer from taking the final steps to war. 'Hitler is very cordial,' noted Ciano in his diary, 'but he, too, is impassive and implacable in his decision.' Surrounded by maps, immersed in military calculations Hitler showed what Ciano called 'a truly profound military knowledge'. In demonstrating the superiority of Germany's strategic position, he declared that after the conquest of Poland, which could be expected in a short time, Germany would be able to assemble a hundred divisions on the West Wall for a general conflict.* Hitler was soon to have further cause for such confidence. The Wehrmacht had certainly undergone an unprecedented expansion against the General Staff's advice. It had taken on tasks which might have been judged quite beyond its resources. The risks were undeniable. Yet when eventually the only test that counted was applied to it, the test of war, the Wehrmacht turned out to be one of the most efficient, adaptable and successful military machines the world had seen. There were many causes for it. New weapons, sound and original tactics, a different brand of commander, Hitler's own will-power and drive coupled with a bold strategy, the total commitment of the soldiers themselves. But it was not any single one of these which made the Wehrmacht so irresistible a force. It was in the combination of planning, weapons, tactics and leadership that its quality was incomparable. There was something more. It was that Seeckt's *Führerheer* had not just survived. It had flourished on the revolutionary spirit of National Socialism. The Wehrmacht was an army of leaders who really believed all the propaganda about *Herrenvolk*. The master race was about to demonstrate to the *Untermenschen* of Poland how rapidly a campaign could be fought and won. Hitler gave it a fortnight. He was only a few days out.

'How good bad reasons and bad music sound,' commented

* By the end of November [1939] Allied intelligence estimated that 97-99 divisions were already concentrated on the western front, facing Holland, Belgium, Luxembourg, and France. *Official History*.

Nietzsche, 'when we march against an enemy.' Hitler had given plenty of bad reasons and no doubt his military bands had played plenty of bad music during their march to the Polish frontier. How good they sounded may be questioned, for the German people did not greet Hitler's war with the enthusiasm they had shown in 1914. Grave, even sullen, silence was their response. But how much better than either reasons or music sounded immediate and total victory.

The principles of blitzkrieg were, as we have seen, surprise, speed and concentration. Each was aided by the other. Surprise made for speed; speed enhanced surprise; concentration bolstered both. In the Polish campaign each had its own particular manifestation. Surprise was achieved by negotiating until the last moment and then attacking without even a declaration of war. Hand in hand with concentrated *Schwerpunkte*, speed was assured firstly because the Luftwaffe eliminated the Polish air forces and disrupted the enemy's command and communications, secondly, as von Manstein has it, because of 'the tearing open of the enemy's front by tank formations which penetrated deep into his rear areas'. This was the very essence of blitzkrieg —the deep breakthrough which paralysed opposition and led to what Clausewitz called the battle of annihilation, when the enemy, with moral and material resources exhausted, is no longer able to wage war.

The truth was, of course, that the Poles were from the start in a strategically hopeless position. Germany was able to attack from three sides, and so be well placed to outflank whatever forces Poland might deploy west of the Vistula (the only natural defensive line) in the great salient which stuck out westwards, threatened from the north by Pomerania and East Prussia, from the south by Silesia and Slovakia. Yet not to defend western Poland would be to give up those strategic commodities—coal, oil, armaments, industry—indispensable to defence. As it was the Polish Commander-in-Chief, Marshal Smigly-Rydz, strung his six armies out along the frontier, with some reserves near Warsaw, in an attempt to contest the German advance everywhere, so aggravating his strategic dilemma with a tactical deployment which most suited the German plan of massive *Schwerpunkte* from East Prussia, Pomerania and Silesia-

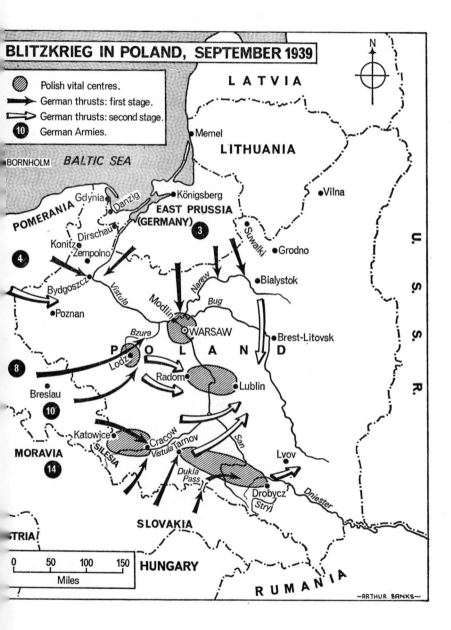

BLITZKRIEG IN POLAND, SEPTEMBER 1939

Polish vital centres.

German thrusts: first stage.

German thrusts: second stage.

10 German Armies.

LATVIA

Memel

LITHUANIA

BORNHOLM *BALTIC SEA*

Vilna

Gdynia Danzig Königsberg

POMERANIA EAST PRUSSIA **3**

(GERMANY)

Suwalki Grodno

Konitz Dirschau

4 Zempolno

Bialystok

Bydgoszcz *Vistula* Modlin *Narew*

Bug

Poznan

Bzura WARSAW

P O L A N D Brest-Litovsk

8 Lodz

Radom Lublin

Breslau

10

Katowice Cracow Tarnov

MORAVIA SILESIA *Vistula* *San* Lvov

14 *Dukla Pass*

Drobycz *Dniester*

Stryj

SLOVAKIA

TRIA

0 50 100 150 HUNGARY

Miles

R U M A N I A

~ARTHUR BANKS~

Moravia-Slovakia. Two great pincer movements were made, employing some 45 divisions, the first to envelop and destroy Polish forces west of the Vistula, the second driving east of Warsaw and cutting off all Poland west of the line Bialystok-Brest Litovsk-River Bug.

One of the formations which tore open the enemy's front was Guderian's XIX Corps, containing one panzer and two motorized infantry divisions, whose task was to advance from Pomerania, cross the Brahe between Zempolno and Konitz, and move as fast as possible to the Vistula thus cutting off enemy forces in the Polish Corridor. He described what it was like at H-hour, and unlike any previous corps commander he accompanied the leading tanks in an armoured command vehicle, enabling him to keep in touch with his own headquarters and the divisions under his command. This first experiment in commanding from the front had an unfortunate beginning:

> On 1 September at 0445 hrs the whole corps moved simultaneously over the frontier. There was a thick ground mist at first which prevented the air force from giving us any support. I accompanied the 3rd Panzer Brigade, in the first wave, as far as the area north of Zempelburg where the preliminary fighting took place. Unfortunately the heavy artillery of the 3rd Panzer Division felt itself compelled to fire into the mist, despite having received precise orders not to do so. The first shell landed 50 yards ahead of my command vehicle, the second 50 yards behind it. I reckoned that the next one was bound to be a direct hit and ordered my driver to turn about and drive off. The unaccustomed noise had made him nervous, however, and he drove straight into a ditch at full speed.

But this uncharacteristic incident did not alter the nature and the devastation of blitzkrieg. All that Liddell Hart had supposed, all that Guderian had trained for, came about. The Luftwaffe commanded the skies, reconnoitring, bombing, terrorizing, paralysing, the Stukas screaming and shooting, supporting the panzer units, which easily broke through the Polish lines and drove deep into enemy territory. Nor were they alone on the ground. Mechanized artillery, motorized infantry kept up; even the marching infantry seemed to advance with terrifying speed. It was all too much for the Poles. They were simply overwhelmed. Courage, however, they were not short of. Guderian reported that on 3 September during the battle for the Corridor some of his panzers had been charged by a Polish Cavalry Brigade with sword and lance. Their losses were appalling. So were those of a Polish artillery regiment overrun by panzers (Hitler himself was astonished by the destruction when he visited on 5 September), of Polish infantry and of their supply columns. In annihilating these another part of the blitzkrieg doctrine came to pass.

All was over in about two weeks as Hitler had prophesied. The first of the two great pincers had done its work during the first week. On 7 September Halder was already making plans to move divisions to the West Wall. The second pincer closed on 17 September when Guderian's XIX Corps joined hands with the spearheads of General List's 14th Army. They met 50 miles south of Brest-Litovsk, and it was at this town, where more than 20 years before Imperial Germany had imposed peace on the newly formed Soviet Republic, that the Russian and German armies effected the last partition of Poland. Russia had not exactly shown herself 'disinterested' in Poland's destruction. Stalin's bill was a heavy one—half Poland and the three Baltic States of Estonia, Latvia and Lithuania. But from Hitler's point of view the 'final solution' of the Eastern problem could wait. Having won his first campaign in the east, it would now be necessary to turn his attention to the west.

There were plenty of tactical lessons from this campaign for the world to take note of. The peerless pair, Panzer and Stuka, had prevailed not so much because of numbers but because together their velocity had been irresistible, especially so by a defence which had been essentially linear. In this one key circumstance was revealed, or concealed (according to who was examining it), all that mattered about the tactical handling and control of large armoured forces, and the antidote thereto. Mobility could only be matched by mobility; deep penetration could only be countered by great depth and adaptability in defence; panzers must be met by anti-tank guns, which were themselves partnered by tanks, infantry and guns; integration of all arms, including aircraft, had come to stay; command itself took on new horizons, for much more detailed decision-making had to be left to those executing the plan, which itself should be general, but with an overall tactical purpose clear and common to all. Reliable communications were paramount. Above all leadership at every level had to be resolute, fast-thinking and dynamic—like blitzkrieg itself.

Hitler's part in all this had been considerable. Indeed but for him it clearly would not have come about. He had seen early on the potential of blitzkrieg, then set about creating a Wehrmacht which could make war *blitzartig schnell*. He had then contrived to bring about the political and strategic conditions which made possible the nature of the Polish campaign itself, that is to say three-directional *Schwerpunkte* to pulverize Poland while the West sat and watched, and Russia, as Seeckt had predicted and Hitler himself had arranged, helped him to make Poland disappear. He had achieved the isolation of Poland as he said he would. He had put Germany in an unassailable strategic position—for the duration of a blitzkrieg. Next, in his directives—and they were his—Hitler laid down objectives, the aims which were to be realized by military action. He went further as to method and timing, all-important factors. They really were Directives for the Conduct of the War. In short his grip of strategy was complete. He determined what the armed forces were to do and when they were to do it.

But he went still further than this. To the consternation of the General Staff, for by doing this Hitler was invading a province they thought of as peculiarly, indeed exclusively, their own, he said how they were to do it. It will be remembered that when Hitler issued his directive for *Fall Weiss* in April 1939, he called for detailed military plans to be submitted to OKW, that is to him, a month later. For this first operation of war he was not content to confine his control of affairs to political and strategic considerations. He went through all the orders, down to regimental level, for the first three days of the operation. Worse, he criticized and even altered them. He was now dictating to the General Staff on matters of tactics. How different might have been the subsequent history of his interference in the broader battlefields of Africa, Italy, Normandy and Russia if he had made a hash of it. But he did not. He was right again.

In particular Hitler had completely altered the plan for

capturing the key bridge at Dirschau and had personally worked out all the details. It was a much bolder plan than that recommended by the General Staff, and foresaw a speed of advance into Poland far greater than the generals thought possible. Yet in the event the breakthrough was even faster than Hitler had supposed. His alterations to tactical planning had been more than justified by the battle itself—a circumstance hardly calculated either to reconcile the generals to Hitler's interference or to restore Hitler's dwindling confidence in the generals' mastery of their profession. When the campaign was over, therefore, and the completeness of its success is perhaps best illustrated by numbers and time—the Polish air force destroyed in two days; the Polish Army disrupted as a fighting force within a week; all resistance at an end in less than a month; cost to the Germans some 10,000 killed, 30,000 wounded with half Poland as the prize—when all this was over, Hitler was in no mood to be 'lectured' by the generals. Yet this is precisely what they tried to do. This further confrontation was provoked by the Führer's intention, as soon as it became clear that the Allies were not prepared to make peace, to attack in the west at the earliest possible date.

On 27 September, the day Warsaw capitulated after being subjected to savage bombing, Hitler informed the Wehrmacht Commanders-in-Chief of this intended attack 'since the Franco-British army is not yet prepared for it'. He went so far as to select a date—12 November. The response from his Commanders-in-Chief was that no plans had been made for such an operation, and von Brauchitsch and Halder even submitted a memorandum three days later giving their reasons for conducting a defensive war in the west. True to his custom of exploring all avenues before making a final decision, Hitler accepted the memorandum without exploding, and on 6 October told the Reichstag that he had offered peace to the West provided they recognized his conquest of Poland. Even before the predictably unenthusiastic replies from France and Britain, he seemed to have abandoned this peace offensive, for on 10 October he again summoned his senior commanders and read them a memorandum which he had drawn up the previous day. Its language was uncompromising. The German war aim was military settlement with the West, and by settlement he meant the destruction of their ability to interfere with German domination of Europe. His War Directive No 6 gave further planning guidance:

1. Should it become evident in the near future that England, and, under her influence, France also, are not disposed to bring the war to an end, I have decided, without further loss of time, to go over to the offensive. . . .

3. I therefore issue the following orders for the further conduct of military operations:

(a) An offensive will be planned on the northern flank of the Western front, through Luxembourg, Belgium, and Holland. This offensive must be launched at the earliest possible moment and in greatest possible strength.

(b) The purpose of this offensive will be to defeat as much as possible of the French Army and of the forces of the allies fighting on her side, and at the same time to win as much territory as possible in Holland, Belgium, and Northern France, to serve as a base for the successful prosecution of the air and sea war against England and as a wide protective area for the economically vital Ruhr.

(c) The time of the attack will depend upon the readiness for action of the armoured and motorized units involved. These units are to be made ready with all speed. It will depend also upon the weather conditions obtaining and foreseeable at the time . . . .

8. I request Commanders-in-Chief to submit to me their detailed plans based on this directive at the earliest moment . . .

No one could complain about the strategy envisaged here. It was when Hitler on 27 September confirmed that X-day for this operation, *Fall Gelb,* would be 12 November that he brought to a head once more the opposition of the generals, who were convinced that it could not succeed at that time. It was not the idea of extending the war to the West that they jibbed at; it was Hitler's evident determination to commit the Army to an operation which they believed was bound to fail. Von Brauchitsch, Army Commander-in-Chief was given the unenviable task of making two petitions to the Führer—first that a major offensive was out of the question during the fogs and bogs of autumn; second, and here he was treading on even more dangerous ground, OKH, ever-sensitive about Hitler's interference in the Polish campaign, would be glad of an assurance that in future they alone would be responsible for conducting military operations. Neither proposition was to the Führer's liking. But when von Brauchitsch made the error of casting aspersions on the fighting spirit of the German soldier in Poland, the storm broke. Hitler accused the Army of cowardice, of disloyalty, of sabotaging his efforts to rearm the Wehrmacht, of defeatism, of no proper belief in his genius. He poured every piece of invective he could think of on the unfortunate Brauchitsch, who bent before the storm and retired to Zossen, OKH headquarters, vanquished, in a state of severe shock, and incoherent.

Hitler was never one to forego an advantage. Although he postponed Operation Yellow because of bad weather (and went on postponing it throughout the winter) he once more sent for the generals to his Chancellory on 23 November and treated them to another tirade, whose principal purport was the need for belief in victory and for absolute unity of purpose. The trouble with German leaders in the past, men like Bismarck and Moltke, was that they had not been hard enough, unlike himself—'the hardest man in centuries'. Military solutions were only found by striking at favourable moments. At present, while Germany enjoyed the advantage of a one-front war, such moments were at hand. Russia was not a danger for the time being and Russia in any case could be dealt with when Germany was free in the west:

> Everything is determined by the fact that the moment is favourable now.... As the last factor I must in all modesty name my own person: irreplaceable. Neither a military nor a civil person could replace me.... I am convinced of my powers of intellect and decision.... My decision is unchangeable. I shall attack France and England at the most favourable and quickest moment.... Every hope of compromise is childish.... I have to choose between victory and destruction. I choose victory.... As long as I live I shall think only of the victory of my people. I shall shrink from nothing and shall destroy everyone who is opposed to me.... If we come through this struggle victoriously—and we shall—our time will enter into the history of our people. I shall stand or fall in this struggle. I shall never survive the defeat of my people. No capitulation to the forces outside; no revolution from within.

Hitler may have been a consummate liar. But just as he was

able to forecast strategic dispositions with uncanny accuracy, so some of his more frenzied exhortations had an astonishingly prophetic ring. This one did more and rallied the generals to his views. Von Hassell reported that the majority of those present were convinced, deeply moved and full of enthusiasm.

The ideas Hitler had written about in *Mein Kampf* and discussed with Rauschning were now being translated into reality. Smash Poland; then turn West and destroy the enemy there; then turn back East again for a final solution to the problem of *Lebensraum*. But since the origin of these ideas, how solidly circumstances seemed to be lining up with him—total vindication of blitzkrieg in Poland; no interference by the West either during the campaign or since, indeed on land a passive France and England; the East secure. His attack in the West, moreover, would be 'the end of the World War, not just a single action'. Much of what Hitler had to say about strategy was sound, even brilliant, but here he was on less sure ground. For by attacking in the west he would be embarking on the first of the real battles for Europe. Far from ending the world war, it was exactly this that it would lead to. The matter of timing, however, had still to be resolved.

War Directive No 8, issued on 20 November, ordered that a high state of preparedness must be maintained so that the offensive could be mounted at a moment's notice and thus take immediate advantage of favourable weather. This directive, which supplemented the previous Operation Order, contains one significant modification to the planning for land operations. 'All precautions will be taken to enable the main weight of attack to be switched from Army Group B to Army Group A should the disposition of enemy forces at any time suggest that Army Group A could achieve greater success.' When *Fall Gelb* was finally executed it was to be this very point which was decisive in bringing about Hitler's most startling victory, and since by then he had convinced himself—not wholly without reason—that it was his own plan, one more step was taken on the road to infallibility, megalomania and ruin. But first there was to be what Hitler had called for in *Mein Kampf*—one last decisive battle with France.

5

Sichelschnitt—Cut of the Sickle

I place a low value on the French Army's will to fight. Every
army is a mirror of its people. . . . After the first setbacks it will
swiftly crack up.

Hitler, November 1939

'The best thing between France and England,' was Jerrold's
comment on the Anglo-French alliance, 'is the sea'—a far cry,
much earlier delivered, from Churchill's thanking God for the
French Army. But Churchill was thinking primarily of its size
and armaments rather than its quality or tactical dexterity. In
this respect it was by the 1930s moribund. If a soldier were
required to point at the one single feature of military activity
which is of overriding importance, from which all else stems, it
would be command he would point at. It is the commander
who applies his imagination in making strategic plans, who
organizes and trains his armed forces, who sees to it that they
are properly equipped and administered, who makes them
capable of anything, and then who inspires and leads them,
above all who imbues them with the offensive spirit, the will, as
well as the skill, to win. To win demands success in combat,
and combat, as we have seen, means moving about, controlling,
and applying agents of violence. Macaulay wrote of Hampden
that he knew the essence of war to be violence and that 'moderation in war is imbecility'. Yet the whole of France's Maginot
Line policy preached the deterring of violence and the practice
of moderation. 'Phoney War'—the *drôle de guerre*—was the
result.

After Poland's capitulation, Gamelin, Supreme Commander

of the French Armies, decided to pull back to the Maginot Line. 'What else did you expect?' asked one of his subordinate generals. His question embodied the French Army's defensive stance. Vercors with his battalion at Embrun recalled that inactivity created 'a lazy scepticism and a comforting thought that things would turn out all right without any actual scrapping'. When his commanding officer spoke to the men it was as if the German Army and its likely intentions did not exist. No martial spirit was abroad. When the battalion moved to Romans he noted that 'the important thing was to kill time—for want of an enemy'. He observed without being reassured some of his elderly brother officers—'veterans of the Great War, bemedalled down to their bellies, but a bit flabby with wine and fat, and I was worried how they would manage against the steely-eyed athletic young SS men whom I had seen on the Kehl Bridge'. Two British soldiers, who were to find great renown in the war, had comparable misgivings. Alan Brooke, a Corps Commander at the time, could find little comfort in the security of the Maginot Line. If it broke, he suspected, the French fighting spirit might break too. Montgomery, commanding the 3rd Division, noted that offensive action against Germany was confined to bombing with propaganda leaflets. 'If this was war, I did not understand it.' What sort of plans were there for dealing with blitzkrieg should it come, or were the Allies so possessed by their defensive thinking that they believed the Sitzkrieg would go on for ever? As has been shown, it was not for want of trying to persuade his commanders that Hitler had not yet attacked. What about the French command?

Alistair Horne sums up the weakness of the French position when he says that they had learned nothing and forgotten everything. French strategy had not changed in 20 years. It was still to preserve the integrity of both French manpower and French soil until Allied military strength could be built up sufficiently to think about an offensive. This might be all right as long as there was no fighting to do. But what if there were blitzkrieg in the west? Would the Maginot Line be proof against Panzer and Stuka? Or if Hitler violated the neutrality of Belgium and Holland—a breach he had already dismissed as 'meaningless'

—and swept through to northern France in a repetition of the Schlieffen Plan, how would the integrity of French soil be preserved without stopping the Germans in Belgium?

In his masterly analysis of what was wrong, Alistair Horne explains that Gamelin was incapable of exercising command which would be effective in countering the type of battle that the Germans were planning. Not only was his area of command far too wide—so much so indeed that he later delegated the north-eastern front to General Georges—but he actually had no radio communications in his remote headquarters at Vincennes. So little notice was he prepared to take of what had happened in Poland, of the new tactics and method of command demonstrated there, that he was convinced of the Wehrmacht's being at a serious disadvantage because its generals had not been generals in 1914-18. He might have done well to remember France's own greatest soldier—only 27 when he beat the Austrians in Italy, only 31 at Marengo and 36 at Austerlitz, while the experienced generals who went down to him were between 60 and 70. In 1940 Gamelin was 68.

He set infinite store by experience, yet totally misunderstood its nature. Wilde called experience another name for mistakes, and Frederick the Great made it clear that it was only of any value if the right conclusions were drawn from it. Gamelin's 'experience' of war had been on Joffre's operations staff and as a divisional commander. Before the Polish campaign he had maintained that tank breakthroughs were impossible; anti-tank guns would always stop them. After this had been shown to be nonsense, he rejected the 'experience' of Poland as inapplicable. What had happened there could not happen in France. The whole concept of blitzkrieg—armoured and air breakthrough supported by mechanized and dismounted follow-up formations to widen and deepen the penetration, while air forces disrupted the enemy's command and communication systems—all this was ignored, dismissed or simply miscomprehended by the tactical doctrinaires of the French High Command. It might have worked in practice; but how could it work in theory? The purpose of tanks was still to support methodical infantry advances, and that was that.

Having closed their eyes to tactical realities, they proceeded to do the same with strategic ones. Since a German attack was most likely to come through Belgium, they argued, the invasion must be met there. The only question was where. Gamelin's proposal to base his master plan on the Dyle line, extended towards Breda, brought a strong protest from General Georges who pointed to that very weakness which in the event the Germans were to exploit so drastically. The way in which you conduct defence is, of course, always affected more by what forces are available than is the way in which you attack. You must guard against more contingencies; freedom of choice is forfeit; compromise is apt to speak with too loud a voice; reserves disappear; adaptability goes out of the window. What Georges feared was committing so much strength to the Low Countries that there would be no adequate reserves left if a German attack there turned out to be no more than secondary, a diversion to facilitate the success of a 'force breaking out in the centre, on our front between the Meuse and Moselle'. Might not the supposed German intention to attack in the north be, in short, another gigantic piece of bluff?

Gamelin's doubts were put at rest by the capture of German documents at Mechelen in January 1940, which gave the operational plans for invading Holland and Belgium. The main thrust would come that way. Gamelin's final deployment of his 100-odd divisions (including the British Expeditionary Force) therefore allowed for a strong right flank based on the Maginot Line, a strong left flank for the Dyle-Breda position, and a weak centre opposite the Belgian Ardennes, with nothing behind it. 'What a standing temptation,' writes Alistair Horne, 'the spectacle of this French line, then, so weak in the centre, might present to an opposing captain of audacity and genius!'

It was as just such a captain that Hitler, Commander-in-Chief of the Wehrmacht, saw himself, and there were two main reasons for his succumbing to the temptation. There has been much controversy as to who was responsible for *Sichelschnitt*, Cut of the Sickle, the plan so fittingly named which won the Battle for France. There were many hands in it, it is true, but principal credit must go to four men: von Manstein as the detailed architect; von Rundstedt, who commanded Army Group A, as the fervent backer and ultimate executor of the plan; Halder, once convinced—and this took a long time—of the plan's soundness, for the thoroughness and excellence of his organization; and Hitler himself, because he was thinking along similar lines, because he insisted that Manstein's ideas be effected, and because responsibility for the plan, as Supreme Commander, was ultimately his. The first reason therefore in yielding to this temptation was that a plan to burst through the French centre and thereby destroy their whole Army coincided exactly with Hitler's own ideas about the value of surprise, of boldness, of risk, of sudden, unexpected, hammer-like blows, paralysing in their strength and velocity. All that he had so often said about planning campaigns which would utterly smash all resistance and be totally decisive was borne out by von Manstein's concept of defeating and annihilating the whole of the enemy force fighting in Belgium, or north of the Somme, and not just throwing them back frontally. *Sichelschnitt*'s final form was many months in evolving and was further influenced by Hitler's second reason—capture of the top secret documents at Mechelen—thereby putting paid to any notion that an offensive whose principal *Schwerpunkt* would in fact (as opposed to what the Allies might be deceived into anticipating) be through Belgium and Holland could produce the decisive results he was set on.

The first indication Hitler gave that he was thinking like this was as early as October 1939 when he confounded Brauchitsch and Halder by suggesting that a main attack from south of Namur to Amiens might 'cut off and annihilate the enemy'. A few days later, dissatisfied with OKH's plans which were still for limited, frontal attacks, he mentioned to Jodl, OKW Chief of Operations, a new 'brainwave'. This supplemented his former one, and its originality lay in his proposal that one *Schwerpunkt* should strike through the Ardennes to Sedan—sinister locality in the annals of Franco-Prussian conflict—and on from there.

Von Manstein's ideas—he was at this time Chief of Staff to von Rundstedt, commander of Army Group A—also sprang from his conviction that a main thrust in the north against what was expected to be a powerful Allied defence could not lead to decisive victory. By shifting the main weight further south, however, it might be possible to penetrate behind the Allied defences in Belgium. It was the difference between pushing against the maximum opposition and cutting it off at the roots, as a sickle does with corn. While Hitler was still toying with his new idea and allotting Guderian's XIX Corps (of two panzer and one motor divisions) to the southern thrust at Sedan, von Manstein, constantly reviewing and revising his plan and following discussions with Guderian, plumped firmly in a memorandum dated 6 December for the main *Schwerpunkt* to be von Rundstedt's Army Group A. When therefore von Manstein was finally able to pour out his theories to Hitler himself on 17 February 1940, by which time *Gelb* had been indefinitely postponed, it is hardly surprising that the Führer listened with rapt enthusiasm. A new directive instantly emerged:

> The objective of offensive 'Yellow' is to deny Holland and Belgium to the English by swiftly occupying them; to defeat, by an attack through Belgian and Luxembourg territory, the largest possible forces of the Anglo-French army; and thereby to pave the way for the destruction of the military strength of the enemy. The main weight of the attack across Belgium and Luxembourg will be south of the line Liege-Charleroi.

When this directive had been translated into an actual plan, it was clear that the modification foreseen in War Directive No. 8, which we glanced at in the last chapter, had come to pass. Von Bock's Army Group B, with some 29 divisions including 3 panzer divisions, was to be the bait, a powerful fighting bait, which would draw the Anglo-French forces into Holland and Northern Belgium, and allow von Rundstedt's Army Group A of 45 divisions, including 7 *panzer divisions*, to smash through the Ardennes and swarm over the Meuse between Dinant and Sedan. The *Schwerpunkt* of *Schwerpunkte* would fittingly enough be Guderian's XIX Corps at Sedan. Meanwhile von Leeb's Army Group C would threaten the Maginot Line.

Hitler did not confine himself to the grand tactical plan. As in the Polish campaign he got down to detail. At his insistence most of the powerful Mark III and IV panzers were to be transferred from Army Group B to Army Group A, where their fire power could hardly have been dispensed with. It seems extra-

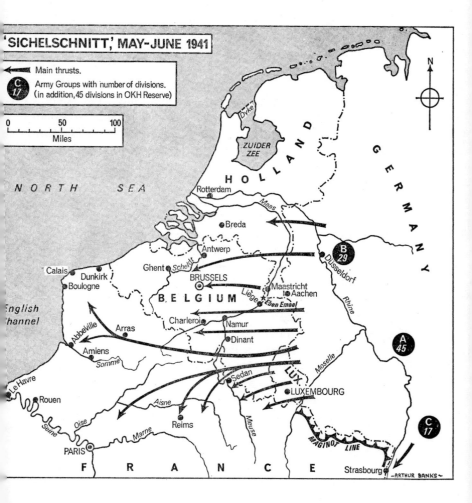

'SICHELSCHNITT', MAY-JUNE 1941

Main thrusts.

C 17 Army Groups with number of divisions.
(in addition, 45 divisions in OKH Reserve)

0   50   100
Miles

NORTH   SEA

HOLLAND

GERMANY

Dyke

ZUIDER ZEE

Maas

Rotterdam

Breda

Antwerp

B 29 Düsseldorf

Calais
Dunkirk
Boulogne

Ghent *Scheldt*

BRUSSELS

Maastricht
Liège Aachen
Eben Emael

Rhine

BELGIUM

English Channel

Abbeville
Arras
Charleroi   Namur
Dinant

Amiens
Somme

A 45

Moselle

LUX.

Le Havre
Rouen
Sedan
LUXEMBOURG

Seine   *Oise*   *Aisne*

Reims

Marne

Meuse

C 17

PARIS

MAGINOT LINE

F   R   A   N   C   E
Strasbourg

—ARTHUR BANKS—

ordinary that so obvious an adjustment was left to the Supreme Commander. Moreover Hitler personally worked out highly unorthodox plans for such special operations as capturing the vital Eben-Emael fort by glider and parachute assault and other airborne exploits to seize bridges and forts on the line of advance. For once his own confidence was matched by that of the General Staff, all of whom took pleasure in the singularity, simplicity and sheer beauty of the plan. It was, as we have noted, one of the occasions when Hitler and the General Staff had worked together in something like harmony. The Führer's intuition together with his determination to get von Manstein's plan adopted were matched by OKH's professional excellence and the thoroughness with which they turned strategic opportunity into the tactical means of defeating France with a single blow.

The plan is not without its critics, however. It did not go far enough for some, did not envisage how to exploit its own success, how to end the war, that is to say, assuming always that the Allied armies were destroyed, how to knock England out, and so fulfil Hitler's claim that an attack in the west would put a stop to the world war. But to defeat England, Hitler had to defeat also the Royal Navy and the Royal Air Force. *Sichelschnitt* could scarcely comprehend so wholly different a strategic operation. Hitler failed to end the war in 1940 not by winning the Battle of France, but by losing the Battle of Britain. Had Göring gone about this latter undertaking in another way, who knows what the outcome might have been. Moreover, such criticism ignores the nature of blitzkrieg, and the whole opportunistic character of Operation Yellow. The breakthrough was everything, for it was this, Hitler believed, that would dismay the French Army—'after the first setbacks it will swiftly crack up'. Curiously enough Hitler was the one to put his finger on this very omission of planning, of not seeing the operation right through to the end. In March 1940 at a conference in the Chancellory, Guderian was explaining his plans to Hitler and the generals of Army Group A:

On the fourth day I would arrive at the Meuse; on the fifth day I would cross it. By the evening of the fifth day I hoped to have established a bridgehead on the far bank. Hitler asked: 'And then what are you going to do?' He was the first person who had thought to ask me this vital question. I replied: 'Unless I receive orders to the contrary, I intend on the next day to continue my advance westwards. The supreme leadership must decide whether my objective is to be Amiens or Paris. In my opinion the correct course is to drive past Amiens to the English channel.' Hitler nodded and said nothing more.

Something else was afoot in March 1940, and was further evidence of Hitler's boldness as a strategist, of the risks he was prepared to take once he had made his mind up. On 1 March he had signed his directive for the occupation of Denmark and Norway. Its purpose was to forestall British action in Scandinavia and the Baltic, secure Swedish ore for Germany and provide the Luftwaffe and Navy with additional bases to operate against England. As few forces as possible were to be used. Surprise, speed and skill were to make up for numbers. The success of these operations was remarkable in two respects— first it seemed to demonstrate in general that Germany could do what she liked, when she liked, and that the Allies, dithering in decision, feeble in conflict, were helpless to stop her; second it looked, despite severe German naval losses, as if even Britain's traditional naval omnipotence went for nothing in the face of the Wehrmacht.

What is more, in the first major clash with Germany, British arms, their achievements at Narvik and at sea notwithstanding, had suffered a serious reverse. They had, as in Pitt's day, been put ashore on the continent of Europe only to be beaten and chased out again. They had seen—although the lesson took long to sink in—that without proper air support, navies and armies could not effectively conduct amphibious operations. Not that Norway's acquisition was strategically so important for Germany, indeed it was the beginning of a process by which Hitler became prisoner of his own conquests, but psychologically this further display of invincibility fortified Germany and dismayed the Allies. The First Lord of the Admiralty, however, was not dismayed by failure of his first strategic project. He drew comfort from the losses suffered by the German Navy, which as he later recorded could be 'no factor in the supreme

issue of the invasion of Britain'. There was another result of
the Norwegian campaign from which Churchill and his country-
men could draw comfort—he became Prime Minister on 10
May, the very day that the sickle began cutting the Allies down.

The story of the battle for France has been told many times,
perhaps never more elegantly or more satisfactorily than by
Alistair Horne. We may therefore confine ourselves here to
tracing broadly what happened, what to some the battle was
like, and, most pertinent to our purpose, what Hitler's part in
it had been. What happened can really be told in three words.
The plan worked. It worked far better and far faster than
the Germans could ever have believed likely in spite of General
Fromm's confident claim that 'we shall push through Holland
and Belgium at one stroke, and finish off France in 14 days'.
Holland was swiftly occupied and capitulated. Hitler's ideas
about special operations to seize forts were completely vindicated. Eben-Emael fell to airborne attack in little more than
a day's fighting. The main thrust of Army Group A to the
Meuse and beyond was overwhelmingly successful; Guderian's
Corps poured through a hole made in the French line; Panzer
and Stuka demonstrated once more their peerlessness. In ten
days German spearheads reached Abbeville, three days later
Boulogne. On 27 May Belgium gave in. British forces, sandwiched between Army Groups A and B, fell back on Dunkirk,
from which, together with many French units, they were
evacuated by 4 June. The Germans then set about finishing off
the French who, true to Hitler's prediction that they would not
have the will to withstand setbacks, surrendered on 16 June.
Churchill's 'Thank God for the French Army' might almost be
said to have an undreamed of connotation in that Hitler's
decision to destroy it assisted the escape of the British Army.
Meanwhile Italy, eager to be in at the kill, had declared war on
10 June.

Perhaps the most far-reaching of tactical successes was
Guderian's crossing of the Meuse on 13 May and the subsequent expansion of this hole into a huge 50-mile gap through
which the panzers flooded, reaching the Channel a week later
and cutting the Allied armies in half. Rommel's 7th Panzer
Division on the right, that is the north, of von Kleist's Panzer

Group, reached the Meuse on the afternoon of 12 May. It was no picnic. He had to fight for a crossing:

> At Leffe weir we took a quick look at the footbridge, which had been barred by the enemy with a spiked steel plate. The firing in the Meuse valley had ceased for the moment and we moved off to the right through some houses to the crossing point proper. The crossing had now come to a complete standstill, with the officers badly shaken by the casualties which their men had suffered. On the opposite bank we could see several men of the company which was already across, among them many wounded.... Several of our tanks and heavy weapons were in position on the embankment east of the houses, but had seemingly already fired off almost all their ammunition. However, the tanks I had ordered to the crossing point soon arrived, to be followed shortly afterwards by two field howitzers ... soon the aimed fire of all weapons was pouring into rocks and buildings.... Under cover of this fire the crossing slowly got going again.... I now took over personal command of the 2nd Battalion of 7th Rifle Regiment and for some time directed operations myself.

Rommel was never one to lead from behind, and as Liddell Hart commented on this action, the assault thus boldly led was able 'to prise open the defence once they had gained sufficient space on the west bank to develop a manoeuvring leverage'.

Sichelschnitt was the ultimate justification of all that Guderian had ever claimed for the decisive nature of blitzkrieg. It must have given him infinite satisfaction to be in the van of his irresistible panzers. On 16 May all was going well:

> The fog of war that had confused us soon lifted. We were in the open now.... I passed an advancing column of the 1st Panzer Division. The men were wide awake and aware that we had achieved a complete victory, a breakthrough. They cheered and shouted remarks: 'Well done, old boy' and 'There's our old man' and 'Did you see him? That was hurrying Heinz' and so on.... Now roads had to be allotted among the three panzer divisions— the 6th, 2nd and 1st—which were pouring through the town [Montcornet] in their headlong drive towards the west.

Guderian goes on to explain that he now fully expected to put into practice all the ideas he had expressed to Hitler in March, to go on and on until they reached the English Channel. He simply could not believe that his superiors would be satisfied with deep bridgeheads over the Meuse or that they would want to halt the advance until the infantry formations came up. Least of all could he imagine that Hitler who had seemed to endorse his proposals for exploitation and who had been fascinated by the very boldness of Manstein's plan would be unnerved by his own risk-taking. But to his surprise and chagrin von Kleist, commanding the whole Panzer Group, directly ordered him to halt the advance. After a good deal of threats, 'resignations' and interventions, he was permitted to carry out further 'reconnaissance in force'. This was all he needed. A reconnaissance in force is open to all sorts of interpretation. By 18 May his panzers reached St Quentin; next day they were forcing the Somme; on 20 May Guderian himself was on the outskirts of Amiens watching 1st Panzer Division's attack; the day after that a unit of 2nd Panzer Division was at the Atlantic coast. Then, as neither he nor von Kleist had been told where to go next, they had to wait for orders, 'so the 21st of May was wasted'.

If this day was thrown away by Guderian's Corps, it was more actively and profitably spent by General Martel's force from 151st Infantry Brigade and 1st Army Tank Brigade, which in a battle near Arras held up the German attempt to cut off the BEF's withdrawal. Sergeant Hepple of the 7th Royal Tank Regiment sustained an exciting encounter with a German group of infantry and anti-tank guns:

> Near the main road west of Achincourt we came under anti-tank fire and received three hits. The effect was that of hitting a large stone at speed, and the track on the right-hand side was seen a yard or two in front of the tank. Two more shots followed, and then the guns were silenced by our fire, and that of the I tanks.... We were subjected to intense rifle fire for some minutes, and then left alone, apparently in the belief that we were all killed. After five or ten minutes about thirty to fifty Germans were congregated in groups on the road and to the right of us. We estimated the range of each group, and then opened fire. Many of the enemy fell, but some doubtless, were unhurt. Later an abandoned anti-tank gun, about 800 yards to our right front, was re-manned, but was seen to be deserted after we fired upon it.

This scrappy action, one of many such, does not sound all that formidable. But the mere fact of having to defend themselves against an attack at all threw the Germans off balance—Rommel thought that five British divisions were engaged—and delayed their advance.

What of the French? It was General Corap's 9th Army which was unfortunate enough to find itself in the path of von Rundstedt's *Schwerpunkt*. Vercors summed up the disaster which overtook Corap and the rest of them:

> This time, Giraudoux's* talent would have been incapable of keeping such illusions alive for long. After a period during which we kept victoriously 'containing' pockets and breaches in our positions, he was obliged to announce the disintegration of General Corap's army.... The wholesale retreat towards Dunkirk turned into an epic, but it was a sombre epic. The disaster was immeasurable. The French Army was smashed to pieces, cut to shreds by the tanks, nailed to the ground by the enemy's Stukas. A hundred miles from the front dazed soldiers were still streaming back.

Why had it happened? The truth was that the German superiority—not in numbers, where they were slightly inferior, but in leadership, training, tactics and spirit—was overwhelming. The Allied forces, strung out along the front with no depth, no proper reserves, no means of rapid movement, concentration or co-ordination, were no match for, simply had no chance against, fast, integrated, Luftwaffe-supported and supplied, armoured columns which struck hard and deep into Allied territory. On 5 June Hitler issued an order of the day: 'Dunkirk has fallen ... with it has ended the greatest battle of world history. Soldiers! My confidence in you knew no bounds. You have not disappointed me.' He was certainly right in saying that the battle had ended, for the final weeks before the French capitulated, in spite of some unexpectedly fierce fighting, was best summed up by Rommel—'the war has gradually turned into a lightning tour of France'.

Hitler then had not been disappointed in the Wehrmacht. Had, however, the Wehrmacht been disappointed in its Supreme Commander? There are two points we might examine here: his orders on 16 May to halt the panzer divisions, which so in-

* Chief of the Information Service.

furiated Guderian; second his alleged halting of the whole
advance on 24 May which led to the 'miracle' of Dunkirk. We
shall probably find him guilty on the first count, and in one
sense not guilty on the second. Ironically enough the former
did not much matter; the latter turned out to be a blunder of
incalculable proportions.

When Hitler became concerned about Guderian's flanks and
the danger of a counter-attack against them from the south, his
behaviour in the Führer HQ at Münstereifel was not that of a
commander who having given his orders, and supremely confident in them, in himself and his subordinates, retires to sleep
as Montgomery did. Excitable, talkative and always ready to
blame others, it appeared that the hardest man in centuries lost
his nerve for a day or two, not because things were going wrong,
but at a time when they were going superlatively well. The
central point of all that Guderian had for so long been trying
to persuade the sceptics was that once a panzer thrust had got
going, it must maintain momentum day and night. It must
never halt—to be located, checked, counter-attacked. The
enemy must be subjected continuously to unexpected, ever-
deepening, ever-broadening thrusts, disrupting reserves, communications, headquarters, supply areas, a never-ending, yet
ever more paralysing flow of integrated panzer, motor infantry,
artillery groups with the Stukas and transport aircraft to keep
them supported and supplied. All this was fundamental.

Yet as Halder recorded in his diary on 17 May: 'Führer is
terribly nervous. Frightened by his own success, he is afraid to
take any chance and so would rather pull the reins on us,' and
again next day: 'Führer keeps worrying about south flank. He
rages and screams that we are on the way to ruin the whole
campaign. He won't have any part in continuing the operation
in a westward direction.' In other words the astonishing success
of *Sichelschnitt*'s opening phases somehow caused Hitler to
forget the actual fount of this success. As it turned out, indeed
as we have seen from Guderian's account of things, Hitler's
interference was evaded and had no real impact in either
upsetting or enhancing the plan's effectiveness.

When we come to halting the panzers on 24 May, the story
is a different one. On 23 May von Kluge, Commander of 4th

Army with the bulk of the panzer divisions, proposed to von Rundstedt that his formations should 'halt and close up'. Von Rundstedt, convinced that the Allied armies were trapped, with his own Army Group well placed to be the anvil and von Bock's from the north, the hammer, agreed. The War Diary of 4th Army noted that the Army 'will, in the main, halt tomorrow [24 May] in accordance with Colonel-General von Rundstedt's order.' Thus it was the Army Group Commander, not Hitler, who gave the order. Hitler, visiting von Rundstedt on 24 May, endorsed it. The fact was, as the *Official History* reminds us, that the various generals concerned disagreed widely. Brauchitsch, Army Commander-in-Chief, wanted to put 4th Army under von Bock who would then continue to attack the Allies from east, south and west. Halder, his Chief of Staff, thought this a mistake. So did von Rundstedt who believed there was world enough and time. Bock himself was immersed in the business of driving a wedge between the Belgian and British armies. So that Hitler, in supporting von Rundstedt, overruled Brauchitsch.

We are now able to see that Hitler's error lay not in *initiating* the order to halt, but in allowing it to stand, in not seeing—after Guderian's triumphant demonstration of how right he had been all along—that the one thing, as Supreme Commander, he must not allow to happen was for the panzers to halt. The actual command arrangements were secondary. He should have made certain with the supreme tactical powers he wielded that the drive went on until the enemy annihilation was absolute. In this respect he was guilty. But it was the guilt of inaction, not of action. In continuing to leave the decision whether to go on or not to von Rundstedt, who did not do so, this guilt was prolonged. Yet on 26 May it was Hitler who intervened positively and ordered the attacks to continue. The *Official History* comes down with the view that neither Hitler's nor anyone else's orders allowed the BEF and others to escape. The Wehrmacht, soldiers, airmen and commanders alike tried, but failed. Whoever is to bear the blame, however, this failure was the Third Reich's Military Blunder No 1. Yet it cannot detract from the breathtaking results of *Sichelschnitt*. It had overcome France like a summer's cloud, and warranted special wonder. Sir John Wheeler-Bennett makes the point that when

Hitler, flushed with victory, created 12 Field Marshals on 19 July, having had a continuous run of 'evil good-fortune', he was at the summit of his success. His *Vorhersehung*, his strategy, his tactical instinct, his political intuition, his will-power—all had borne fruit. The generals 'looked upon him as a military genius and also as a fount of honour. There were no doubts in 1940'.

Alistair Horne, however, as we have already seen, contends that *Sichelschnitt*, apart from the tactical error of halting the panzers on 24 May, contained a fatal strategic flaw. No provision was made for finishing off England after defeating the French Army. We have seen too that there are flaws in the argument itself. Hitler had no quarrel with England, provided England gave him a free hand in Europe. He was convinced that England would make peace, and if not he had already outlined air and sea measures which would strangle the island. How was it possible to plan for total victory without first arranging to destroy the Royal Navy and the RAF. 'I do not say they cannot come,' observed St Vincent of Napoleon's Grande Armée, 'I only say they cannot come by sea.' Would the capture of the BEF (and at one time in the battle Churchill judged that only 30,000 might get away)—as many historians assume without examining the military factors—have resulted in Great Britain's surrender? British naval and air forces would presumably have been stronger, not having sustained the losses they did at Dunkirk. Churchill had already made it clear that whatever happened at Dunkirk, 'we shall fight on for ever and ever and ever'. Why should a Battle of Britain fought in June 1940 have been lost, when the Luftwaffe was at the limit of its operational and administrative resources, when it was so convincingly won three months later after the Luftwaffe had had time to recuperate and reorganize? If the same mistakes had been made by Göring in June as he made later, the result, we may surmise, would have been the same too.

Planning for total victory, for a single knock-out campaign, is no easy thing. It may be that the resources for such an undertaking simply are not to hand. Even when they are, it may not be done. Slogging victory at Alamein was followed by dull, inconclusive pursuit; surprise in French North Africa gave way to shocks at Kasserine Pass; when the Allies landed in Sicily in July 1943, the grand strategists had not made up their minds where to go next; Italy's expected capitulation was treated with so much dithering that no decisive strategic gain was wrested from it; the break-out from Normandy in August 1944 sparked off a strategic controversy which robbed it of real dividend. Hitler and the Wehrmacht had no monopoly of failing to plan war-winning campaigns in advance.

The real fault, as we shall see, was not neglecting to plan for a specific operation, the invasion of England. It was failure to plan and secure the resources for a long war. This was the fatal flaw of blitzkrieg, and obliged Hitler to cast about all over Europe to make up for this neglect. Having created the Wehrmacht and so triumphantly demonstrated both the infallibility of his own intuition and the invincibility of the machine which executed his strategy—on the threshold, as it were, of absolute victory, with his mighty armed force (before the Battle for Britain) more or less intact, he set about making plans, as Napoleon had with the Grande Armée, for throwing it away.

Yet no plan, however intuitively brilliant or professionally excellent, could have taken account of Churchill's, and thus England's, defiance in the face of all odds. Hitler, never having met Churchill, thought and talked of him as a superannuated drunkard supported by Jewish gold. In fact he was, like Hitler, one of the hardest men in centuries, or as Sir Isaiah Berlin has it 'a man larger than life, composed of bigger and simpler elements than ordinary men, a gigantic historical figure during his own lifetime, superhumanly bold, strong, and imaginative, one of the two greatest men of action his nation has produced, an orator of prodigious powers, the saviour of his country, a mythical hero who belongs to legend as much as to reality, the largest human being of our time'. If the Führer had realized this it may be doubted whether he would have boasted that he had been selected by Fate to deal the final blow to the great British Empire. Yet it is amazing that two men so wholly different should have had so many accomplishments in common: both were supremely successful amateur strategists, both loved to dabble in and commanded astonishing grasp of military detail, both were remarkable orators, both had strong historical imaginations, both were for ever fighting, neither could give up. But there could at the same time never be any real resemblance between one who loved life, was above all a libertarian, and fought unendingly for freedom and 'this evil man, this monstrous abortion of hatred and defeat'. When in 1947 Vyshinsky compared Churchill to Hitler in a speech at the United Nations, he was simply being absurd. Harold Nicolson reminds us of Hector McNeil's reply 'that in 1940 Winston would walk about under the bombs dropped by the Germans and perhaps served by Russian oil'.

Three days before Hitler created the 12 Field Marshals and made his peace appeal—'I can see no reason why this war must go on'—he issued his War Directive No. 16 for the invasion of England, Operation *Sea Lion*, which he himself pronounced 'an exceptionally bold and daring undertaking'. The directive contained this sentence: 'The English Air Force must be so reduced morally and physically that it is unable to deliver any significant attack against the German crossing.' This prerequisite of air mastery was, of course, never forthcoming. The story of The Few has been related by the many, among them Basil Collier with his *Battle of Britain*. Göring's two fundamental mistakes, first not concentrating on Fighter Command's radar stations, secondly switching his attacks from the fighter airfields to London are well known. The RAF's great victory of 15 September put paid to *Sea Lion*, and two days later Hitler cancelled it. One feature of the Army plan parallels the last successful descent on England 252 years earlier when William of Orange took 8,000 horses with him; the Wehrmacht's requirement was 57,000, but apart from anything else the shipping for them did not exist.

If not to England, where was the Wehrmacht to go? Could it turn east and leave an unsubdued foe behind it? Could indirect attack on England succeed where direct attack had failed? Italy was a partner in the war, fighting somewhat half-heartedly and inconclusively in Greece and North Africa. Would decision in the Mediterranean be a substitute for indecision over the skies of Kent? Or was it rather that Hitler's forthcoming moves in the Mediterranean were purely defensive, to rescue Mussolini and to guard his southern flank while seeking that decision—which had eluded him in the west—in the east? Where was the war's real centre of gravity, where, as Major-General Fuller has it, did the real line of operations which would lead to decisive, total victory lie, through London or through Moscow? When we remember that as early as July 1940, Jodl, Chief of Operations OKW, confided to some senior staff officers that Hitler was considering an attack on Russia in the coming spring, we may perhaps realize in which direction Hitler's mind was already moving. Yet would this be 'a favourable moment'? Would it not contravene his own condition—'only when we are free in the west'.

It is easy to understand Hitler's dilemma. The ultimate aim was unchanged—conquest in the east: but how to achieve it? Britain would not submit. Russia grew stronger. Time could not be induced to return. What then was he to do? War Directive No 18 shows the breadth—a breadth which in this case spoke of indecision—of his strategic thinking:

1. The most urgent duty of the French is to secure their African possessions, offensively and defensively, against England and the de Gaulle movement. From this the full participation of France in the war against England may develop. . . .
2. Political measures to bring about the entry into the war of Spain in the near future have already been initiated. The aim of *German* intervention in the Iberian peninsula will be to drive the English from the Western Mediterranean. To this end Gibraltar is to be captured and the Straits closed. . . .
3. The employment of German forces [to assist the Italian offensive against Egypt] will be considered, if at all, only after the Italians have reached Mersa Matruh. . . . Preparations of the Armed Services for operations in this theatre will be made on the following basis:
    Army: One Panzer Division will stand by for service in North Africa.
    Navy: German ships in Italian ports which are suitable as troopships will be converted to carry the largest possible forces either to Libya or to north-west Africa.
    Air Force: Plans will be made for attacks on Alexandria and on the Suez Canal to close it to English warships.
4. Commander-in-Chief Army will be prepared, if necessary, to occupy from Bulgaria the *Greek mainland* north of the Aegean Sea. . . .

5. Political discussions for the purpose of clarifying Russia's attitude in the immediate future have already begun ... all preparations for the East ... will be continued....
6. Changes in the general situation may make it possible, or necessary, to revert to 'Undertaking Sea-Lion'....
7. I await reports from Commanders-in-Chief on the operations laid down in this directive. I will then issue orders on the manner of execution and the timing of individual operations....

Hitler made it clear from the last sentence quoted above that he did not intend to relax his hold on how and when things were to be done, let alone what was to be done. The directive is dated 12 November 1940. Which was it to be—French North Africa, Gibraltar, Libya, Greece, England or Russia? The first moves were not so much of his choice—and here was the first sign of losing the initiative—but were reactions to what the Greeks and British were doing to the Italians. The Wehrmacht's dissipation was about to begin.

6

Dissipating the Wehrmacht

The Mediterranean question must be liquidated this winter.
... I must have my German troops back in the spring, not
later than May 1st.

Hitler, November 1940

There are two great rules of strategy and each is dependent on
the other. The first is correctly to select your primary object.
This is the master rule. The second rule is so to concentrate and
deploy your forces that you achieve the object. From 1941
onwards these rules were more honoured by Hitler in the breach
than in the observance. Just as Napoleon strung the Grand
Army out between Cadiz and Moscow, so Hitler, in Halder's
words, 'drawn by his will, which refused to acknowledge any
limit to possibility, scattered the formations of the German
Army from the North Pole to the Libyan desert, while failing
to provide any of the increase in strength which they conse-
quently needed'. There are some, however, who might argue,
indeed who have argued, that Hitler's primary object was always
clear—to defeat Russia—and that he concentrated his forces
to do so. The argument falls down when set against the strategic
circumstances of the time. In late 1940 and early 1941 he was
not at war with Russia, and either would not or could not see
that England's subjection was not subsidiary, not a preliminary, to an attack on Russia. It was an indispensable condition
of victory, as Churchill told the world when he said that Hitler
knew he must conquer Britain or lose the war.

Whether Hitler knew it or not, his Naval Commander-in-
Chief, Admiral Raeder, did. He had produced and went on
producing reasons why Germany should concentrate on war
against England, particularly in the Mediterranean which, he

maintained, was the 'pivot of their world empire'. Since Italy was weak, Britain would be bound to try and strangle her first, and to make easier her attacks on Italy would aim to get control of north-west Africa. Therefore Germany must take steps to forestall any such move. In co-operation with Spain and Vichy France, Gibraltar must be seized, and French North Africa secured. Then together with the Italians, German forces should capture the Suez Canal, and advance through Palestine and Syria to Turkey. Nelson and Sir Sydney Smith would have seen much to recommend the programme. 'If we reach that point,' Raeder concluded, 'Turkey will be in our power. The Russian problem will then appear in a different light. Fundamentally Russia is afraid of Germany. It is doubtful whether an advance against Russia in the north will then be necessary.' Göring, a rival Commander-in-Chief who did not often agree with Raeder, thought the same in this case, and five years later he told Ivone Kirkpatrick that the greatest mistake Germany had made was not invading Spain and North Africa in 1940. 'If we had seized Gibraltar, we should have won the war.' Whether this is so may be doubted for even the loss of Gibraltar would not have closed the Mediterranean to the Royal Navy as long as Egypt remained militarily under British control. But in any case Hitler, like Napoleon before him, refused to recognize the importance of sea power until it was too late.

Conscious of the need to subdue England, Hitler certainly was. Yet in his arguments he turned the priorities upside down:

> In the event that invasion does not take place, our efforts must be directed to the elimination of all factors that let England hope for a change in the situation.... Britain's hope lies in Russia and the United States. If Russia drops out of the picture, America, too, is lost for Britain, because the elimination of Russia would greatly increase Japan's power in the Far East.... Decision: Russia's destruction must therefore be made a part of this struggle.... The sooner Russia is crushed the better. The attack will achieve its purpose only if the Russian State can be shattered to its roots with one blow ... if we start in May '41, we will have five months in which to finish the job.
>
> (*Also sprach Hitler*—to his Commanders-in-Chief in July 1940.)

Hitler had already made up his mind what course he wished

to pursue, and in explaining it with the passage just examined, he found all sorts of reasons for it. Intuition, will-power, world-shaking strategic possibilities—this was the way his mind bent. Capabilities and difficulties received shorter shrift. Like so many other military amateurs, he made the plan first and found the justification for it later; not without cause, for how well the system had worked up to now. Yet he did not leave it at that. OKW and OKH were required to get on with the preparation of detailed plans, and as early as the summer of 1940 he actually began to move troops to the east.

In his discourse to the Commanders-in-Chief, Hitler left out what was perhaps the most powerful strategic argument for doing what he proposed. Blitzkrieg in the west had been inconclusive. German naval and air forces were inadequate to crush England. Most of the Third Reich's military strength was tied up in the Army, both men and material. The machine could not suddenly be switched to conduct a wholly different type of war. Moreover it seemed that the war was not to be a short one after all. If so the economic resources needed both for prosecuting a long war and sustaining a largely occupied Europe could only be guaranteed by securing control of the Balkans—in September 1940, for example, Rumania virtually became a German satellite and was occupied by German troops —and ensuring continued supply of oil and grain from the Soviet Union. Some of those being occupied held other views. Vercors' poet friend, Robert Ganzo, was perhaps one of the few who in the autumn of 1940 pronounced the 'Jerries to be washed up ... they've now got to hold down the whole of Europe; they're like the fellow in the story who shouts that he's captured a prisoner. When he's told to bring him in, he says: "I can't, he won't let me go!"' It was this very circumstance, aggravated by Hitler's further, and this time unwanted, conquests in the spring of 1941 which prejudiced so fatally the great enterprise of that summer.

To this enterprise other considerations were now subordinated. Hitler's aims in the Mediterranean were not characterized by the audacity essentially offensive in nature, by the intent utterly to smash resistance and win decisive results which had been features of the campaigns in Poland and France and was to be the aim in Russia. In the Mediterranean his aims were precautionary and protective. It is true that by continuing to harass England, and in particularly attempting to close the Mediterranean to her shipping, he hoped to persuade her to give in. But he can hardly have had much confidence in such an outcome when direct assault had served only to strengthen Britain's resolution and defiance. Much more pertinently he was already concerned about the future integrity of his *Festung Europa*. 'For all her glittering victories,' wrote Arthur Bryant in 1941, 'the Third Reich is encircled by steel. And the instrument of that encirclement is the sea-power of the British Empire and its still passive but very real and potent supporter, the United States of America. Germany must break that ring or go down as surely in the end as she did in 1918.' In the Battle of the Atlantic Hitler tried to break it by offensive means. In his plans for the Mediterranean his ideas were pre-emptive. Block the Western Mediterranean, seize Gibraltar and secure French North Africa—do this and their use would be denied to the British as a stepping stone back into Europe. The spectre of war on two fronts would be laid.

There were two main reasons for things not developing as Hitler wished. Each concerned his 'allies', but whereas in the first case another's prudence robbed him of an opportunity which might have been decisive, in the second another's rashness provoked a rescue operation as untimely as it was expensive. Not only had the Führer broken the first great rule of strategy; he was now obliged to compromise with the second.

In the Western Mediterranean Spain and Vichy France did not play the game he had in mind. Franco's demands were too high and Pétain was better at collaborating in words than in deeds, even though Vichy's defeat of de Gaulle's attempt to seize Dakar with British naval assistance in September 1940 greatly cheered Hitler. At the other end of the Mediterranean Mussolini precipitated the very crisis which Hitler wished to avoid by attacking Greece on 28 October. This unexpected upsetting of equilibrium, so unwelcome to the Führer who was confident of his political ability to absorb the Balkans 'peacefully', was peculiarly welcome to another leader whose strategic dilemma was no less profound—Churchill.

Churchill who had made it known that wars are not won by evacuations (yet was about to arrange for a few more of them) was concerned 'not with avoiding defeat, but inflicting it'. Where could British forces best inflict damage on the Axis? The answer was not hard to find. No sooner had Italy declared war on Great Britain than Great Britain, taking the declaration more seriously than the country which had made it, began to employ her forces in the Mediterranean and Middle East to harass Italy. The Mediterranean Fleet soon established its ascendancy over the Italian Navy whilst the Desert Rats began to plague Graziani's 10th Army. This activity did not greatly harm the principal foe. Only the Royal Navy and Royal Air Force could do that. But North Africa was at this time the only theatre of operations where Great Britain could engage the enemy on land, and before long she would be engaging Panzers and Stukas too.

Churchill therefore began to build up Wavell's forces in the Middle East particularly with armoured formations, and foresaw their strategic use as defensive, at any rate to start with in view of Italy's huge numerical superiority of ground troops. They were to block the Italians on land while British naval and air forces attacked their communications with Africa, a process in which Malta would play a key role. Wavell himself was thinking far more boldly and was contemplating 'such measures of offence as will enable us and our Allies to dominate the Mediterranean at the earliest possible moment; and thereafter take the offensive against Germany in Eastern or SE Europe'. His great offensives against the Italians in Cyrenaica and East Africa together with his containing operations in Iraq and Syria, plus, of course, Admiral Cunningham's triumphs against the Italian Navy at Taranto and off Cape Matapan, did much, if not to dominate at least to contest the Mediterranean. These measures were within his resources and allowed him some freedom of choice both as to timing and objective. But he was not able to choose his time and place in SE Europe. When it came to 'succouring' Greece, his resources, land, sea and air, were desperately overstretched.

Yet the instinct of both Churchill and Wavell to fight for the Middle East as far forward as possible was sound. The mere

fact of British successes in Libya and intervention on the mainland of Europe was so disturbing to Hitler that it had the precise
effect which British strategy in the Mediterranean was intended
to have. It was not here that decision in the struggle for Europe
was to be found. But by persuading Hitler to begin dissipating
the Wehrmacht, by managing to create the opportunity for
attrition, to provide a colossal distraction, to enforce a division
of effort, to pose and go on posing a threat which Germany could
neither eliminate nor ignore—this was to wield sea-power both
traditionally and advantageously. This in the end was not only
to account for as many Axis soldiers as Stalingrad claimed; it
was to provide a springboard from which to arrange and carry
out the violation of a fortress.

Now we must see what Hitler actually did. On 8 and 9
January 1941 he held another of his war councils at the Berghof.
Italy was to be supported in Africa and in Albania; Operation
Marita (this was the attack on Greece, the outline of which—24
divisions to be assembled in Rumania and then advance through
Bulgaria on Greece as soon as the weather was suitable—was
contained in War Directive No 20 dated 13 December) would
start at the end of March; Stalin was a 'cold-blooded black-
mailer' and since Russia would not abandon her claims in
eastern Europe would have to be crushed as soon as possible.
Yet if Russia and the United States made war on Germany
'the situation would become very complicated'. In spite of this
gloomy prognostication, Hitler's review of grand strategy was
wreathed in confidence. 'The situation in Europe can no longer
develop unfavourably for Germany even if we should lose the
whole of North Africa.' The British could only hope to win
by defeating Germany on the Continent, and this the Führer
considered to be out of the question. This review was quickly
turned into yet another directive—No 22.

All Hitler's War Directives are eloquent and No 22 is no
exception. It deals exclusively with German support for battles
in the Mediterranean area. Tripolitania was to be held and a
collapse of the Albanian front averted. German Army units
would therefore be made ready to move to Libya in February.
X Fliegerkorps would remain in Sicily and take on a new
offensive role—to attack British naval forces, communications

and supply installations in the Mediterranean area. An entire
Corps would be made available to stiffen the Albanian front,
enable the Italians to break through the Greek defences, and
support the Army commanded by Field Marshal List which
was moving south into Bulgaria. This Corps was not in the
event used on the Albanian front, but the whole directive shows
the lengths to which Hitler was prepared to go to help his ally.
At the time of Mussolini's compliance with the *Anschluss,*
Hitler had been almost unduly grateful: 'I will never forget,
whatever may happen. If he should ever need any help or be
in any danger, he can be convinced that I shall stick to him,
whatever may happen, even if the whole world were against
him.' Hitler did stick to Mussolini—not that it did him much
good. And coming to the Duce's rescue did Hitler no good
either.

On 19 and 20 January the two men conferred at the Berghof
with Hitler as usual doing most of the talking. Once more he
greatly impressed his audience with his 'mastery' of all strategic
contingencies, which suggested his firm control of any situations
likely to develop. Ciano recorded that Hitler talked for two
hours on his coming intervention in Greece, dealing mainly
with the purely military aspects of the problem but fitting it all
neatly in with the general political circumstances. 'I must admit
that he does this with unusual mastery. Our military experts are
impressed.' While taking up an extremely anti-Russian attitude,
Hitler said nothing to Mussolini or Ciano about his intention
to attack Russia. Yet over a month before the meeting and
some three weeks before War Directive No 22 was issued,
Hitler had signed No 21, Case *Barbarossa,* whose opening
sentence must have sent a shiver down the spine of those who
read it at OKW and the three Service HQ and who remembered
a former war on two fronts: 'The German Armed Forces must
be prepared, even before the conclusion of the war against
England, to crush Soviet Russia in a rapid campaign.' It was,
of course, with this in mind that the Mediterranean question
must be liquidated; it was for this that Hitler's German troops
must be back by May 1941; if he started in May (Directive
No 21 set 15 May as the time to be ready for *Barbarossa*) he
would, as he had said, have five months to finish the job. We

must return to this directive later, but its continuing dominance in Hitler's mind does much to explain the speed and savagery with which he turned to deal with two of the obstacles in its way—British military assistance in Greece and Yugoslavia's refusal to be 'reliable'.

Churchill, with his profound historical instinct, hoped for much from the Balkan distraction. He wanted to form a Balkan front with Greece, Yugoslavia and Turkey, and was thinking of an Allied force totalling 50 divisions—'a nut for the Germans to crack'. In the event the nut was neither large nor solid. Instead there was a number of smaller, softer nuts which were cracked all too easily. Yet after the war Jodl, OKW Chief of Operations, stated that Germany had lost because of having to forfeit both troops and time to deal with the British intervention in Greece. The truth is, however, that no single campaign lost or won the war for either side, although some campaigns were clearly more conclusive than others. Only the sum of circumstances could be truly decisive. If any single thing could be said to have lost the war for Germany, it was, as already suggested, Hitler's breach of the two great rules of strategy. This is not to say that had he observed them faithfully, he would have won. But to infringe them and to go on doing so while he still held the initiative—for once he lost it, choice was no longer his—this was to throw away a winning hand.

Intervention in Greece turned Wavell's winning hand in the desert into two losing ones. He was obliged to rob O'Connor of the strength needed to press his desert victory into Tripolitania, and still had too little strength to stem the German onslaught in Greece. The arrival of Rommel and his Afrika Korps in Libya was further to turn the tables in North Africa. Meanwhile Churchill's hopes to bring in Yugoslavia and Turkey were dwindling. There would be no Balkan front, at least not one which Great Britain led. The Balkan front which was created—by Hitler—was not put together with political persuasion, but hammered out by brute force. In turning to expel the British from Greece and subjugating the Greeks themselves, he required the co-operation, or if not this, the compliance of Hungary, Bulgaria, Rumania and Yugoslavia. The first three complied. It seemed that Yugoslavia would too until a military *coup* in Belgrade seized power at the end of March 1941 and its leaders disassociated themselves from the former government's support of the Axis.

Thereupon matters moved fast. War Directive No 25 dated 27 March branded Yugoslavia as an enemy, and therefore 'must be beaten down as quickly as possible'. Simultaneously Operation *Marita* would be mounted against Greece. The Führer was in such a hurry to revenge himself on Yugoslavia that he ordered Keitel and Jodl to work out detailed plans for the invasion on that very evening of 27 March. At the same time he announced—and here was the rub—that the launching of *Barbarossa* would have to be postponed for up to four weeks. Hitler would no longer have five months to finish the job. Directive No 26 dated 3 April gave details of the campaign against Yugoslavia, and three days later the attacks on this country and Greece began. Belgrade was subjected to three days' intensive bombing. This was part of Hitler's plan to destroy the country 'militarily as well as a national unit'. There were no diplomatic approaches or ultimatums. Yugoslavia was simply to be smashed 'with merciless brutality ... in a lightning operation'. It was certainly *blitzartig schnell*. On 13 April Belgrade was occupied, whilst further east List's 12th Army had entered Macedonia and cut Yugoslavia off from Greece. On 17 April Yugoslavia capitulated, and faced with the entire weight of the German armies there Greece held out only one week longer. The British Army conducted an operation it was getting good at—withdrawal and evacuation.

In their first campaign of the war, the 4th Hussars, Churchill's old regiment of which he was to their great joy about to become Colonel—an appointment he held until his death—had an introduction to blitzkrieg at Ptolemais on 13 April 1941. As part of the 1st Armoured Brigade the regiment conducted a successful delaying action south of the Veve Pass. One of the squadron leaders watched the Germans as they approached the blown bridge at Ptolemais:

> Half an hour passes; we have an early lunch and then we get our first view of the enemy. It's not much different to what we have been watching [he was referring to the British column which

shortly before had withdrawn]. Same pace, same intervals, but all armour and a good deal bigger. I count over two hundred as they disappear into the dip on the far side of Ptolemais, where they are apparently concentrating. Two Panzers and a motor-cyclist come down the road to the blown bridge. As they reach it everything opens up on them from our right, streams of tracer, anti-tank shot and machine-gun bullets. The shot ricochets off the Panzers. The cyclist dismounts and takes notes. More tracer opens up. I suppose the range is about 1,500 yards. The cyclist remounts and rides quietly back, the Panzers lumbering after him. One seems to be slightly lame. An impressive show.

Together with field and anti-tank artillery and the more effective guns of the 3rd Royal Tank Regiment, supported also by RAF Blenheims, the 4th Hussars helped to give the Germans a hot reception. But the collapse of Yugoslav and Greek resistance meant that the British campaign in Greece was simply a withdrawal, not made any more pleasant by the all-powerful Luftwaffe. Between 24 April and 1 May some 50,000 men were evacuated, many from Kalamata, 20 miles west of Sparta. It had been at Calamita Bay in the Crimea that the 4th Light Dragoons, as the 4th Hussars then were, had disembarked 87 years earlier. But the calamity which overtook them at Balaclava was nothing to that which they endured in Greece, where surrounded by Panzers and airborne units they had lost over 400 men and most of the senior officers taken prisoner. British casualties in the Greek campaign were about 12,000; almost as many lorries were lost, while the RAF were 200 aircraft worse off, at a time when the Germans were about to launch the biggest airborne operation that war had yet produced.

For Hitler was not satisfied with capturing Greece. He wanted Crete too, and with Operation *Mercury*, which started on 20 May, seized the island by parachute, transport aircraft and glider assault within a week. *Mercury* was a bold and novel undertaking, yet as far as control of the air went—the Royal Navy effectively put paid to the seaborne part of the attack—such overwhelmingly powerful air forces were assembled (some 700 reconnaissance, fighter and bomber aircraft, 500 transports and 72 gliders) that provided the Germans were quickly able to seize and hold an airfield to accommodate their transports, they were almost bound to win. Their early capture of Maleme airfield ensured a superiority of build-up which the Commonwealth forces could not match. Yet the battle was no walk-over. The Germans lost some 6,000 men killed, wounded and missing, and nearly 400 aircraft destroyed or damaged. General Student's Fliegerkorps XI had ceased to be an operational formation. Had it been worthwhile? The strategic advantages were not inconsiderable; the Royal Navy denied use of the Aegean; Axis sea routes both through the Dardanelles via the Corinth Canal to Italy and from Italy to eastern Cyrenaica much more secure; a further base for harassing British sea communications between Egypt and Malta. Yet in spite of these undeniable gains and in spite too of its being tactically, supremely, almost recklessly offensive in character, *Mercury* was strategically an operation of defensive security, a flank guard. Student had seen the operation far more imaginatively as one in a series of 'Island-hops' that would take him by way of Cyprus to the Suez Canal or in the opposite direction to Malta. But as we have seen in his dealings with Raeder, Hitler was not prepared to sanction a major effort in the south when his mind was made up to press forward with the *Drang nach Osten*.

There was another man who was pressing east, with comparatively almost puny force but by no means negligible results —Rommel. As if demonstration of blitzkrieg in the Balkans, with Stukas calling an uninterrupted tune of success, were not enough, it now came about that in the one place where Britain had seemed to have the upper hand, the Western Desert, Rommel and his panzers brought a new set of rules to desert fighting and between March and April 1941 bundled the British right out of Cyrenaica back into Egypt, leaving of all O'Connor's conquests only the fortress of Tobruk in British hands. Rommel's own letters are as eloquent as any report of this unwelcome reverse to British arms:

We've been attacking since the 31st with dazzling success. There'll be consternation amongst our masters in Tripoli and Rome, perhaps in Berlin too. I took the risk against all orders and instructions because the opportunity seemed favourable. No doubt it will all be pronounced good later and they'll all say they'd have done exactly the same in my place. We've already [his letter is dated 3 April, 1941] reached our first objective [Benghazi] which we weren't supposed to get to until the end of May. The British are falling over each other to get away....

In subsequent letters he notes the Führer's congratulations and a directive which is in accord with his own ideas. Success gives him more room for manoeuvre. He cannot remember the date as they had been attacking for days in endless desert. All idea of space and time have gone. He is as always in the vanguard. His main force is behind him. 'I flew back from the front yesterday to look for them and found them in the desert. You can hardly imagine how pleased I was. It's going to be a "Cannae" modern style.' On 10 April he writes that he has reached the sea after a long desert march. 'It's wonderful to have pulled this off against the British.' When later Rommel recorded what he thought were the lessons of his first African campaign, he had some telling things to say about misdirection of strategy. Germany should have kept her hands off Greece and concentrated on North Africa to drive the British right out of the Mediterranean area. Malta should have been taken, not Crete. Capture of the whole British-held coastline would have isolated SE Europe. It could all have been done for no more than the cost of the Balkan campaign. The prize would have been not just the Balkans but oil and bases for attacking Russia. Rommel and Raeder thought alike.

On 30 May Raeder renewed his proposal for a 'decisive Egypt-Suez offensive for the autumn of 1941 which would be more deadly to the British Empire than the capture of London'. Raeder and his staff accepted Hitler's priorities but insisted that whilst the attack on Russia 'naturally stands in the foreground of the OKW leadership, it must under no circumstances lead to the abandonment of, or to delay in, the conduct of the war in the Mediterranean'. Churchill was in no doubt about the grave consequences of losing Egypt and the Middle East. In a telegram to Roosevelt earlier that month he did not endorse the President's view that such a loss would be 'a mere preliminary to the successful maintenance of a prolonged oceanic war'. Even if the United States entered the war, exclusion of the Allies from Europe and much of Africa and Asia would mean that a war against 'this mighty agglomeration would be a hard, long, and bleak proposition'. Therefore the British would fight 'to the last inch and ounce for Egypt'. The desert flank was in Churchill's view 'the peg on which all else hung' and he was soon to urge Wavell once more to return to the attack there. But Wavell and his fellow Commanders-in-Chief were harder pressed and more stretched in their resources at this time than perhaps at any other. The East African campaign was not quite finished; Greece and Crete had taken their toll of men and material; Malta must be maintained, Tobruk turned into a fortress and supplied; Rashid Ali's pro-German revolt in Iraq had to be suppressed; Syria to be invaded and occupied; Rommel to be attacked. What might not have been achieved by the Wehrmacht if they had been allowed to concentrate their might against the British at this moment?

Yet Hitler refused to see it. Never one to forgo an advantage, he missed here an opportunity that was never to recur. For him tides were not to be taken at the flood; they were to be arranged by himself. Although he gave support, which was insufficient to turn the scales, to Rashid Ali's revolt, anything bigger would have to wait. 'Whether, and if so how,' read Directive No 30, 'it may be possible, in conjunction with an offensive against the Suez Canal, finally to break the British position between the Mediterranean and the Persian Gulf is a question which will be decided only after *Barbarossa*.' This decision, like so many others of Hitler's, was unalterable. If failure to destroy the British Army at Dunkirk had been Blunder No 1, was failure to destroy the British position in the Middle East in mid-1941, just a year later, Blunder No 2? Today it looks very much as if it was. It is true that Britain had been turned out of Egypt and the Mediterranean before—by Napoleon—and had even lost Malta, until Nelson began to rush up and down to restore the supremacy of British sea-power, but that was before the age of air-power. 'Had the Eastern Mediterranean arena not been successfully held during the lean years,' wrote Major-General Playfair, 'in which case, for want of bases, no British fleet or air forces could have even disputed the control of the Mediterranean sea communications, the task of the Allies in gaining a foothold in Europe would have been rendered immensely more difficult; indeed it might well have proved to be beyond their powers.' In other words Hitler's confident prediction that the British could not hope to defeat Germany on the Continent might have had more substance. But if you brush aside the master rule of strategy, you cannot expect to win.

Russia must be defeated first. He had not done what he had told Mussolini must be done. He had failed to 'liquidate' the Mediterranean question, but his immediate aims had nevertheless been realized. Italy's precarious position had been rectified. The English leopards had been thrown back into the sea. The southern flank was secure. What did the balance sheet look like? Between September 1940 and May 1941 Hitler's battles for Europe, political and actual, had vastly spread his control over that continent—Rumania, Hungary, Bulgaria, Yugoslavia, Greece, Crete, to say nothing of all Cyrenaica regained in another continent. The position had been stabilized. But what entry was there on the debit side?

We may perhaps reflect on the irony of circumstances which allowed the Germans to win a series of rapid and startling victories in order to facilitate a campaign which knocked the stuffing out of the Wehrmacht so that defeat became only a matter of time, and allowed the British by instinct, certainly by choice, to indulge in a series of hopeless campaigns, almost to court defeat with results far beyond their expectation or wildest imaginings. In June 1946 Harold Nicolson was talking to Smuts about Nuremberg, and Smuts was commenting on Jodl's view of the immense consequences of British intervention in Greece, which robbed Germany of time—'and with time she lost Moscow, Stalingrad and the war. Smuts recalled the decision which Winston, he and Wavell had made at the time. "We had just won a victory. We knew that if we withdrew divisions from Libya, that victory would be reversed. We knew that only defeat faced us in Greece. But we made our decision, not on military principles, but on moral principles. Now we are proved right by the Director of Operations of the German Army. This shows once again that to do the right thing is generally the right thing to do."' It puts us in mind of Stevenson's point that the mark of a good action is that it appears inevitable in retrospect.

The British may have been in the Mediterranean and Middle East because, as A. J. P. Taylor has it, 'they were there', yet their efforts there in the year since Dunkirk had not been derisory. Italy had been savaged, Germany distracted. Twenty-four divisions had been diverted to the Balkans at a time when Hitler was building up his strength for the great venture in the east. More countries had to be held down. Dissipation of the Wehrmacht was well under way.

During this process Hitler's influence had been as decisive as ever. He had perhaps concerned himself less with the detailed conduct of campaigns and more with strategic decisions leading to a variety of lightning operations. He issued his Directives and they were carried out. More and more they were concerned with the application of force, less and less with 'political' solutions to military problems. Yet there were no real grounds for challenging his 'infallibility', for Germany's intervention in coming to the help of her ally had been crowned with spectacular success. That the Directives themselves might be wrong, however, is perhaps best brought into focus by the fact that decision eluded him still just as it had after the breath-taking triumphs of June 1940. Now, a year later, he was about to embark once more on the personal conduct of a major campaign, so vast in concept, so powerful in execution that the world would hold its breath. Here surely, Hitler told himself, he would find the decision which had eluded him elsewhere.

7

Barbarossa—The Irretrievable Blunder

One of the first rules of war is: don't march on Moscow.
Montgomery

In the 1920s Hitler had said of Russia, 'this colossal empire in the east is ripe for dissolution'; in 1941 he saw himself on the point of making his prediction come true. 'We have only to kick in the door and the whole rotten structure will come crashing down.' Whether Russia was planning to attack Germany or not, and Hitler had convinced himself that this was so, he resolved to make assurance double sure. Negotiations had failed. Only force of arms could weld Europe together.

On 21 June 1941, the day before *Barbarossa* began, an article by Arthur Bryant appeared in the *Illustrated London News*. It analysed the strategic disadvantage under which Germany laboured in spite of all her conquests, all her strength and all her freedom of choice. Hitler had to maintain the offensive; he could not sit back and wait to be attacked; he must himself attack and since he had already overrun so much of Europe, wherever he now advanced would take him further and further from his homeland bases. To break out of Europe meant either wresting mastery of the seas from the British— and this particular battle was already raging in the Atlantic— or thrusting through Russia into Asia and Africa. It seemed to Bryant that Russia was the 'easier' road 'but such desperate steps cannot be taken without evoking human and racial imponderables which may well benefit us far more than the enemy. Hitler knows this, and his hour of decision is at hand. It is his fate to strike, and ours to resist and strike back.'

Thus with the initiative so securely in his hands (and this was the last time that it was, for thereafter Hitler responded more and more to Allied moves) it was peculiarly, supremely important that he used the initiative decisively. We have seen how the two great rules of strategy apply in choosing a campaign. The same rules are equally binding for conducting the campaign once it is chosen. In other words, tactically too—and here the line between strategy and tactics is a fine one—the decisive objective must be unerringly chosen and relentlessly pursued. No sideshows, however glittering they may be in terms of political propaganda or personal prestige, must be allowed to distract from it.

It seemed from his Directive No 21 that Hitler had fully grasped this fundamental point. When faced with the seemingly invincible armies of Napoleon, Czar Alexander I refused to be dismayed. In spite of them, he declared, in spite of the world's greatest captain, the most valiant lieutenants, space was a barrier, and by leaving his defence to the climate, he might yet have the last word. In short, refusal to concede defeat, as long as he could keep a Russian army in being, was everything. If, in being obliged to postpone his attack until 22 June, Hitler allowed himself a reflection on the coincidence that it was almost exactly the same time of year as Napoleon's invasion of Russia had begun 129 years earlier, history has not revealed what it was. But so aware was he that the Russians, Borodino always excepted, had simply retreated in front of Napoleon's advance that the general intention contained in Directive No 21 was designed precisely to prevent this happening a second time: 'The Bulk of the Russian Army stationed in Western Russia will be destroyed by daring operations led by deeply penetrating armoured spearheads. Russian forces still capable of giving battle will be prevented from withdrawing into the depths of Russia.' In spite of laying down a final objective—to erect a barrier against Asiatic Russia on the general line Caspian Sea to Archangel—the directive did not say exactly where and how the Russian armies were to be destroyed. But then of course it was not meant to. This was for detailed military planning. On the other hand the directive did outline generally how operations were to be conducted.

North of the Pripet Marshes two Army Groups would deliver the main weight of the attack to destroy all enemy forces in White Russia and the Baltic area; south of the marshes a third Army Group would account for all Russian forces west of the Dnieper in the Ukraine. When these battles were ended, and the northern one was to include capturing Leningrad and Kronstadt, then, and only then, would the pursuit be ordered, a pursuit whose aims were Moscow, 'an important centre of communications and of the armaments industry' and the Donets Basin. As usual the directive ended with instructions for the Commanders-in-Chief to submit their detailed plans.

When Hitler first saw these plans on 3 February 1941, he reiterated the overriding need to 'wipe out large sections of the enemy and not put them to flight', yet added the not altogether compatible footnote that the main aim was to 'gain possession of the Baltic States and Leningrad'. Here we may see, early as it was in the planning stage and over four months before Barbarossa began, an illustration of the ruinous condition which was constantly to recur and more than any other robbed Hitler of decision in Russia—no absolutely fixed and immutable purpose to which all other considerations were subordinated. This is not to argue for inflexibility of mind and method. Nothing could be more foreign either to the grand strategist or the fighting soldier. But it is to say that between June and December 1941 in the Supreme Commander's handling of his struggle for Russia, singleness of aim—a necessary end, and beginning, for concentration of forces—was absent without leave. The struggle became a gigantic encounter battle which, for all the vast distances covered, for all the unthinkable destruction or capture of Russian men and material, was marred by fatal compromises.

This was to be the blitzkrieg to end all blitzkriegs, to shackle accidents and bolt up change. With Russia struck down, Britain impotent and the United States unwilling actually to enter the war, the Thousand Year Reich was assured. Excluding Finnish and Rumanian forces, 120 divisions, 17 of which were panzer and 12 motorized, were organized into three Army Groups, von Leeb in the north, von Bock in the centre (it was here that the main panzer groups were—one commanded by Guderian)

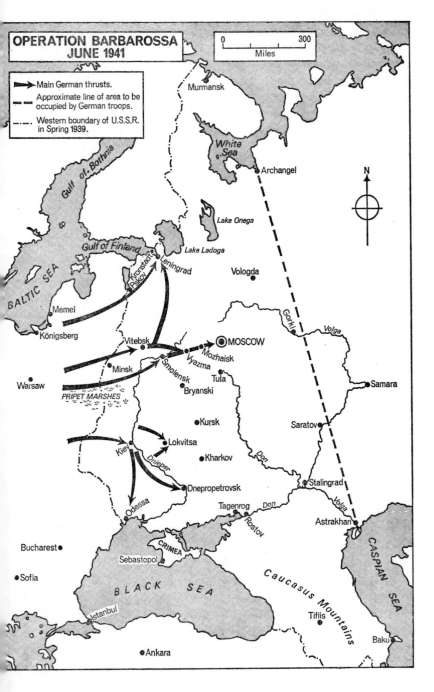

OPERATION BARBAROSSA
JUNE 1941

0 — 300
Miles

➤ Main German thrusts.

— ■ — Approximate line of area to be occupied by German troops.

— ■■ — Western boundary of U.S.S.R. in Spring 1939.

and von Rundstedt in the south, three great *Schwerpunkte* directed roughly at Leningrad, Smolensk and Kiev. They were the same three Army Group commanders who had destroyed the French Army. But whereas *Sichelschnitt* had been a battle of manoeuvre which led to annihilation, which had worked, *Barbarossa* was designed as a battle of annihilation which would facilitate manoeuvre, and therefore depended upon two conditions, without which it could not work and which in the event did not obtain—that the Russians would be encircled and once encircled would give up. At dawn on 22 June 1941 Panzer and Stuka swept forward. 'What an appalling moment in time this is,' writes Alan Clark in his masterly study of the whole Russian-German conflict, 'the head-on crash of the two greatest armies, the two most absolute systems, in the world. No battle in history compares with it. . . . In terms of numbers of men, weight of ammunition, length of front, the desperate *crescendo* of fighting, there will never be another day like the 22nd June 1941.'

Eleven days previously Hitler had issued one of the most remarkable of his many directives—No 32—remarkable not for its execution, but for its conception. It laid down how the war was to be conducted after Russia had been conquered. In other words Hitler was planning to fulfil his former promise to Raeder to finish England. The British position in the Middle East would be strangled by converging attacks from Libya through Egypt, from Bulgaria through Turkey, and from Transcaucasia through Iran. In addition the Western Mediterranean would be closed by seizing Gibraltar. Planning was to begin 'so that I may issue final directives before the campaign in the east is over'.

Now that the results are known how easy it is to call *Barbarossa* Blunder No 3, the greatest one of all, the irretrievable blunder. The reaction of those at the time with no real means of knowing is likely to carry more weight. Vercors could hardly believe his ears when he heard news of the attack, yet he was not at first reassured. Hitler, he told himself (and there were many in Europe, in America and even in England who thought alike) had never attacked any country without first making sure that the enemy had been destroyed from within, and here Vercors had in mind his own country, which collapsed almost at once.

> Might Hitler not thrust his army, like a knife into butter, right into the heart of a country that had been politically undermined, decomposed by treachery, where a rebel Fascist government, after overthrowing Stalin, would be ready to capitulate without a fight—as Vichy had done—and go over to the enemy? If this catastrophe were to happen, what hope would be left for Europe, for France? With a whole continent behind him, assured of raw materials and industrial products, of oil, cereals, fats, perhaps of manpower and fresh troops, in almost infinite quantities, who could still hope to defeat Hitler?

Vercors' friend, Leon Motchane, himself a Russian, ridiculed such pessimism: 'What an idea!' he cried.

> You don't know the Russians. Never mind if they like or dislike Stalin and his régime, that doesn't count any more: Holy Russia is attacked, and they'll defend it. To the last man! And they're invincible! When an army can manoeuvre over a territory covering two-thirds of Europe and half of Asia, it can't be destroyed. Hitler has repeated Napoleon's mistake. Even if he gets away with some early successes, he has flung himself into a bottomless pit. He's doomed. Let's drink to victory!

This utter contradiction of Hitler's insistence that the whole rotten structure would come crashing down was soon to be confirmed. In spite of huge advances and sensational victories, it was clear almost from the start that this was no blitzkrieg on the lines of those that had gone before. The Russian Army, also a mirror of its people, did not crack up after the first setbacks, and there was no shortage of these. It fought back wherever and whenever it could. Von Bock in the centre executed a gigantic pincer movement which converged on Minsk and on 10 July the Germans claimed over 300,000 prisoners. A week later the battle for Smolensk was joined and lasted three weeks; a further 300,000 prisoners, but von Bock's armies had suffered such losses that they had to refit and regroup. There was no advance from Smolensk before 2 October. In the north von Leeb pushed through Estonia, reaching Nava and Pskov by 20 August, but he was repulsed at

Leningrad in mid-September, and, after capturing Schlüssel-berg to the east, had to be content with investing Leningrad. In the south during the first two weeks of September the great encirclement of Kiev took place. Two Army Groups were involved—from von Bock's command north of Kiev were Weich's army and Guderian's panzer group, and from von Rundstedt's to the south were Reichenau's army and Kleist's panzer group. The pincers closed at Lokvitsa on 14 September when Guderian and Kleist joined hands—120 miles east of Kiev. The bag was nearly 700,000 prisoners. Hitler called it 'the greatest battle in the history of the world'; Halder, for reasons which we shall presently see, condemned it as the principal strategic blunder of the campaign. Yet earlier Halder, in spite of all his caution, had judged that in a mere two weeks from the outset of the campaign, it had been won, and that in a few more weeks all would be over.

There followed further advances and further spectacular successes—von Manstein, for example, got as far as Sevastopol; Kleist reached Rostov; von Rundstedt's Army Group occupied the general line Tagenrog-Kharkov-Khursk; Bock set off from Smolensk on 2 October, trapped another 600,000 Russians between Vyazma and Bryansk, and actually got to Klin, only 35 miles west of Moscow, by 5 December. But, despite all this, despite perhaps a total of two million Russian soldiers killed or captured and Otto Dietrich's sensational announcement on 8 October that Soviet Russia as a military power was done for, that the war in the east was over, none of the basic aims which Hitler had laid down were achieved. Moscow had not been captured, nor Leningrad, nor the Caucasian oilfields, nor the Archangel railway; above all the Russian armies as a whole had not been destroyed nor prevented from withdrawing. The very diversity of these aims was the cause, and diversity itself was well nigh inevitable because of sheer width of front. Yet as early as 3 February when plans were first being discussed, Hitler had answered the General Staff's objection that a success-ful advance to a general line from the Black Sea to the Gulf of Finland would double the frontage by claiming that since the entire Russian armies would by that time have ceased to exist, it did not matter how wide the front or how great the distance beyond, for there would be nothing to stop them.

How different was the Russians' behaviour in reality. Not only was the individual Russian soldier as fanatically tough and as careless of death as the most ardent Nazi; not only were the partisans already fighting in the areas from which the Red Army itself had withdrawn; not only was the organization from which the partisans came, the Osoaviakhim, 36 million strong and spread over the whole nation; not only was the raising of new armies done at prodigious speed and their equipment as efficient as it was seemingly endless—but the proof of the pudding was such that on 6 December Marshal Zhukov counter-attacked in the central sector of the front with 17 armies;* and winter had set in. It seemed that all the conditions, which Alexander I had stipulated as being necessary for him to have the last word, now prevailed.

What had Hitler's part in it been? The first point is that his interference in this campaign, whether from his East Prussia headquarters, *Wolfsschanze*†, near Rastenburg, or when visiting commanders at their headquarters, was more radical and more continuous than in any that had gone before. Before long it was to become absolute. During the first weeks of spectacular success there was no cause for major disagreement between Hitler and tne generals. But when it came to deciding what to do after the great Smolensk battle, the scene changes. Hitler's original directive had laid down, leaving aside for a moment the ever-present requirement of destroying Russia's armies, that in the north Moscow would be occupied only after the capture of Leningrad, whilst in the south the Ukraine with its large industrial and agricultural resources would be seized. The question in August, with these three possible objectives, was which of them—singly or together—to go for.

The professional soldiers, Brauchitsch, Halder, Bock, Guderian among them, were convinced that by concentrating their effort and pushing on to Moscow, they would not only be aiming at a great communications, armaments and political centre, but would also stand the best chance of achieving the

---

* A Russian army was roughly the equivalent of a German corps; Zhukov had about 100 divisions.

† Wolf's lair.

primary object—destruction of the main Russian armies including the newly formed ones which would dispute their passage. Hitler disagreed. He had his eye on political and economic objectives—Leningrad and the Ukraine. 'Only completely ossified brains, absorbed in the ideas of past centuries,' he angrily declared, 'could see any worthwhile objective in taking the capital'. Brauchitsch's objection that the main Russian armies contesting the road to Moscow could not be destroyed by any other means than engaging them—a reasonable argument—was brushed impatiently aside. The fact was that by mid-July so confident was Hitler, as a result of the Wehrmacht's initial successes, that Russia's defeat was assured that he supplemented Directive No 32 with another, which actually proposed to reduce the Army, limit naval activity to what was necessary for prosecuting the war against England (and possibly America), and greatly strengthen the Luftwaffe. Yet the first of a series of crises was about to break over Hitler's head, crises which only an infinitely more powerful Army could have resolved.

In the event the controversy as to which objectives were to be pursued was, not surprisingly, decided by Hitler. The Ukraine and Leningrad gave way to the Ukraine alone. This was to receive the main attention and the results, as we have seen, were dazzling. Halder's comment that it was the greatest strategic error of the campaign must be put into context. Possession of the Ukraine and 665,000 prisoners cannot be thought of as anything but significant, even in relation to the primary object of smashing Russia's ability to resist. It is when this stroke is looked at in conjunction with Hitler's second refusal to concentrate on one objective that we see how fatal his repudiation of strategy's master rules could be.

On 2 October von Bock's Central Army Group resumed the advance. Within a week another huge pincer movement had accounted for another 600,000 Russian soldiers between Vyazma and Bryansk, and by 15 October the panzer spearheads were at Mozhaisk, a mere 65 miles from Moscow. It was then that the supreme tactical error was made. At this point, in spite of the time the Russians had been given, in spite of deteriorating weather, victory, if by victory we mean what the

German General Staff meant—destruction of the Russian armies disputing the road to Moscow and capture of the capital itself—was probably still in Hitler's grasp. But failing once more to observe those prime principles of war—singleness of aim, concentration of forces—failing to select the decisive objective and go for it with all the terrifying weight of fire-power that was available (and this time, unlike the Kiev/Moscow controversy, there could be no real doubt as to which this objective was), Hitler chose to go for three, absurd in their dispersion and sheer unattainability.

Von Leeb was to capture Leningrad and having linked up with the Finnish Army under Mannerheim push on to the Murmansk railway; von Bock was to press forward to Moscow; von Rundstedt, who records that he laughed aloud when he received the orders, so unrealistic were they, was to clear the Black Sea coast and advance beyond Rostov to the Caucasus. There were many obstacles to the second of these objectives, the critical one, Moscow. October rains and new Russian armies had clearly made the defences more formidable. Winter was coming on. Hitler's interference in the detailed conduct of operations, formerly infrequent, had become a daily affair. Yet despite these drawbacks it is hard to believe that if every ounce of effort had been concentrated from mid-October on-wards on von Bock's drive to Moscow, with von Leeb's and von Rundstedt's front relegated to holding operations, and the entire weight of the Panzer Groups welded into one *Schwerpunkt*, Moscow could not have been taken. Even with the crazy dispersion that Hitler insisted on, the city's suburbs were reached. Had the effort been trebled, Moscow must have fallen, and 'the greatest battle in world history' have gained, if not absolute decision, a victory so great that the future shape of the war must have been altered.

Instead Hitler preferred to pursue many objectives simultaneously, to reject out of hand the advice of his professional soldiers who in this case knew what they were talking about, and to fritter away his resources chasing chimerical victories. He doubled his frontage against an enemy whose army was larger than his own. He trebled his purpose and trisected the forces to achieve it. He ignored the almost immediately evident fact that the whole rotten structure was *not* crashing down, that the Russian soldier was brave, tough and well-equipped, that the Red Army's will to fight was very different from that of the French and would not swiftly crack up. Hitler knew better, and here perhaps was Blunder No 4.

Nonetheless he had told his people that 'the enemy in the east has been struck down and will never rise again'. Just as well perhaps for the enemy in the west was reviving. On 22 June Churchill had told his people and his new found allies:

> Any man or state who fights on against Nazidom will have our aid.... It follows, therefore, that we shall give whatever help we can to Russia and the Russian people.... Hitler wishes to destroy the Russian power because he hopes that if he succeeds in this he will be able to bring back the main strength of his army and air force from the East and hurl it upon this island, which he knows he must conquer or suffer the penalty of his crimes*.... The Russian danger is, therefore, our danger, and the danger of the United States.... Let us redouble our exertions, and strike with united strength while life and power remain.

In August Churchill met Roosevelt, and the Atlantic Charter, 'a resounding declaration of principle', was the result. Strategic discussions yielded less. Some of the American military men regarded the Middle East as 'a liability from which they [the British] should withdraw'. Yet Hitler's turning away from the Mediterranean had given the British just the respite they needed in the Middle East to strengthen Malta and Tobruk, win the race of supplies against Rommel and embark on another desert offensive in November which turned Rommel out of Cyrenaica and regained the airfields so vital further to reinforce Malta and harass Axis communications. The consequences of *Barbarossa* were certainly not confined to Russia. Yet except for supplies, Britain was unable to come to her new ally's aid. The greatest battles in world history were being fought by the Wehrmacht and the Red Army alone. What were they like?

Halder recalled early on in the campaign that it was quite unlike 'manoeuvres with live ammunition' which they had enjoyed in the west a year before. The Russians' determination

---

* How well Churchill foresaw Hitler's Directives Nos 32 and 32a.

and heroism was something the Germans had not encountered before. Alan Clark's great survey contains many such stories. One of them is of a wounded Russian tank crew, thought by the Germans to be dead within their knocked-out tank, who somehow, with no hope of ultimate rescue or survival, managed to live long enough to call down artillery fire on the not-distant German positions for days on end, always choosing moments such as supply and maintenance periods when their enemies were most vulnerable. The mystery of this unerring bombardment is only cleared up when a German soldier forces open and looks into the derelict Russian tank. 'Half overcome by the stench which escaped from it, he saw two squatting skeletons. We were able to get them out. Can you imagine the guts of those two men, one of whom, a captain, had lost an eye— cloistered up with a corpse among so much filth. Some provisions . . . helped them to endure and, although they were wounded, to send information to their troops by means of their wireless set.' Another account tells of a Russian cavalry regiment setting off on a fighting reconnaissance south-west of Kiev at the end of August. Evading both the Luftwaffe and the fighting elements of von Reichenau's 6th Army, they fell upon a non-combatant survey unit whose men thought the front to be miles away. One of them recalled that the village where they were billeted suddenly became empty as the inhabitants withdrew to their houses. Then 'there was the sound of horses, and . . . they were upon us . . . sturdy little horses riding at a gallop through our camp. Some of the Russians were using submachine guns, others were swinging sabres. I saw two men killed by the sword less than ten metres from me . . . think of that, eighty years after Sadowa! They had towed up a number of those heavy, two-wheeled machine guns; after a few minutes whistles began to blow and the horsemen faded away; the machine gunners started blazing away at very close range with enfilade fire.' And then the Russians' endurance, indifference to pain and death, their almost inscrutable stubbornness and silence was such that an SS major recorded that even after five campaigns he had never seen anything to equal it.

This almost inhuman resistance had its effect not only on the Wehrmacht's material, but on their morale as well. Even the great Panzer Leader, Guderian, was deeply depressed during the drive on Moscow in November. The cold, like the Russians, affected men and machines. Special fittings were required for the tank tracks and these had not turned up; the gun sights were useless; fuel froze; the machine guns would not fire. Worse, the Russian T-34 tank seemed to be impenetrable when engaged by the German 37-mm gun. For once Guderian saw no way to carry out his orders, as his panzer troops 'had reached their end'. In a letter written on 21 November he noted: 'The icy cold, the lack of shelter, the shortage of clothing, the heavy losses of men and equipment, the wretched state of our fuel supplies—all this makes the duties of a commander a misery, and the longer it goes on the more I am crushed by the enormous responsibility I have to bear.' Writing about the campaign after it was all over he maintained that it was only possible to judge what those events were like for him 'who saw the endless expanse of Russian snow during the winter of our misery and felt the icy wind that blew across it, burying in snow every object in its path; who drove for hour after hour through the no-man's land only at last to find too thin shelter with in-sufficiently clothed, half-starved men; and who also saw by contrast the well-fed, warmly clad and fresh Siberians, fully equipped for winter fighting'.

Guderian did not exaggerate. When Kluge's 4th Army, in spite of reaching the outskirts of Moscow, was obliged to retire during the first week of December, and this failure to realize their objective was at once followed by a massive Russian counter-attack on the whole central front, the Wehrmacht wavered. Something like despair swept over the ordinary soldier, something like the paralysis which blitzkrieg was supposed to induce in others gripped the High Command. More than five months had passed, but the job was not yet finished. The great *Drang nach Osten* was not just bogged down; it looked peril-ously like turning into another retreat from Moscow, another panic, another rout. Hitler, however, did not despair; he showed once again that will-power is all. It is hard to better Alan Bullock's succinct estimate of his remedy. 'Hitler,' he writes, 'rose to the occasion. By a remarkable display of determination he succeeded in holding the German lines firm. Whatever his

19   Russian tommy-gunners in the
     Ukraine

20   German infantry in Russia, 1941

21   Red Army infantry attack near Stalingrad

22   Soviet T-34 towing a captured German tank, July 1943

responsibility for the desperate situation in which the German Army now found itself, and whatever the ultimate consequences of his intervention, in its immediate effects it was his greatest achievement as a war-leader.'

Not that there was anything clever about the action he took. But then cleverness, as Napoleon reminded Talleyrand, is not needed in war. Simplicity and character are greater military virtues. Hitler's orders conformed. There was to be no withdrawal. Nothing could have been simpler than that. And so in keeping with Hitler's character was the enforcement of this order that there was nothing he would not sacrifice to see that it was obeyed. Thousands of German soldiers, scores of German generals whose loyalty or obedience was in question—these could be dispensed with, but not an inch of ground was to be given up.

The month of December saw a good many changes in the Army's High Command. Rundstedt was replaced by Reichenau, Bock by Kluge, Guderian and Höppner were dismissed, numerous corps and divisional commanders despatched home in disgrace. The cause was usually either for tactical withdrawals without obtaining the Führer's agreement or for arguing the case with him. Even Keitel, whose normal stance was that the Führer could do no wrong, plucked up the courage to recommend a general withdrawal and received such a flogging from the Führer's tongue that Jodl found him writing out his resignation, a loaded pistol at his side. But Keitel was persuaded to stay on. Not so the Army Commander-in-Chief, von Brauchitsch, who tried to resign on 7 December, only to be told by Hitler, who was already issuing orders direct to Army Commanders without reference to OKH, that he was too busy to discuss the matter; and then again on 17 December. This time Hitler accepted, and two days later took over command of the Army himself. Halder remained as Chief of the General Staff. This fateful step meant that Hitler now had formalized his supreme control of all military operations. On the one hand as Commander-in-Chief of the Army with the staff of OKH he directly conducted the war in Russia; on the other hand as Commander-in-Chief of the Armed Forces with the staff of OKW he ran operations on all other fronts. This division of responsibility between the staffs meant that Hitler alone retained strategic grasp of the war as a whole.

By assuming command of the Army Hitler transferred himself formally from the realms of strategy to those of day-to-day operations, not that he had been slow in usurping this particular office on many previous occasions. But now, as he told Halder: 'This little affair of operational command is something that anybody can do. The task of the Commander-in-Chief is to educate the Army in the idea of National Socialism, and I know of no General who could do this in the way I want it done.' Accordingly he would do it himself. Yet whereas Hitler's gifts did in some respects fit him for the role of a Supreme Commander concerned primarily with strategic decisions, his faults as a military leader were precisely those which should have excluded him from translating strategic 'intuition' into hard and fast, methodical and proven military practice. In his chosen position as the greatest strategic genius of all time, his sheer love of the unorthodox, of the psychologically crippling value of surprise, of audacious strokes which would yield real decision, all these were advantages. But preoccupation with detail, whether of weapons, of fortifications or of deployment, when unaccompanied by acquaintance with the technique of command, with the actual handling and supply of armies in the field, with the tactical principles and drills which do so much to win battles at the low level, was a handicap. It was out of place. It warped his judgement of and took his mind off those matters which his overall direction of operations demanded he concentrate on. As Speer put it, he knew too much for one in so exalted a position.

Opinion as to his initial command of the Army varies. Halder, his immediate subordinate and writing eight years afterwards, condemns it absolutely. He maintains that what Army Group and Army commanders required above all were long-term orders enabling them to make their own plans with a degree of independence within the framework of a general unified plan. Moreover the essence of tactical operations was movement. Thus Hitler's rejection of a planned withdrawal to more suitable defensive positions was absurd: 'he ordered the Army to fight to the last man where it stood, even where its positions were tactically impossible to hold . . . in consequence there were heavy losses in men and material which could, without the slightest doubt, have been avoided . . . this order shows the quality of Hitler's leadership.' Blumentritt, who was Kluge's Chief of Staff in the battle, thought otherwise. He regarded Hitler's order to stand fast and hold every position irrespective of circumstances as 'undoubtedly correct'. As there were no prepared positions to withdraw to, no proper line to re-establish, a withdrawal across open country, for roads and tracks were snow-blocked, would, he believes, have led to just the sort of dissolution of the Army and total cracking of the front which the Grand Army suffered. One of the corps commanders, von Tippelskirch, supports Blumentritt and thought of it as Hitler's one great achievement. Alan Clark's judgment is similar: 'As for Hitler, it was his finest hour. He had done more than save the German Army; he had achieved a complete personal ascendancy over its ruling class.'

Yet this very ascendancy was greatly to contribute to his undoing. Impatient of the General Staff's professionalism, its conservatism, its readiness to point the difficulties and disregard his own genius, he had always been. He consistently underrated the importance of turning grandiose plans of campaign into practical staff propositions. His own ability to reduce all problems to simple terms, his own iron will-power, indispensable though they may have been for his way of conducting war, were no substitutes for careful analyses of relative strengths by which capabilities could be assessed, of enemy intentions, of logistic considerations, of the effect time and space invariably wielded over the deployment and capacity of armies, above all of selecting objectives that were at once attainable and decisive, and then concentrating all efforts to attain them. Incapable of seeing any point of view which ran contrary to his own, with ever mounting confidence in his own military genius, his own infallibility, the consequence of his success in holding firm the German Army's line in the winter of 1941-42 was twofold. It convinced him that the failure of 1941 had been that of the General Staff, not his own in setting the Wehrmacht a task beyond their means; and it convinced him of the feasibility of a new offensive in 1942 which under his own direction would be the knock-out blow to end the war in the east.

Further east still it appeared that events were moving to Hitler's aid. On 7 December 1941 Japan attacked both the United States at Pearl Harbor and the United Kingdom in Malaya, Hong Kong and Singapore. Japan would be able to keep both of the democracies busy in the Far East. If ever there were a time to wring the maximum benefit from this un-looked for bonus, if ever there were a time to forgo an advant-age, or if not forgo it blow it up to unimagined proportions by demanding a Japanese offensive against Russia in exchange for Germany's active support, it was now. Yet Hitler, for a number of reasons—the United States' undisguised support for Britain, his belief that this was one more decadent and un-military democracy whose defeat would be swift, and by further stimulation of his own historic destiny in deciding the fate of the world—declared war on the United States four days after Pearl Harbor.

In his book, *Origins of the Second World War*, A. J. P. Taylor concludes that when the British people, having defied Hitler, found they were not strong enough to unseat him, he himself came to their assistance. 'His success depended on the isolation of Europe from the rest of the world. He gratuitously destroyed the source of this success. In 1941 he attacked Soviet Russia and declared war on the United States, two World Powers who asked only to be left alone. In this way a real World War began'. If attacking Russia was the irretrievable blunder, de-claring war on the United States must run it a close second.

Yet constantly when we examine Hitler's conversation or his speeches of this period we are struck with the extraordinary contrast between megalomaniac claptrap and strategic vision of the first order. One day, 11 December in his speech declaring war on America he is buoyed up by his great role as Man of Destiny: 'I can only be grateful to Providence that it entrusted me with the leadership in this historic struggle which, for the next five hundred or a thousand years, will be described as decisive, not only for the history of Germany, but for the whole of Europe and indeed the whole world. . . . A historical revision on a unique scale has been imposed on us by the Creator.' It is strange and somehow ridiculous to find Hitler putting forward the determinist view of history when no better example exists of events being subordinated to human will than his own. Next day, however, at the Führer Naval Conference of 12 December, we find him talking in very different vein to Raeder. 'Is there any possibility,' he asks, 'that the United States and Britain will abandon East Asia for a time in order to crush Germany and Italy first?' (Within a matter of weeks the US and UK Combined Chiefs of Staff are endorsing just such a strategy— Japan will be denied the means to wage war while the Allies concentrate on Germany's defeat, tightening the ring round her by sustaining Russia, strengthening the Middle East and getting hold of the whole North African coast.) Whilst Raeder reassures the Führer that the British cannot put India at risk nor the Americans abandon the Pacific to the Japanese Navy, he takes the opportunity to press his former strategy; while the Allies are preoccupied elsewhere now is the time to seize Malta and the Suez Canal, so preparing for a great linking-up with the Japanese in the Indian Ocean. 'The favourable situation in the Mediterranean, so pronounced at the present time, will probably never occur again.' It was in fact to occur once more, but then as now Hitler was not interested. The struggle with Russia had him in thrall.

If in 1941 Hitler's pretensions to generalship had been justified by his prevention of the Army's disintegration, it was but slight consolation for what was to happen in 1942. Despite the most spectacular advances, perhaps of the whole war, in both Russia and Africa, and visions of the most gigantic pincer movement that Panza and Stuka had ever executed, 1942 was to witness Hitler's final forfeiture of the initiative and the imposition of irreparable losses.

Not that the losses of *Barbarossa* had been negligible. Between 22 June, when the panzers in their thousands had cut through the Russian defenders and galloped across the Russian plains while the Stukas above destroyed aircraft, tanks, fuel dumps and soldiers on the march, and February the following year, when the Russian counter-offensive had died down and Halder, worried about the sagging front, had complained that troops do not hold ground when the temperature is 30 below, the Germans had lost over a million men killed, wounded and

missing, almost a third of what they had started the campaign
with. What had started out as a five months' battle of conquest
was beginning to turn into a four-year struggle of attrition. The
tide had not yet turned, but when it did there would be no shortage of the promised shallows and miseries. There were in
Hitler's view still some tides to be taken at the flood. Even
before the near-débâcle in front of Moscow, he had recognized
that his gamble of conquering Russia by blitzkrieg had not
come off. Halder recorded on 19 November 1941 that the
Führer's goals for 1942 were the Caucasus in March or April,
and Vologda or Gorki (respectively 300 miles northeast and
east of Moscow) in May. The question of building an 'East
Wall' remained open. So that Hitler's battles for Europe were
in 1942 still to be ones of conquest. Indeed he would reach a
very zenith of conquest coincident with the peak and turning
point of his career. Then the rot would set in and the battles of
resistance begin.

8

The Tide Turns

It's a thousand times easier to storm forward with an army and gain victories, than to bring an army back in an orderly condition after a reverse or a defeat.
Hitler, December 1942

By the spring of 1942 the fallacy of blitzkrieg was being exposed. The illusion of a short war was gone for ever. 1939 had given Hitler the satisfaction of smashing the Poles, together with some *Lebensraum* and a temporary guarantee of neutrality in the east; 1940 was the year of triumph and security—not unmixed with frustration—in the west. Two truths had been told as happy prologues to the swelling act of the imperial theme; in 1941 Hitler grasped for and muffed the third truth, a final solution in the East. 1942 therefore was the year for putting all to rights. Up to now he had been able to turn East or West as he chose without serious thought that the other front would erupt and interfere. But now that Hitler was bogged down in the East, it could not be long before the West once more took a hand in the affair. In 1942 then he would need to bend up each corporal agent to a terrible feat—the supreme fling at decision in the East, before the United States and Great Britain could open another front in the West, to say nothing of the south. Besides Germany had to have more oil. On the eve of the offensive by which he hoped to gain it, he told Paulus, commander of the 6th Army (which was to perish in the attempt), that if he did not get the Caucasus oil, he must end the war.

In making plans to do so, however, Hitler began more than ever before to close his eyes to hard military facts and rely instead upon his own intuition and will. He refused to see that however well will-power might complement military strength, it was no substitute. Yet all reference to the Russians' growing numbers of soldiers plus tanks and other weapons to equip them, all estimates of the enemy's capabilities, let alone intentions, roused him to a very ecstasy of fury.

When he was read a statement [Halder remembered], compiled from unimpeachable sources which showed that in 1942 Stalin would still be able to muster another 1 to $1\frac{1}{4}$ million men in the region north of Stalingrad and west of the Volga, and at least $\frac{1}{2}$ million more in the eastern Caucasus and the region to its north, and which proved moreover that the Russian output of first line tanks amounted to at least 1,200 a month, Hitler flew with clenched fists and foam in the corners of his mouth at the one who was reading this statement, and forbade such idiotic twaddle.

Like Louis Trevelyan in Trollope's novel Hitler had 'the philosopher's stone of madness, the power of transmuting all new facts into evidence for his fixed idea'. He knew he was right.

Refusal to contemplate the enemy's strength—'the Russians are dead'—was matched by reluctance to acknowledge the weakness of the Germans' own position. At the end of March 1942 only eight out of 162 divisions on the Eastern front were operationally ready, and the 16 panzer divisions could muster between them fewer than 150 tanks. But whereas in the first case nothing could shake Hitler's confidence that the Russians' winter offensive had used up their strength and with one more push the whole structure would at last come crashing down— for this after all was a factor in the equation which he could not influence except by battle, and therefore prior to battle, simply talked about—the state of the Wehrmacht, in respect of both equipment and men, was something he could directly affect and he proceeded to do so. In the matter of equipment and war production generally Hitler had already made an appointment which perhaps more than any other enabled him to go on waging war beyond the point in 1943 when many of his associates pronounced it lost. Albert Speer, a man quite unlike the general run of Nazi ruffians, became Minister of Armaments and Munitions in February 1942. Speer had an astonishing flair for organization, for mustering labour and for methods of production. Faced with ever-increasing difficulties he actually succeeded in expanding the output of arms in 1942 and 1943.*

To get more troops Hitler called upon his 'allies'—and so successful were he and his agents, Göring and Keitel among them, that for the coming summer campaign over 50 divisions were raised mainly from Rumania, Hungary and Italy. Mussolini, disturbed by Germany's setback in Russia, was subjected to another interminable lecture from Hitler when the two dictators met at Salzburg on 29-30 April. 'Hitler talks, talks, talks, talks,' recorded Ciano, 'Mussolini suffers—he, who is in the habit of talking himself, and who, instead, has to remain silent.' But the Duce was sufficiently reassured to provide nine divisions. Not all these 'foreign' divisions were to take part in the actual offensive, but some twenty of them were positioned in the southern sector of the front where the main German effort was to be made. What exactly was the Führer trying to achieve this time?

His principal objectives were no less than the Caucasus oil, the Donbass industry and Stalingrad. War Directive No 41 spelled out the details:

> Our aim is to wipe out the entire defence potential remaining to the Soviets, and to cut them off, as far as possible, from their most important centres of war industry. All available forces, German and allied, will be employed in this task. At the same time, the security of occupied territories in Western and Northern Europe ... will be ensured.... In pursuit of the original plan for the Eastern campaign, the armies of the Central sector will stand fast, those in the North will capture Leningrad and link up with the Finns, while those on the southern flank will break through into the Caucasus ... all available forces will be concentrated on the main operations in the Southern sector, with the aim of destroying the enemy before the Don, in order to secure the Caucasian oilfields and the passes through the Caucasus mountains themselves.

These were formidable tasks, but the fault of this directive

---

* But even Speer could not alter the fact that the Russian T-34 was the best all-round tank on either side.

was not so much because of this; rather it was that the kernel of Hitler's strategy was never made wholly clear to those who had to execute it. The master plan was never revealed. This is not to say that had it been known to all, the offensive would have succeeded in realizing Hitler's real objective, but at least it is more likely that the various armies would have operated in a way designed to contribute to this ultimate aim. What Hitler had in mind was that if he succeeded in destroying the Russian armies of the south and accounting for their oil and war economy, he would then have a choice—he could either exploit further south to Baku, or, much more promising for a conclusion, turn north, outflanking and dealing with the Russian forces in the centre protecting Moscow. In this way he might smash Russian resistance once and for all.

Perhaps the main, and in the end fatal, misunderstanding which arose was the role of Stalingrad. At first to Hitler it was subsidiary, a place to pin and block Soviet forces, while the main Axis thrust swept forward to the north or south; OKH, on the other hand, saw Stalingrad as the objective. Later these separate ideas may have come together, but by then the campaign had withered. From the very outset, from the moment that Hitler's intention to conduct an offensive at all was made known, it was opposed by the General Staff who maintained that the resources, German and allied, to undertake anything of the sort were inadequate. Hitler rejected the advice with scorn and contumely. He was having no truck with such cowardice and defeatism. If will-power could prevail in the defensive of 1941, it would prevail in the offensive of 1942. Besides there was no stopping now. To stand on the strategic defensive in the east was tantamount to admitting that the war could not be won, that force of arms must give way to negotiation. Such weakness was no part of Hitler's nihilistic philosophy. *Weltmacht oder Niedergang!* Victory or defeat! No compromise. Possessed by his conviction that decision in the east would rescue him from growing dangers to the west and south, unable to take in the war as a whole or genuinely to think in continents, the measure of Hitler's failure as a strategist, even while he still possessed some initiative, may best be measured by considering not so much what might have happened elsewhere had he grasped his opportunities, but by what actually did happen elsewhere even though he forwent them. That he was now free, however, to pursue policies which both strategically and tactically were at odds with the advice of his military commanders, that he was able once more to set the Wehrmacht to do things which the generals did not believe could be done, illustrates how absolute was the grip he had of both it and them.

We have seen that Hitler had made promises to Raeder for the execution of his 'Great Plan'—a gigantic pincer movement whose left-hand thrust would destroy Russian resistance in the Caucasus and sweep on towards Persia, meeting there the right hand which would already have gained possession of the Suez Canal; then the whole would link up with the Japanese in the Indian Ocean. He had agreed that Operation *Herkules*, the seizure of Malta, and *Aida*, the desert offensive, would be mounted in the summer of 1942, but *Herkules* was to wait until Rommel had driven the British from Cyrenaica and captured Tobruk. Rommel's success, perhaps the greatest of his career, was dazzling. Starting his advance on 18 January 1942 with no more than a spoiling attack in view, he converted immediate, yet limited, gains into a great victory culminating in the fall of Tobruk on 21 June. 'Soldiers!' read his Order of the Day,

> The great battle in the Marmarica has been crowned by your quick conquest of Tobruk. We have taken in all over 45,000 prisoners and destroyed or captured more than 1,000 armoured fighting vehicles and nearly 400 guns ... you have through your incomparable courage and tenacity dealt the enemy blow upon blow. Your spirit of attack has cost him the core of his field army ... Now for the complete destruction of the enemy. We will not rest until we have shattered the last remnants of the British Eighth Army. During the days to come, I shall call on you for one more great effort to bring us to this final goal.

Yet it was the very magnitude of his achievement which blinded Rommel to the true priorities. Having Tobruk in his hands, with all the fuel and trucks and stores his *Panzerarmee* so badly needed, closed his ears and mind to the absolute necessity of having Malta too, if his supply and reinforcement prospects were to have even a chance of matching those of the

British, so much closer to their well-nigh invulnerable lines of communication. Thus the key to mastery in the desert, the tiny fortress of Malta, was chucked aside at the very moment when its possession might indeed have opened the gates of Egypt, the Suez Canal and the Persian Gulf, with all its oil so priceless to the Axis. Ironically, it was the very ease and speed of Tobruk's capture that reprieved Malta. Rommel and Hitler may have had few qualities of character in common, but they did have one of inclination. They were both opportunists, both gamblers. When Rommel therefore claimed that his unlooked-for haul of enemy supplies was sufficient to carry him into the Delta, the Führer, ever reluctant to undertake an assault on Malta, supported him.

Here we have another example of Hitler's shortcomings as a strategist. To be a successful opportunist in a war involving the world, your opportunism must be on a grand scale. Yet quite apart from Hitler's inability to grasp the global nature of the conflict, or the supreme importance of war at sea and in the air, or the unique opportunity of severing the Allied link between the Pacific and the Atlantic—quite apart from this, reinforcement of success is fundamental to decision in war. Far from sticking to the rules, Hitler was bent on reinforcing failure. He promised Rommel everything, but gave him nothing, and with Malta revived, the 8th Army growing daily stronger, the Desert Air Force becoming more and more arbiter of the skies, and new management under Montgomery and Alexander, it was soon to become clear that, robbed of the men and material he could not do without, Rommel had shot his bolt in Africa. When we remember that a few months later Hitler poured his troops and aircraft into Tunisia—again by way of bolstering up failure—we can see how this particular tide of June 1942, having been neglected, was faithful in its subsequent delivery of shallows and miseries. The Desert Fox was no longer to be in search of quarry; he was to be the quarry himself.

Hitler and Raeder were not the only ones to have conceived a Great Plan. The Allies had one too. Like the German plan it concerned the Mediterranean—not because the Mediterranean was for the Allies *the* decisive theatre, but because it was not. President Roosevelt had determined to send American ground troops into battle against the Germans on land some-where in 1942. The leading strategists in the United States, General Marshall amongst them, believed in the direct approach. Roundabout methods, use of sea power on the peri-phery of Nazi Europe, savaging Italy first, possessing them-selves of Africa—such devious British ideas cut little ice with them. A knock-out blow at Germany itself was what they wanted, and they were at first reluctant to settle for anything less. Operation *Sledgehammer*, codename for the invasion of Western Europe in 1942, was the plan they had set their hearts on. But early that year it was made plain to them by the British Joint Planning Staff that the troops and support available to the Allies throughout 1942 were so limited that to put them ashore on the Continent of Europe would be to invite their elimination by German forces already deployed for the pur-pose. There would be no question of bringing relief to Russia, no question of opening and holding a second front which would be able to take on the German armies in the West, let alone what reserves and reinforcements they could call on. It would mean a bloody repulse—as the Dieppe raid was to be in August—whose psychological effect on the Axis and Grand Alliance alike might be incalculably more damaging than the loss of soldiers and weapons could be to the Allied cause.

Gradually the Americans came to see this. But whilst con-verted to the view that a landing on the mainland of Europe was not to be contemplated as a sensible operation of war in 1942, they were by no means ready to prejudice hopes and plans to do so in 1943. Indeed during the early months of 1942 British and American military opinion was unanimous that nothing must be done to interfere with this goal. The invasion of Western Europe in 1943 had a codename too, more modest than *Sledgehammer*, yet with almost too facile a connotation —it was known as *Round-Up*. It was true that a number of Axis soldiers were to be rounded up in 1943, but it would not be in Western Europe. Churchill, like Hitler, had long had his eye on French North Africa, and although his initial proposal to Roosevelt that it should be seized had foundered, when in July 1942 he renewed it, the President eagerly embraced the idea. Moreover Roosevelt, despite profound opposition from

Marshall and Eisenhower, both of whom regarded it as an unwarranted dissipation of effort away from the decisive theatre of operations, pushed it through. The notion of lighting a *Torch* (final codename for the Anglo-US landings in November 1942) became a firm strategic commitment.

It is curious that the Americans to some extent shared Hitler's view of the Mediterranean, and failed to appreciate its critical importance. Marshall, and as Chief of US General Staff his opinion carried weight, saw the possession of North Africa merely as a means of establishing a defensive circle round continental Europe. He could not at first see the immense advantages both of security—the Middle East itself, the oil, to say nothing of the benefit to shipping (a factor which proved more handcuffing to Allied military ambitions than any single other) —and of offensive potential, a springboard from which to threaten and actually attack southern Europe. Churchill was in no doubt that to lay hands on the whole of the North African coastline would lend reality to his strategic dream of being able to deliver blows at the Axis, either from the Atlantic or the Mediterranean or both simultaneously, with but a single aim—throttling and extinguishing the Third Reich. The result of all Anglo-American discussion and argument was that when Churchill set out for Cairo and Moscow on 2 August 1942, he had obtained Roosevelt's agreement to *Torch* and so would be able to report to Stalin that a second front, however remote from the mainland of Europe it might be, would be opened in 1942. Some ten days later he did so, and recounts that, as he explained the plan, Stalin became intensely interested. Churchill listed the advantages of freeing the Mediterranean and emphasized that once this was done yet another front could be opened from it. The Allies would be able to threaten the southern part of *Festung Europa*. He even went so far as to draw a picture of a crocodile for the Russian Premier and illustrated his intention to attack the soft belly of the reptile at the same time as hitting it on the snout. What grist for the amateur strategists' mills was to come from this harmless demonstration! Churchill then explained that with the ever-present aim of taking the strain off the Red Army, whereas a descent on Northern France would simply be rebuffed, North

Africa beckoned with solid promises of victory. 'Then we could help in Europe. If we could gain North Africa Hitler would have to bring his Air Force back, or otherwise we would destroy his allies, even, for instance, Italy, and make a landing ... !' Churchill was impressed by Stalin's rapid grasp of the strategic advantages of *Torch*—that Rommel would be sandwiched, Spain overawed, Frenchmen and Germans set in conflict in France, Italy exposed to the full weight of attack. 'I was deeply impressed.... It showed the Russian Dictator's swift and complete mastery of a problem hitherto novel to him. Very few people alive could have comprehended in so few minutes the reasons which we had all so busily been wrestling with for months. He saw it all in a flash.' This volume of Churchill's was published in 1950. Everyone likes flattery; and when you come to Russian Dictators you should lay it on with a trowel. Later in their discussions Stalin confidently predicted that he would successfully defend the Caucasus against the German advance.

We must now consider how were these ideas of the two war leaders turned into fact on the battlefields of Asia and Africa. The two Great Plans went in such a way that Hitler's ability to mount offensives, other than those of short-lived desperation, came to an end. He ceased to call the tune and began to dance to it. He lost the initiative not on one front, but on all three, east, west and south, in Russia, the Atlantic and North Africa.

It will be as well to sketch the main events before seeing what they seemed like to those who took part in them. On 28 June, when the 8th Army was withdrawing to Alamein, the German offensive in the east began. Army Group B under von Bock was directed on Stalingrad with 4th Panzer Army and von Paulus's 6th Army; Army Group A under List was headed south-east through the Caucasus with Baku as a final objective. Three weeks later when Hitler confidently asserted, so well were the advances going, that the Russian was finished, General Halder, ever cautious, ever circumspect, was moved to concede that it looked uncommonly like it. In fact Hitler had already made the tactical blunder which was to ensure that the Russian was not finished. July 1942 was the month which some observers have regarded as the turning of the tide. Rommel's repulse at Alamein—by Auchinleck, not Montgomery—was certainly a check, but the German armies in Russia had not yet come to a halt. All in all October 1942 is a better month to mark the change—Rommel's defeat at Alamein and the Germans' final failure to wrest Stalingrad from the grip of Stalin's armies. Yet the initial success of Hitler's Russian offensive led him into exactly the same error as he had been guilty of a year earlier.

Instead of sticking to his plan that the whole weight of Army Group B should concentrate on establishing the 'block' at Stalingrad before deciding what Hoth's 4th Panzer Army would do next—and had he stuck to the plan it is probable that Stalingrad would have fallen, for the Russians would have had far less time to strengthen its defences—instead of this, Hitler diverted Hoth before the Stalingrad battle was joined; what is more, diverted it to help Army Group A which at that time did not need help, and then as resistance at Stalingrad stiffened, re-directed Hoth there when it was already too late. This chopping and changing reminds us of D'Erlon's Reserve Corps at Waterloo, which marched and counter-marched between Ligny and Quatre Bras, unable to influence either battle. For Hitler it was the old story—no patient concentration, either of mind or material, on one objective at a time, but a wild dilettantism at its worst, dashing forward for all objectives at once, grossly exaggerating his own strength and the enemy's weakness, doubling the aim whilst halving the forces to achieve each one, and by doing so, achieving neither.

By September the struggle for Stalingrad, the battle that saved the world, as Edward Sammis has it, was raging, and the thrust to the Caucasus had been halted by the Russians short of the main oilfields. The Wehrmacht's tide was as high as it had ever been or ever would be. Henceforth it would ebb.

Hitler, who in August had moved from his East Prussian headquarters to a new one at Vinnitsa in the Ukraine, urged his armies on, sacked Halder and appointed Zeitzler in his place. Halder had consistently protested against what he regarded as wastage of men in the battle for Stalingrad and its taking on a mystic importance for Hitler quite at odds with the price it was exacting. When Halder recommended that the

23   Street fighting in Stalingrad

24   German dead in Stalingrad

25   A German sentry guards the Atlantic Wall

battle be broken off, he was dismissed. In blaming Halder for the state of nervous exhaustion they were both in, the Führer made a most revealing comment to the effect that it was not professional ability which was required, but National Socialist ardour. 'So passed from the scene Franz Halder,' observed John Wheeler-Bennett, 'the man who could have been a Yorck or a Lafayette, and had not the courage to be either.' Halder was not the only general to be out of favour. List's failure to overcome the increasing enemy resistance in the Caucasus turned Hitler's displeasure not only on himself, but on the unfortunate Jodl who was unwise enough to point out that List had simply been carrying out the Supreme Commander's orders.

Halder is not always just in his condemnation of Hitler's handling of the Wehrmacht for he allots him no credit for successes in face of General Staff advice and all blame for failures. But his comments on the 1942 offensive are fair:

> While the attack was moving forward, Hitler's pre-conceived idea that all Russian resistance was finally broken led him to pull out the bulk of the Sixth Army's tank formations—just when they were particularly required to deal with stiffening Russian resistance west of Stalingrad—and to send them to the south over the Don. He then gave the forces assembled there a new assignment—the conquest of the Caucasus and a push through to the line Batoum-Baku! That was something completely new. In place of one single operation, directed uniformly to the East and with its main weight towards Stalingrad, which moreover as far as the south was concerned merely needed sealing off, there were now to be two separate and diverging operations.... But there was worse to come.... Hitler suddenly gave orders for particularly valuable motorized formations to be moved off to the West. As for the Crimean Army ... he unexpectedly ordered them north with the task of taking Leningrad. These decisions had ceased to have anything in common with the principles of strategy.... They were the product of a violent nature following its momentary impulses, a nature which acknowledged no bounds to possibility....

Yet the possibility of further offensives no longer existed. List's Army Group in the Caucasus, von Weichs' at Stalingrad, Rommel's *Panzerarmee* in Africa—all had gone over to the defensive. November 1942 was the climacteric month at Stalin-

grad and Alamein alike. The armies of General Vatutin from
the north and General Eremenko from the south joined hands
at Kalach, some 50 miles west of Stalingrad. Over 300,000
German soldiers were trapped. Rommel, despite all handicaps
of denied supplies and limited support, enjoyed one incalculable
advantage. Führer HQ was not just behind him. He was able
to reinforce his own tactical instinct with the disobedience
which sheer distance allowed him. In spite of huge losses—
perhaps half his army—and of Hitler's absurd order to stand
fast (a repetition of his successful demonstration of what will-
power alone had done in December 1941, for an order which
held good in the snow would presumably hold good in the
sand), Rommel extracted his depleted forces to fight another
day—and by now there was an Allied Army on either side of
him. There would be no shortage of fighting to do. Nor was
there in Russia. Von Manstein's great drive from the south to
relieve Stalingrad was countered and checked by Malinovsky in
December. Early in January Army Group A began to withdraw
from the Caucasus, and the Russians captured Pitomnik airfield through which the Luftwaffe had kept Paulus' 6th Army
supplied. At the end of the month, in spite of all Hitler's orders
—'Capitulation is impossible. The 6th Army will do its historic
duty at Stalingrad until the last man, in order to make possible
the reconstruction of the Eastern Front'—in spite even of
being promoted to Field-Marshal—'There is no record in
military history,' Hitler told Jodl, 'of a German Field-Marshal
being taken prisoner'—Paulus gave up. The battle of Stalingrad
was over, and with it some 250,000 Germans had been accounted
for.

> What hurts me most personally [Hitler declared] is that I pro-
> moted him to Field-Marshal. I wanted to give him this final
> satisfaction. That's the last Field-Marshal I shall appoint in this
> war. You mustn't count your chickens before they are hatched.
> I don't understand that at all. So many people have to die, and
> then a man like that besmirches the heroism of so many others
> at the last minute. He could have freed himself from all sorrow
> and ascended into eternity and national immortality, but he pre-
> fers to go to Moscow. What kind of choice is that? It just doesn't
> make sense.

Alan Bullock called this declaration the comment of a supreme egoist, the sign that Hitler was beginning to think the German nation unworthy of his own genius. When it came to his own turn Hitler preferred to free himself from sorrow and descend into eternity. His national immortality is not in doubt.

The Eastern front was no joke. Alan Clark emphasizes that for the German nation all the other campaigns, at sea, in Africa, even the bombing of Germany itself, were side-shows. Two million soldiers were in Russia. To say that you were off to the Eastern front, a young soldier remembered, was like admitting that you had contracted some fatal disease, like being a man condemned to death. And Werner von Ebrennac, in *Le Silence de la Mer*, is struck with incredulity and horror when he hears from a former friend what the Nazi plans for Europe really are—'We have the chance to destroy France, and destroy her we will.... We'll turn her rotten with our smiles and our forbearance. We'll make a grovelling bitch out of her.... We'll buy their souls for a mess of pottage.... We've got to build for a thousand years hence: first we must destroy.' He stands on his rights, demands despite his wounds to be sent back to a fighting unit. He tells his host in France: ' "I am authorized to set off tomorrow." I thought I saw the ghost of a smile on his lips when he amplified this with: "Off to Hell." He raised his arm towards the East—towards those vast plains where the wheat of the future will be nourished on corpses.'

We must go back to Hitler in his headquarters at Vinnitsa on 12 September 1942. Since April, by Reichstag decree, Supreme War Lord, *Oberster Feldherr*,* he was telling two generals, von Weichs and von Paulus, that the vital thing was to concentrate every available man in order to capture as quickly as possible the whole of Stalingrad and the banks of the Volga. From now until the end of the war he was frequently to call for every man and every tank and every aircraft to make a supreme effort for one or other vital objective. But it was nearly always too late. The Wehrmacht, in spite of immense defensive power, was going into a decline; its tasks were, like its enemies, too numerous. Tempt not a desperate man, cried

---

* In fact Hitler was named *Oberster Gerichtsherr* (Supreme Law-Lord), but it amounted to the same thing—absolute power of life or death.

Romeo. In the autumn of 1942 Stalingrad was Hitler's temptation. Here the war would be decided. The street fighting in
Stalingrad was as different as it could be from the approaches
to Moscow almost a year before. But the two battles had something in common. Once again it was Hitler versus Zhukov, and
Zhukov had never lost a battle. General Doerr recalled that
the situation map at GHQ had condensed itself into one of the
city itself:

> For every house, workshop, water-tower, railway embankment,
> wall, cellar and every pile of ruins, a bitter battle was waged,
> without equal even in the First World War with its vast expendi-
> ture of munitions. The distance between the enemy's army and
> ours was as small as it could possibly be. Despite the concentrated
> activity of aircraft and artillery, it was impossible to break out
> of the area of close fighting. The Russians surpassed the Germans
> in their use of the terrain and in camouflage and were more
> experienced in barricade warfare for individual buildings.

One Russian soldier of the 42nd Regiment remembered turning
a building at a crossroads in the city into a final stronghold
when surrounded by the Germans. In the basement were the
wounded; just above it he sited their one remaining heavy
machine-gun with the last belt of ammunition they had. There
was no water, and but a few handfuls of grain.

> The Germans attacked again. I ran upstairs with my men and
> could see their thin, blackened and strained faces, the bandages
> on their wounds, dirty and clotted with blood, their guns held
> firmly in their hands. There was no fear in their eyes.... We beat
> off the next attack with stones, firing occasionally and throwing
> our last grenades.... This time, reckoning that we had run out
> of ammunition, they came impudently out of their shelter, stand-
> ing up and shouting. They came down the street in a column. I
> put the last belt in the heavy machine-gun at the semi-basement
> window and sent the whole of the 250 bullets into the yelling,
> dirty-grey Nazi mob.... Again we heard the ominous sound of
> tanks. From behind a neighbouring block stocky German tanks
> began to crawl out. This, clearly, was the end.

Resistance of this sort was something the Wehrmacht had
not come across before. The comments and diaries of German
soldiers are full of references to barbarians, wild beasts, fanatics,

soldiers who were not men but creatures made of cast-iron, possessed of a stubbornness which enabled them to see themselves as already condemned to die. 'If all the buildings of Stalingrad are defended like this then none of our soldiers will get back to Germany.' 'Imagine Stalingrad,' another young officer wrote, 'eighty days and eighty nights of hand-to-hand struggles. The street is no longer measured by metres but by corpses ... when night arrives, one of those scorching howling bleeding nights, the dogs plunge into the Volga and swim desperately to gain the other bank ... Animals flee this hell; the hardest stones cannot bear it for long; only men endure.'

The German soldiers had a good deal more to endure before the questionable release of a Soviet prisoner of war camp. Neither the closing of the trap at Kalach nor the failure of von Manstein's drive to relieve the trapped could move Hitler from his determination not to retire an inch. As if it were not enough to throw away the 6th Army, Hitler was repeating the pattern in Africa. The mere fact that Roosevelt had fulfilled his pledge and landed American troops in North Africa without molestation from the U-boats or the Luftwaffe underlined the degree to which the Allies held the initiative in the west. Yet at the very moment when it seemed certain that his grip on Africa was being prized loose, Hitler reinforced it. So swift and effective was this reinforcement that the Axis was able to prolong the battle there for six months. But it was a losing game. To the quarter of a million soldiers he sacrificed at Stalingrad, Hitler threw in a similar number in Tunisia. Napoleon had once boasted that he had an income of 100,000 soldiers a year. It was not large enough for Hitler, who in 1942 overspent an even larger income. One hundred and thirty years earlier Napoleon had confided in Marmont that his game was going wrong. So was Hitler's. On all fronts he had been stopped. The initiative would never return.

'It had been a remarkable career,' writes Allan Bullock, 'while it lasted. At the moment when the tide turned in the autumn of 1942 Hitler was undisputed master of the greater part of continental Europe, with his armies threatening the Volga, the Caucasus, and the Nile. For the man who had begun by peddling third-rate sketches in the back-streets of Vienna this was no small achievement. But now the price had to be paid for the methods of treachery and violence by which it had been accomplished—and it was relentlessly exacted.'

Hitler's War Directive No 47, dated 28 December 1942, so different in character from those which had gone before, shows at once that from 1943 onwards Germany was on the strategic defensive: 'The situation in the Mediterranean makes it possible that an attack may be made in the foreseeable future on Crete and on German and Italian bases in the Aegean Sea and the Balkan peninsula.' This sentence sets the tone. The directive is full of the words 'defence' and talks of the need to prepare for 'defensive battles'.

With the initiative gone, it would no longer be a question of the world asking itself where Hitler was going to strike next. Now he was compelled to ask himself where the Allies would strike next. All the old arguments as to the advantages of operating on internal lines on the one hand, and the supremacy of air and sea power on the other would recur; the Germans' inherent capability of moving powerfully to counter an attack anywhere together with the grievous necessity of keeping up a guard everywhere was one problem; the Allies' flexibility and freedom of choice together with the absolute need to concentrate on a single and limited objective was another; between them the battles of 1943 and 1944 would be resolved. In the event 1943 saw no spectacular descents from the sea or air. Sicily was taken; Italy invested. The heart of Germany was not threatened, although it was being made to beat a little faster by the combined efforts of the RAF and US Air Force. What mattered was that the integrity of *Festung Europa* was disturbed.

As might have been expected when the tide of fortune turned against Germany, Hitler's relations with the generals worsened. This time there was no doubt where the responsibility rested. 'To many he now was revealed not as the most brilliant strategist of all time, but as a megalomaniac corporal, whose lucky gambles had hitherto been justified by a few intuitive master strokes and the incompetence and unpreparedness of his opponents.' Yet he did not cease to keep all the power of decision in his own hands. Indeed so great did his suspicions of the military men around him become that he took upon himself more and more work—methodical, routine work which was not his forte. Gone were the grand intuitive ideas which had paid such dividends in the past. Intuition now contradicted facts, was a substitute for professional skill which in the grave circumstances of 1943 was more necessary than ever. Hitler's military assets had been those which went hand in hand with his extraordinary political talents—a taste for surprise, the unorthodox, the knack of exploiting weakness and taking huge risks when the initiative was wholly in his hands. None of these conditions now prevailed. His interference in the day-to-day tactical battle—and at his twice-daily conferences he would issue orders relating to battalion objectives or defensive positions—was not only disastrous in itself, but meant that he had no time for matters of strategy, which as Supreme Commander were peculiarly his concern. This total over-burdening of the day's business meant that important decisions were often not made at all. Yet the generals went on obeying. It was not only a question of their oath to the Führer. They knew that he still commanded support from the masses, support which increased, rather than dwindled, as Germany itself was more and more under threat.

Certainly the battles of conquest were over; those of resistance were about to begin. Yet in many ways it was in adversity that the Wehrmacht was most to be admired. 'Loss of hope, rather than loss of life,' said Liddell Hart, 'is the factor that really decides wars, battles, and even the smallest combats.' And it was a factor which Hitler, 'the common soldier of the 1914-18 War', had in abundance; so did the soldiers who fought for him in the 1939-45 War. Neither he nor they abandoned hope. Hitler might call it a thousand times easier to storm forward and gain victories—so it was against inferior, unprepared, almost unworthy opponents—but fighting on, when this factor of all factors, hope, was in doubt, this was far more remarkable. To contend every inch of the way back as tenaciously as it had ever stormed forward, against opponents whose ironmongery in the air and everywhere else was overwhelming; to show not just the unchanging military virtues of courage and determination, but also skill, craft and economy; to substitute tactical brilliance for strategic aridity at a time when the Panzers were robbed of their partner, the Stuka—to do all this was to give an account of themselves which every soldier is constrained to applaud.

9

Violation of a Fortress

The Italian front proved to be a far greater drain on Germany than on the Allies. In October [1943] Eisenhower's eleven divisions were holding down a German force double that size in Italy alone. By his decision to fight south of Naples, Hitler was compelled to keep ten divisions idle in Northern Italy.

Chester Wilmot

In January 1943 Churchill and Roosevelt, with the Combined Chiefs of Staff, conferred at Casablanca. Out of this meeting came the Allied blueprint for prosecuting the war that year. It was agreed that the Allies should continue to concentrate on Germany first, and that since the Tunisian campaign was unlikely to end before May, no invasion of Western Europe which could lead both to its liberation and to striking mortal blows at Germany itself would be possible before 1944. The main Mediterranean consideration therefore was how to make use of North Africa, once it was in their hands, to hasten Germany's defeat, to lend further weight to the whole idea of forcing Hitler to bolster up Italy in Europe as he had done in Africa, to facilitate the great cross-Channel enterprise when it was launched. Three special objectives were to be pursued: to open the Mediterranean and release shipping, to divert German pressure from Russia, and to persuade Italy to give in. All this was to be done—by invading Sicily! Beyond this, apart from vague and illusory prospects of manufacturing circumstances in which Turkey would agree to enter the war on the Allied side, offensive plans in the Mediterranean did not go. This being so, there could be little expectation, in spite of the Chiefs' of Staff express intentions, of defeating Germany in 1943, whatever Italy's fate might be. Elsewhere, therefore, major preparations were to go forward.

First, the Allies determined, and there was no doubt of their getting priorities right here, that defeating the U-boats must have a heavy claim on resources; second, severe blows would be directed against Germany from the air; third, the most powerful forces that could be mustered would be assembled in the United Kingdom ready to re-enter the continent as soon as resistance there was sufficiently written down to allow this re-entry to strike at the very heart of the Third Reich. There was not at first unanimity of view between the United States and British military experts. Whereas the British were anxious to keep Hitler fighting in the Mediterranean during the time that must pass before they could mount an attack in the west, in fact to descend on Italy and oblige the Germans to conduct another major campaign in addition to the Eastern one, the Americans thought differently. Reverting to their pre-*Torch* point of view, they saw the Mediterranean as the very distraction to their efforts which the British intended should be to Hitler's. In fairness to them, the Americans were deeply concerned about Japan and reasoned that, if no proper offensive could be mounted against Germany in 1943, then the Far East should have first title to their resources. But they were in the end persuaded to see that it would not be possible to stand on the strategic defensive against Hitler throughout one whole year and expect either that the Wehrmacht's entire weight would not be turned on Russia with results perhaps as far-reaching as a separate peace, or that Germany's position in the west would be so substantially weakened that the cross-Channel venture's probable success could be furthered. The grinding down process had to go on. It was for precisely this that the so-called Mediterranean strategy had been designed. The Chiefs' of Staff report at Casablanca was thus clear as to priorities and as to objectives:

> Operations in the Pacific and Far East shall continue with the object of maintaining pressure on Japan, and for the full scale offensive against Japan as soon as Germany is defeated. These operations must be kept within such limits as will not, in the opinion of the Joint Chiefs of Staff, jeopardize the capacity of the United Nations to take advantage of any favourable opportunity for the decisive defeat of Germany in 1943.

It was, of course, the Americans' scepticism as to the likely dividends of a Mediterranean campaign which explains the incompleteness of their plans there. While agreeing that Churchill should make approaches to Turkey and that Operation *Husky*—the invasion of Sicily—should be mounted in July, no comprehensive long-term plans were discussed or developed. Indeed Marshall believed that Hitler would give up southern Italy when Sicily had been captured. Yet in harbouring such a belief he underlined the paradox of looking for such gains when his own strategic notions had so little faith in their probability that no plans were made to exploit opportunity should it be presented to them. Nor was there anything in either Hitler's character or his recent conduct of war to suggest that he would give up what he could hold on to. If Hitler was to be surprised at all, it was not that the Allies would aim to smash Italy's will to continue with the struggle, it was that having done so they were totally unprepared to wrest real advantage from it.

If there were doubts in Allied counsels as to the wisdom and promise of attacking southern Europe, there were none in the German High Command as to its certainty or imminence. Only the actual place was in question. And now, as earlier in the war, the Balkans were for Hitler a peculiarly sensitive spot— a flank which had been of such concern to him before *Barbarossa* began that he had been willing to pay a high price in troops and time to seal it off. Now once again, with *Barbarossa* bogged down and the Allies on the point of possessing all North Africa, this flank would be exposed. It must be made secure. Hence the Führer's War Directive No 47:

As a result of developments in North Africa, I transfer the defence of the South-east area ... to Commander Armed Forces South-east who will be directly subordinate to me as Commander-in-Chief South-east (Army Group E).... In preparing for a defensive battle of this kind, Commander-in-Chief South-east will have the following tasks:

1. Preparation of coastal defences with the main emphasis in the Dodecanese, Crete and the Peloponnese, which will be developed as fortresses....

2. The final pacification of the hinterland and the destruction of rebels and bandits of all kinds ....

3. The preparation of all necessary measures to meet an enemy attack in the Balkans which is helped or condoned by Turkey....

The practical demonstration of this directive was that throughout the summer of 1943 the Germans disposed twice as many divisions in South-east Europe as in Italy. Europe's under-belly was certainly proving to be a distraction, even though in spite of initial successes it could hardly be called soft. Meanwhile, in his headquarters at *Wolfsschanze*, Hitler was already beginning to have new ideas about the war. Military decision is eluding him, with present resources is unattainable, but just as 'space for living' had once been a purpose in itself, the be-all and end-all of finishing the war, so now space for another design, for manoeuvre, was to be the means of prolonging it. It was time Hitler wanted now, time to get new weapons and to use them, time with which to pluck victory from stalemate, before he himself was checkmated. 'Space is one of the most important military factors,' he told Jodl (how some of the generals must have longed to tell him that it was not always necessary to state the obvious), 'you can conduct military operations only if you have space ... in this huge space one can hold on and on. If we had a crisis like this last one, on the old German border along the Oder-Warthe curve, Germany would have been finished. Here in the East we were able to cushion the blow. We have a battlefield here that has room for strategical operations.'

Despite this opportunity the greatest strategical genius of all time was not at the moment proposing to avail himself of it. He virtually handed over control of operations in the southern wing of the Eastern front to OKH and von Manstein. Manstein favoured flexible defence and was permitted to adjust the dispositions of his Don Army Group so that he could conduct it. In short Hitler was being reasonable for once. When he saw von Manstein at *Wolfsschanze* on 5 February, he began with an admission of failure and responsibility quite foreign to his customary form: 'I alone bear the responsibility for Stalingrad.' Manstein recorded that at this time he had the impression that the tragedy of Stalingrad had deeply affected Hitler—not just because of the blow it dealt his leadership, but because so many soldiers who had believed in him and fought for him with such courage and devotion had lost their lives or liberty. Manstein's later and revised opinion was perhaps nearer the mark, that soldiers of the Reich, field-marshals or privates, all were 'mere tools of his war aims'. But given this exceptionally self-deprecatory prologue to their conference, Manstein wished to discuss two critical matters with the Führer—the business of Supreme Command and the future handling of operations in South Russia. He drew blank on the first; got some of his way on the second.

Accepting that Hitler would never relinquish his position as Supreme Commander of the Wehrmacht and as Commander-in-Chief of the Army, von Manstein tried to persuade him to guarantee uniformity of command by appointing 'one Chief of Staff whom he must trust implicitly, and at the same time vest with the appropriate responsibility and authority'. But Hitler hedged. Disappointments with former Chiefs of Staff and Commanders-in-Chief, the difficulty of Göring's position—his own appointed successor and as such impossible to subordinate to the sort of Chief which Manstein had in mind—and his own unexpressed determination to keep final arbitration of strategy in his own hands, the thing could not be done. That Hitler was prepared to discuss the matter at all shows how adaptable he could be when he wanted to get the most out of an acknowledged critic whose services he nevertheless could not dispense with. On the second point von Manstein succeeded in getting agreement that it might be necessary to withdraw from the east of the Donetz basin to ease the threat menacing the whole of the German Army's southern wing.

Hitler was in a giving vein. Von Manstein noted that the Führer 'always did have a masterly knack of adapting his manner to his interlocutor'. He had partially removed the wind from von Manstein's sails by assuming unqualified responsibility for Stalingrad. Now he was to be similarly ingratiating with Guderian, whom he wanted to reorganize the Panzer arm. When the two men met at Vinnitsa on 20 February 1943, Guderian had not seen Hitler since his dismissal in December

1941. He found the Führer greatly changed and greatly aged—
a less assured manner, hesitant speech, a trembling left hand.
But his desk was covered with Guderian's books and his opening words were irresistible: 'Since 1941 our ways have parted;
there were numerous misunderstandings at that time which I
much regret.' This was something, but the admission which no
soldier could have heard unmoved from a Commander-in-Chief
when things were going badly for his country was perhaps what
ensured Guderian's co-operation—'I need you'. He became
Inspector General of Armoured Troops with wide respon-
sibilities and direct access to Hitler. Guderian's powers of
command were equivalent to those of an Army Commander;
he was required to turn the panzer troops into a 'decisive weapon
for winning the war'; he was able to deal direct with Speer, in
charge of Armaments and Munitions; most surprising of all
perhaps, he was authorized to direct the armoured troops of
the Waffen-SS and the Luftwaffe as far as organization and
training were concerned. Guderian was to serve his Führer with
fidelity until the end. It was ironic that he should have been
Inspector General of Armoured Troops when the 'greatest tank
battle in history' at Kursk dealt those troops a blow from which
they never really recovered.

On 17 February Hitler and von Manstein conferred again,
this time at Zaporozhe, as close to the front line as Hitler ever
came, the bunker in Berlin always excepted. Their three day
discussion underlined once more the extraordinary dichotomy
of Hitler's military qualifications. On the one hand he was
almost always more than a match for the most professional of
his professionals when it came to discussing grand strategy, for
his own strategic experience was almost unparalleled. Besides he
alone had all the facts. At the same time he was a master of such
tactical detail as how to site an 88-mm gun, capture a fort or
calculate the logistic needs of forward troops. But on the other
hand he knew little or nothing about actually commanding
armies in the field, and his first attempt to do so with the stand
fast order of December 1941 had, by virtue of its very success,
taught him a false and fatal lesson. What had worked in 1941—
'this little matter of operational command is something that
anyone can do'—had led in 1942 to the unmitigated catastrophe

of Stalingrad. Hence his willingness to allow von Manstein to conduct a mobile defensive battle in the early part of 1943. And what had happened? More ground had been lost and the front was almost collapsing. What was the use of it? Fluid defence might have its advocates. But if it meant endless loss of prestige, territory and troops, Hitler was not one of them. This was not his idea of strategical operations which screwed every benefit out of space. At Zaporozhe, Hitler called a halt once more, and ordered Manstein to stop withdrawing and retake Kharkov. Manstein did.

Several factors came to his aid. The Russian armies holding Kharkov were at the end of their tether, both logistically and physically; the SS Panzer Corps, which co-operated with Hoth's Panzer Army, was equipped with the Tiger tank whose agility, by virtue of its very broad tracks, and its gun-armour combination (it mounted the 88-mm gun) outclassed the formerly undisputed master of the battlefield, the T-34. By the end of the second week in March, the Russians were turned out of Kharkov and the German Army had succeeded in re-establishing itself more or less on the line from which the 1942 offensive had been launched. The power of the Wehrmacht was not to be sneezed at. This success made possible the very thing which Guderian was later to contemplate with incredulous aversion—even Hitler admitted that his stomach turned over at the thought of it— an offensive in the East in 1943. Why then did he plan and order it? It seemed to some of his staff that he could think of no alternative. He seemed to have run out of ideas. Not so some of those officers who were resolved to be rid of him. Yet the brandy bottle bomb which Tresckow and Schlabrendorff secreted into Hitler's aircraft failed to explode during his flight from Smolensk to Rastenburg. 'The Devil's hand', as Clark puts it, may have protected Hitler. It was not to protect the 4th Panzer Army when it took part in *Fall Zitadelle*; this greatest of all tank battles in the history of war would put an end to consolidation in the east and herald the arrival of a Russian tide whose ultimate ability to surmount even the high shore of the Wehrmacht was not long to be in doubt.

Zitadelle was the German attack on the Kursk Salient at the beginning of July. The basic fault of the operation was that it

was delayed for so long—apart from indecision, Hitler wanted
the new Panther tanks to take part—that by the time it came,
the Russians were not merely ready for it; they were wholly
prepared to defeat it; they might almost be said to have
welcomed it, for having defeated it, they at once seized the
initiative, never again to lose it. By 5 July when this last German
offensive in Russia began, on the other side everything was
ready. The Russian defensive zone contained eight belts with
a depth of about 200 miles. Every form of defensive device—
mines, anti-tank guns, tank-killing teams, armour itself including the T-34 and new tank destroyers mounting 122-mm and
152-mm guns, whole divisions of artillery (the Russians were
masters at using massed artillery) and perhaps a million soldiers.
It was like Alam el Halfa blown up a thousand times. Against
this formidable array the cream of the Wehrmacht, half a
million men, with no less than 17 panzer divisions, went forward. Model's 9th Army contained three Panzer Corps and
two Infantry Corps in support; Hoth's 4th Panzer Army, operating on a frontage of only 30 miles, had the unprecedented total
of nine panzer divisions, and what divisions they were—SS
Totenkopf, SS *Leibstandarte*, SS *Das Reich*, *Gross Deutschland*,
3rd, 6th, 7th, 11th and 19th Panzer. The general feeling was
that, if a force of such veterans as this could not smash the
Russians, nothing could. Hitler believed that he would not
just smash them, but by driving them back to the Don, the
Volga even, he would at last be able to sweep up from the
south-east behind Moscow and capture it. His Order of the Day
was at once an appeal and a confession:

> Soldiers of the Reich! This day you are about to take part in an
> offensive of such importance that the whole future of the war
> may depend on its outcome. More than anything else, your vic-
> tory will show the whole world that resistance to the power of
> the German Army is hopeless.

In the event it was the German Army's defeat which showed the
world that resistance to it was full of hope. Blitzkrieg could
not work against a determined and prepared enemy whose
depth, concentration and reserves seemed to be limitless. The
battle was one of senseless battering against defences which
were too strong and numbers which were too great. A week

after the attack had begun a panzer NCO recorded that they had found themselves taking on inexhaustible masses of enemy tanks which streamed 'like rats' all over the battlefield. Never had he had so overwhelming an impression of Russian numbers and strength. Even the new Panther tank did not come up to expectation. Mechanically not as reliable as they should have been, vulnerable to flank fire and easily set ablaze, their crews inadequately trained, neither they nor the Tigers could turn the scales. The veterans of Hoth's 4th Panzer Army had simply indulged in a 'death ride'. Hitler called off the offensive. Guderian's panzers had been cut to pieces and the Inspector General of Armoured Troops himself retired to a sick bed with dysentry.

Hitler's principal concern, however, was not that so many of Guderian's precious panzers had been destroyed. It was that another attack, where space was at a premium, had taken place. The Allies had landed in Sicily on 10 July. In spite of all the setbacks, there might still be plenty of room for manoeuvre in Russia, plenty of space for 'strategical operations', but the Allies rapid descent on and capture of Sicily brought the war on land closer to *Festung Europa* than at any time since its establishment. On 9 July Hitler again rang the bell for Mussolini and the two men duly met in northern Italy. As usual the talk was one-sided; its content was familiar too. There was nothing to be done but to go on fighting—in Russia, in Italy, on all fronts, everywhere. It was the will to resist, the will to conquer that mattered. Mussolini sat silent. He could not argue with 'the voice of History'. Within a week, however, other voices had their say. The Fascist Grand Council met; the King dismissed the Duce; Badoglio formed a new Government. Like other régimes before and since it was founded on the twin authorities of Army and Monarchy.

That a dictator, like himself, could be so quickly, with such absurd ease, dismissed and shorn of all power was a serious political blow to Hitler. It seemed that it was after all but a step from the sublime to the ridiculous. But the military implications of this upheaval were what possessed him most nearly. It might mean the loss of Italy itself and such a loss could bring the struggle for Europe to the very doorstep of the Greater

Reich. As was customary with him in a time of crisis he acted swiftly, decisively, ruthlessly. In January 1943 the Allied leaders, Roosevelt and Churchill, had called for 'Unconditional Surrender' and perhaps more has been made of its effect than it warranted, for as Professor Trevor-Roper points out there were probably few Germans who, choosing Nazi rule rather than unconditional surrender, 'would have been inspired to rebellion by an Allied assurance of moderation'. Yet Hitler suspected, and rightly, that Badoglio was above all set on surrender of one sort or another, and he was therefore determined not so much to prevent it as to prevent its allowing the military situation in the Italian peninsula to get out of hand. His judgement, as in the old days, was cold, clear and sound. He did not require further reports of what was happening in Rome, as Jodl urged, to show him what he should do: 'We still have to plan ahead [this on the very day that Mussolini fell]. Undoubtedly in their treachery they will proclaim that they will remain loyal to us. Of course they won't remain loyal. . . . We'll play the same game while preparing everything to take over the whole area with one stroke, and capture all that riffraff.' Even the Vatican could not embarrass Hitler. It could be taken over right away, the entire rabble of a diplomatic corps as well. He would get 'that bunch of swine' out. Later apologies could be made.

One of Hitler's principal worries was, of course, that the Allies would take full advantage of Italy's 'treachery'. He overestimated both their boldness and their readiness to act quickly. Six weeks passed between Mussolini's dismissal and publication of an armistice with Badoglio's Government, six weeks in which Hitler had tightened his hold on Italy to the extent that he would now have a choice as to how and where to conduct its defence, six weeks in which the Allies had talked much and done little. Although British and American troops set foot on the Italian peninsula on 3 September—four years exactly since the outbreak of war—8th Army on the toe of Italy, 5th Army at Salerno, all the German fears of audacious action (the sort Hitler himself would have chosen) to seize Rome and exploit Allied command of sea and air were put to rest. By 10 September 16 German divisions were in control of two-thirds of the peninsula. The Italian Army was disarmed and immobilized.

In a broadcast speech that day Hitler referred to the facility with which the Germans would now be able to carry on the struggle 'free of all burdensome encumbrances.... Tactical necessity may compel us once and again to give up something on some front in this gigantic struggle, but it will never break the ring of steel that protects the Reich.' In fact he would not be giving up much ground on this front for many months to come. Yet by holding fast here he was obliged to remove divisions from the Russian front; in short Hitler was conforming to Allied Mediterranean strategy—the southern front had become the very distraction which Churchill and his advisers had always hoped it would.

Kesselring, who was commanding in southern Italy, was a man after the Führer's heart; he believed in hanging on to territory which could be properly defended and he was not easily dismayed. When to his astonishment—in spite of Churchill's 'Why crawl up the leg like a harvest bug from the ankle upwards? Let us rather strike at the knee!'—and delight, both Allied landings were south of Naples, when further by the end of the year he had successfully delayed their advance so that they were still but 70 miles north of Salerno, Hitler agreed that Kesselring should establish the Winter Line across the peninsula only just north of Naples. More than six months would pass before the Allies captured Rome, and before they did, one more of those battles which possessed the world's imagination, Cassino, would have been fought, lost and won.

Hitler's next step was to rescue Mussolini. Once more he fulfilled his promise of five years' standing, 'If he should ever need any help or be in any danger, he can be convinced that I shall stick to him, whatever may happen, even if the whole world were against him'—not that its fulfilment was unmixed with political expediency. After Skorzeny's daring airborne rescue on 13 September, the two men met once more at Hitler's headquarters. Mussolini was no longer 'the greatest son of Italian soil since the collapse of the Roman Empire'. He was a broken old man who desired nothing more than to quit the political stage for ever and be permitted to go home to the Romagna. This, however, Hitler could not allow. The Duce must play his part. He was restored as Fascist Leader and became nominal head of the new Italian Socialist Republic. In his villa at Lake Garda he was a prisoner of the SS, held in hatred by his countrymen, contempt by his gaolers. He was even required to hand over his son-in-law, Ciano, to the Germans who had the former Foreign Minister shot by a Fascist firing squad. Ciano's final entry in his Diary is eloquent both as to Italy's tragedy and Germany's disingenuousness:

> The Italian tragedy, in my opinion, had its beginnings in August 1939, when, having gone to Salzburg on my own initiative, I suddenly found myself face to face with the cynical German determination to provoke the conflict. The Alliance had been signed in May ... [it] had a clause that for a period of three or four years neither Italy nor Germany would create controversies capable of disturbing the peace of Europe.... Instead, in the summer of 1939 Germany advanced its anti-Polish claims.... 'Well, Ribbentrop,' I asked, as we were walking together in the garden, 'what do you want? The Corridor or Danzig?' 'Not that any more,' he said, gazing at me with his cold metallic eyes. 'We want war!'
>
> From Salzburg on, during the period of Italian neutrality and during the war, the policy of Berlin towards Italy was nothing but a network of lies, intrigue, and deceit.... The attack on Russia was brought to our knowledge half an hour after the German troops had passed the eastern border.... The preceding Sunday, on June 16th, I was with von Ribbentrop in Venice.... 'Dear Ciano,' said von Ribbentrop, 'I cannot tell you anything as yet because every decision is locked in the impenetrable bosom of the Führer. However, one thing is certain: if we attack, the Russia of Stalin will be erased from the map within eight weeks.' Thus, in addition to a notable case of bad faith against Italy, there is a conspicuous misunderstanding of realities sufficient at least to help lose a war....

In another theatre of war, a theatre where perhaps with more economy of effort than any other, Hitler could, had he realized its importance in time, have avoided losing it—the Atlantic—there was more conspicuous misunderstanding of realities and things were going badly for Germany. In January 1943 Raeder, for all his strategic grasp, had been allowed to resign his command of the German Navy after a furious disagreement with the Führer, and Doenitz, the U-boat man, was appointed in his place. In 1942 the U-boats had sunk over 6 million tons of

Allied shipping—a tonnage greater than could at that rate be replaced. But 1943 told a different story. Aircraft carriers and long-range shore-based aircraft, which gave the Allied convoys continuous air cover, together with radar in the surface escorts able to find the submarines before the submarines found them, turned the tables. Between February and May 1943 Doenitz lost 87 U-boats. He could not sustain such losses and withdrew his submarines from the North Atlantic. Hitler, as unwilling to give up a fathom of sea as he was to concede an inch of ground, ordered them back again. 'There can be no talk of a let-up in submarine warfare,' he shouted at Doenitz. 'The Atlantic is my first line of defence in the West.' In September back the U-boats went, and in that single month 64 of them were sunk. True, they had accounted for 67 Allied vessels, but this was a ratio which merely illustrated their failure and doom. By November Doenitz was in despair: 'the enemy holds every trump card, knows all our secrets and we know none of his.' He spoke more truth than he knew. The Allied trump card for 1944 was played in 1943—ferrying the men, the weapons and the stores which were to break down the Atlantic Wall. Unmolested by U-boats, their numbers multiplied.

What then, with the game going wrong everywhere, in the East, in Italy, in the Atlantic, was Hitler to do? The war on two fronts, that dreaded chimera, was no longer so fanciful, could not now be far off. Hitler's Directive No 51 dated 3 November 1943, the last of his numbered ones, as if to signify a final loss of the initiative, a final surrendering of the control of strategic affairs, for thereafter the Directives were largely to counter Allied blows, anticipated the deeds of dreadful note which were about to be performed:

The hard and costly struggle against Bolshevism during the last two and a half years, which has involved the bulk of our military strength in the East, has demanded extreme exertions. The greatness of the danger and the general situation demanded it. But the situation has since changed. The danger in the East remains, but a greater danger now appears in the West: an Anglo-Saxon landing! In the East, the vast extent of the territory makes it possible for us to lose ground, even on a large scale, without a fatal blow being dealt to the nervous system of Germany.

It is very different in the West! Should the enemy succeed in breaching our defences on a wide front here, the immediate consequences would be unpredictable. Everything indicates that the enemy will launch an offensive against the Western front of Europe, at the latest in the spring, perhaps even earlier.

A shrill note of alarm enters here, a suggestion of apology, almost of helplessness, in this preamble to the actual measures to be taken for strengthening the West. But there is nothing uncertain about the measures themselves. Panzer and Panzer Grenadier Divisions are to be equipped with 93 Mark IV panzers; the 20th Luftwaffe Field Division will be converted to the role of mobile attack by the end of the year; this number of heavy anti-tank guns will be allocated to formations in the West; details of machine guns, of coastal defences, of training and preparing reinforcements abound; units here, there and everywhere are to do this and that; no unit will be moved without the Führer's approval. As usual plans are called for.

Yet the truth was that by the end of 1943 the war was lost. In the East after the failure of *Zitadelle* at Kursk, the Russians began to advance and went on advancing. Towns, which the Germans had taken so easily before, now went down like ninepins in face of the sheer weight of Russian attack—Orel and Kharkov in August, Poltava and Smolensk in September, Kiev in November, Zhitomir on the last day of the year. Objectives like the Donetz basin and the Crimea, which Hitler had put so much store by, were either lost or cut off. The consequences were grave enough militarily when as a result of his continued inflexible defence and implacable refusal to give up a yard without a fight, hundreds of thousands more soldiers, many of them from the satellite armies, were captured. But this price he willingly paid in the hope that by hanging on in strength he would not be required to pay an even higher political price— the defection of his allies, or Turkey's turning away from neutrality. He would give up nothing voluntarily: not Italy, nor Greece, nor Crete, nor the Crimea. No one could say that the Mediterranean Strategy was not paying off. And then not only was the Battle of the Atlantic lost as well; the battle for Germany, albeit at this time from the skies only, was going heavily against him. In three months the RAF dropped over 20,000 tons of bombs on Berlin alone.

Hitler refused to recognize that the sacrifice was in vain. What might not the Secret Weapons do? In his austere head-quarters at *Wolfsschanze*, 'a mixture of cloister and concentra-tion camp' as Jodl had it, where reports from military fronts were almost the sum of the news, the Führer sat in his bunker, held his military conferences, heard the reports from each front, announced his decisions, reflected on destiny and history, worried, went for short walks with his Alsatian bitch, Blondi, and brooded on. What was happening at the fronts?

Manstein was desperately trying to extract his hard-pressed troops from the Dnieper bend. The story of the entrapped 'pocket' at Korsun-Shevchenkovski and its attempted escape along a narrow corridor held open by a few panzers puts us in mind of the Grand Army's terrible plight, plagued by Cossacks and the cold; almost Ney's crossing of the Dnieper, not frozen enough to hold the baggage or guns, but all right for men if they jumped from floe to floe, was re-enacted:

> The artillery teams which had escaped destruction plunged first into the waves and ice floes. The banks of the river were steep, the horses turned back and were drowned. Men then threw themselves in to cross the river by swimming. But hardly had they got to the other side than they were transformed into blocks of ice, and their clothes frozen to their bodies. Some fell down dead. Most of the soldiers preferred to get rid of their clothes. They tried to throw their equipment over the river [it was eight metres wide and two deep] but often their uniforms fell into the current. Soon hundreds of soldiers, completely naked and red as lobsters, were thronging the other bank. Many soldiers did not know how to swim. Maddened by the approach of the Russian armour which was coming down the slope and firing at them, they threw themselves pell-mell into the icy water. Some escaped death by clinging to trees which had been hastily felled.... But hun-dreds were drowned. Under the fire of tanks thousands upon thousands of soldiers, half clothed, streaming with icy water or naked as the day they were born, ran through the snow towards the distant cottages of Lysianka.

During the early months of 1944 two separate battles were raging for the possession of Rome, one at Anzio, another at

Cassino. Raleigh Trevelyan at Anzio remembered that his slit trench was so close to the German positions that he and his companions were not much bothered by mortars:

> Snipers and hand grenades were the main worry, not counting shells falling short and airbursts. All night long the artillery and mortars of both sides kept up a non-stop barrage. The screeching and whirring of the shells over our heads might have been some furious gathering of witches on Walpurgis Night. Sometimes the explosions were close enough for us to see shreds of flame spurting upwards in the dark, and the shrapnel would come hissing at us on all sides. We grew to distinguish the sound of various guns, as if they were voices—some were alto, some bass, some grumbly, some like baying wolves, some as retchy as the cough of a tubercular in his last stages. But all these were more or less noises off; nearer to hand were the staccato *eugh-eugh* of two-inch mortars, the snarly spandau-ripple, the more deliberate bren-crackle, and the swift searing whine past of a single bullet, generally tracer and half-seen like a miniature comet....

Fred Majdalany remembered Cassino. 'It was ours—the Monastery, the mountain, the smells. A cemetery for the living.' His battalion too was close to the enemy, so close that neither had to move very far to get to grips with the other. Hills which were key positions in the defence often found themselves occupied by British and German soldiers—one dug in on the near side of it, the other on the far side. Movement by day was not recommended. Enemy OPs would not take long to bring down an unpleasant 'stonk'. At night it was different. Movement was easier and far harder to identify.

> Being attacked at night is particularly unnerving because you cannot tell if there are twenty of the enemy or a whole battalion. If two machine-guns can infiltrate through your positions and open fire from behind, the most dogged temperament finds it hard to resist the impression that it is surrounded.... At any moment we expected to hear our machine-guns get to work—if it was a big attack they would be bound to go for the ridge overlooking us. Messages were flashed to the mortars and guns to stand by ready to bring down fire on all the SOS targets. The tension of total alertness temporarily eclipsed one's tiredness. Nobody spoke, unless it was to pass a message on the telephone

or wireless. You just stood or leaned or sat motionless—and fancied you could hear your heartbeats. Then the firing seemed to die down slightly—or was it that you wanted it to die down? No, it was definitely easing off. People began to talk again. They made the rather forced little jokes which always follow a period of fear. We still had no idea whether the attack had been made by twenty or two hundred. Twenty minutes later we heard that it had in fact been made by twelve men. One of them had been wounded and taken prisoner. He said it was a fighting patrol of twelve. Its object had been to get a prisoner. One suddenly felt very, very tired.

The battalion was to be tireder still before the Monastery disappeared behind them as they travelled the road to Rome, and even when they got there, their triumph would be overshadowed by yet greater events elsewhere, events which would rob Alexander of the strength required to inflict a really decisive defeat on the German armies in Italy. For at Teheran the Americans and the British committed themselves not just to the invasion of Western France, *Overlord*, but to a landing in Southern France, *Anvil*, as well. Stalin did not want his allies interfering in the Balkans and Western Europe, particularly as the Mediterranean Strategy had already weakened that area by the despatch of no fewer than 15 German divisions from it to Italy. *Overlord* and *Anvil* would be the Combined Chiefs' of Staff 'supreme operations for 1944'; Eisenhower was appointed to command and directed to 'enter the continent of Europe' with a view to destroying the armed forces of Germany.

10

The Atlantic Wall Crumbles

We Germans do not indulge in the tired Maginot Spirit.
von Rundstedt

Far from dreading the prospect of an Allied assault from the West, Hitler actually seemed to welcome it, for in it he saw a possible solution to his strategic dilemma. Such a view of things cannot be shrugged aside as mere self-delusion. What he knew at this time—December 1943—of Anglo-American amphibious operations did not alarm him; rather the reverse. The landings in North Africa had met with light or no opposition; those in Sicily and Italy had been possible only, as he put it, with the help of traitors; at Dieppe in August 1942 the Canadians had suffered a bloody repulse; why, a year or two back even the forces of Vichy France had succeeded in defeating a joint Anglo-Free French attempt to seize Dakar. No—let them come. Hang out our banners on the outward walls! What might not be done when the much-heralded invasion of France had battered itself into a costly failure against the Atlantic defences. He would be able then to transfer such a weight of Army and Luftwaffe units to the East that at last the decision which had so long eluded him there would be realized. As for the Western Allies, beaten back and deprived of invasion, they would be kept quiet by the new V weapons, masses of jet aircraft and the submarines which could remain submerged without the need to surface for battery charging and could move below the water as fast as they could on it.

Hitler's optimism was enthusiastically endorsed by Himmler, and Himmler, having with the aid of Schellenberg replaced the discredited Canaris as head of the intelligence service, should have been well placed to make a sound estimate. Yet for sheer bombast and refusal to face military realities he almost outdid his master.

> There was no room for defeatism now, he said; great things were coming. The Führer was inspired as never before; his statesmanship, skill and intuitive wisdom were yet to exhibit their masterpiece. He prayed that the infatuated plutocrats of the West might be foolish enough to invade the Continent. They would be hurled back and drowned in the seas of their own blood. Then it would be the turn of the East. Within a year the Russians were to be chased headlong across the Volga, over the Urals, and into Asia, their barbarian home, whence a Chinese Wall, built by Slavonic slave-labour, would prevent them from ever returning.

This remarkable forecast was made by Himmler to his subordinates in the intelligence service—just two weeks before D-Day.

That the Führer should pin his hopes on these new weapons may readily be comprehended for they gave promise not just of stemming defeat but of so dismaying the Allies that they might after all leave him alone with his conquests. What is less easy to understand is how he could be so confident of defeating the cross-Channel enterprise without guaranteeing the one military condition indispensable to such confidence—strong, fast-moving and sensibly placed reserves able to go at once to the point of landing or penetration and eject the invaders before reinforcement made them too strong to be pushed back into the sea. In making this point—and it was a simple, sound estimate of the problem—Jodl was insistent that any weakening of these reserves would result in a risk so acute that the entire Western situation might get out of hand. Yet this is precisely what transpired.

To see the reason for it we must remember that just as space had been a barrier for Hitler's adventures in the East, so now space—in spite of its assets, the fact that much of it provided him with an income of resources, of labour or of manoeuvre— was so ravenous in its demands for military security that his position began to resemble that of many another tyrant. His conquests were sticking on his hands. There were just not enough forces to go round. Yet if the world required a demonstration of how to rob Peter in order to pay Paul and how to fight, a war not on two fronts but three, it was about to get it. There was perhaps no more remarkable a contrast to the French and Italian Armies' ignominious collapses as soon as their homelands were seriously threatened than the way the German Army, deprived of most of that air support which had made Panzer and Stuka so matchless a combination, could by sheer determination and skill prolong a conflict whose result was no longer in doubt.

Before we look at the way in which the Axis forces were positioned to counter the Allies' invincible might, it will be well to recall that although all Allied strategy since and even before the North African landings of November 1942 had had as its great purpose the relief of Russia, the assaults and advances arising from this strategy were themselves only possible because of Russian resistance. It was to this point that *Barbarossa* had brought Hitler. He had given to the Allies the very initiative which he himself had forfeited. And now 18 months after *Torch*, it was only Russia's resurgence which made the invasion of France a practicable military proposition in the first place. All Churchill's talk of a strategy, both Mediterranean and Atlantic borne, sound though it was, was also wholly dependent on the inexorable grip which the Red Army had fastened upon so many of the forces at Hitler's disposal.* It is this which explains why the Atlantic Wall could be pushed down almost anywhere and why, once down, it could not readily be shored up again.

Field-Marshal von Rundstedt, who had been recalled by Hitler to be Commander-in-Chief, West in order to prepare for the expected invasion had little faith in fixed, linear fortifications. He had pushed through them so often himself. Yet while it was true, as Jodl had said, that 'along a front of 2,600 kilometres it is impossible to reinforce the coastal front with a system of fortifications in depth at all points', to throw away advantage, not to wrest every trick from what was after all a formidable natural defence, would have been to misplay a strong hand. Water obstacles like the Channel were not presented to military commanders more than once. It was not a

---

* In June 1944 Germany had some 60 divisions on the western front, over 200 divisions fighting the Russians, and about 20 in Italy.

question of indulging in the 'tired Maginot Spirit'. Time, as we know, has a wallet at his back in which he puts alms for oblivion. For von Rundstedt not to seize with both hands all the alms which Time was offering him was to invite his own oblivion; to encourage penetration everywhere. His plan was to defend strongly those important areas which were most vulnerable, to deny ports through which the Allies would seek to build up their strength, and by having powerful armoured counter-attack forces together with enough air support to facilitate their rapid movement to enemy bridgeheads, drive back any successful footholds soon after they were gained. All this made sense in theory; it made none at all in practice, for the conditions on which it depended—panzer troops and air cover of requisite strength—simply did not exist. Rundstedt had some 60 divisions to defend his 2,000 miles of coastline, but half of these against his will and on the Führer's direct orders were manning the Atlantic Wall. Many of the rest were weak, worn out formations from the Eastern front; others were busily engaged in supplying reinforcements for that front, whose demands were insatiable. Rundstedt constantly pressed for more men and more weapons and was as consistently refused. Instead he received the not wholly welcome reinforcement of another field-marshal—Rommel.

Rommel was appointed to command Army Group B, which contained 7th Army responsible for the sector from the Orne to the Loire, 15th Army from the Orne to Antwerp, and 88 Corps in Holland, in other words the very sector which the Allies were going to invade. Rommel had very different ideas from von Rundstedt. He believed that the invasion must be defeated on the beaches for the plain reason that Allied air supremacy would never allow mobile reserves to intervene if they were held too far back. 'In the short time left before the great offensive starts,' he told his Army Commanders in February 1944,

We must succeed in bringing all defences to such a standard that they will hold up against the strongest attacks. Never in history was there a defence of such an extent with such an obstacle as the sea. The enemy must be annihilated before he reaches our main battlefield.... We must stop him in the water, not only delaying him but destroying all his equipment while it is still afloat.

The old Reichswehr generals regarded Rommel as an upstart. His rapid rise from the rank of Colonel to Field-Marshal which took only three years they put down to his popularity with the Nazi Party and because he was such a superb showman. They failed to see that whilst he might have neither the training nor the aptitude for grand strategy, his common sense, his flair for originality, the uncanny instinct for extracting every advantage from tactical boldness, his thrusting leadership and complete identity with both the philosophy and execution of blitzkrieg made him a field commander of no ordinary value. Traditional teachings, conservative caution, political aloofness might have had their day; they were totally irrelevant to the circumstances of 1944. That he was one of Hitler's favourites was not surprising. He too was intuitive; he too had shown the General Staff that many of their ideas were out of date; certainly what was needed to counter the overwhelming weight of fire power and flexibility of movement that the Allies would be able to bring to bear on the Atlantic Wall would not be forthcoming without exceptional energy, imagination and capacity for inspiring its defenders. Perhaps the best tribute to Rommel's talents in the matter of his ideas about what was to be essentially a defensive battle is that had he, instead of von Rundstedt, been Commander-in-Chief, West from the beginning, the Allies might have had serious difficulties in getting ashore, certainly greater difficulties than in the event they did have.

Even in the short time that he was there he made a world of difference. Every ingenious device for defending the coastline with obstacles underneath the water, minefields on the beaches, coastal batteries reinforced with steel and concrete to immunize them from air and naval bombardment, wire, pillboxes with machine-guns, the 88-mm guns which he had made so famous in the desert—all would combine to contest the landings of the boats, vehicles, weapons and men. To discourage airborne troops he flooded low-lying ground and covered suitable landing zones with booby-trapped posts driven into the earth. More-

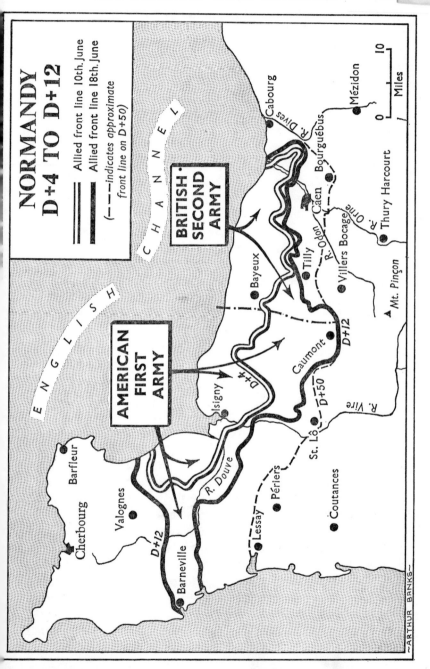

NORMANDY
D+4 TO D+12

Allied front line 10th June
Allied front line 18th June
(— — — indicates approximate
front line on D+50)

ENGLISH CHANNEL

BRITISH SECOND ARMY

AMERICAN FIRST ARMY

Cabourg
R. Dives
Mézidon
Bourguébus
Caen
Tilly
R. Odon
R. Orne
Thury Harcourt
Bayeux
Villers Bocage
▲ Mt. Pinçon
D+12
Caumont
D+50
R. Vire
Isigny
D+4
St. Lô
Périers
Coutances
R. Douve
Lessay
Barfleur
Cherbourg
Valognes
D+12
Barneville

0   10
Miles

~ARTHUR BANKS~

over he was determined—for in the end only bullets and shells would stop the invaders—to put as many soldiers and weapons in the shop window as he could. Just as the British in their numerous internal security undertakings had always argued that a company today was better than a battalion tomorrow, so Rommel maintained that it was more important to have one panzer division on D-Day at the place where the assault came in than to have thrice the strength three days later. It would be the first 24 hours, he maintained, which would decide the issue. Therefore as many panzer troops as possible should be right up in the front line. Such unconventional ideas made little appeal to Geyr von Schweppenburg, the tactically traditional commander of Panzer Group West. Like his superior, von Rundstedt, he predictably favoured defence in depth and wanted to hold back the principal panzer reserves until the Allied assault points had been positively identified. So bitter was the controversy about the armoured reserves that it was referred to Hitler himself.

In spite of his sympathy with Rommel's intention to contest every inch of territory, even at the water's edge, Hitler compromised, and compromised fatally. A really powerful panzer force centrally positioned in depth and supported by the Luftwaffe units to enable it to move might have done great things; smaller but immediately available tactical reserves close to likely landing places was the obvious alternative; yet by splitting control of the panzer reserves Hitler achieved neither the one nor the other, and satisfied neither Rommel nor Geyr. Rommel's impact on the soldiers was as usual both immediate and profound. A new spirit—of purpose, of confidence, of urgency—seemed to take hold of those responsible for preparing and improving the defences. His efforts caused the Allies great concern, and it required all Major-General Sir Percy Hobart's imagination and drive to design and perfect the antidotes. DD tanks to swim ashore, flail tanks to detonate mines, 'bobbins' to lay a firm carpet so that the following tanks would not be bogged in soft clay—these were some of the fruits of his ingenuity.

All this, of course, was technical detail to overcome technical obstacles. Of far greater moment to the Allies was the likely

26 The ruins of Monte Cassino

27 Normandy, 6 June 1944: Allied troops and supplies come ashore

28   The Ardennes: US air power

29   The Ardennes: German troops, December 1944

German deployment in the West. And just as in the earlier years of the war Hitler had been obliged to denude the West in order to subdue the East, and then relax in the East so that he could triumph in the West, so now the full circle had been drawn and he was required to shore up first one at the expense of the other, then the other at the expense of the one. Brigadier Williams, Montgomery's chief intelligence adviser, is eloquent on the point. In his review of the situation early in April 1944 he observed that Hitler was prepared to accept greater losses in the East in order to hang on to the option of significant gains in the West—'more and more Stalingrads in the hope of one Dunkirk'. But unknown to Williams at his moment of writing, the eastern danger was already beginning to render the western adventure more susceptible to good fortune. Shortly before Williams had made this estimate, the Russian threat to the frontiers of Poland and even the passes leading to Rumania's oilfields had caused a switch; no fewer than four of Rundstedt's divisions, three panzer and one infantry, were on the march from west to east. The penalty of too much conquered territory, which allowed the Allies to make war on three fronts, was becoming a fearful reality. There was no longer any question of Hitler's being able to keep a quiet guard on one sector while he dealt a decisive blow elsewhere. Rather it was the Allies who were dealing decisive blows and he was doing his best to parry them. The implacability of priorities was thrusting home.

Williams summed up the global nature of the conflict, which Hitler had ignored until it was too late, by showing how the dependence on each other of the Allies' various attacks against *Festung Europa* contributed first to one success, then to another:

A break through at Lwov affects a division at Lisieux ... the Russian advance was made possible by the Allied bombing of Germany, by the containing actions in the Mediterranean and by the imminence of invasion in the West. Two-thirds of the German Air Force and 100 German divisions were kept pre-occupied. Thus was the Red Army given opportunity. They grasped it with both mighty hands. Making the weather their ally, first they divided the Southern German Sector from the Centre and the North; next they rent it in twain; now they tear these twain in pieces. So in their doughty turn, the Russians make *Overlord* more possible.

The question persisted however—where? Immense, subtle and laborious efforts by the Allies were made to deceive the German intelligence service as to where the main landings would be. Some of the devices used were so fanciful that they inspired Duff Cooper to fictionalize one of them in his *Operation Heartbreak*. Much of this effort to deceive was intended to lead the Wehrmacht into believing that whatever diversionary assaults there might be, the *Schwerpunkt* would be at the Pas de Calais. There was good reason to suppose that their deceptive measures were being successful until the middle of April 1944 when German reinforcement of the Caen-Falaise area seriously alarmed the Allied Intelligence officers. From a former comforting situation when in Normandy there had been but a small armoured force, suddenly the three most formidable panzer divisions that von Rundstedt had at his disposal found themselves shifted to the critical sector between the Seine and the Loire. Moreover during the next month more moves of infantry, parachute and panzer units to Normandy made it seem probable that the Germans had guessed or learned the truth—that Normandy was the place. In fact, the explanation was much simpler, much more in keeping with the way the Wehrmacht was manipulated; Hitler's intuition had once more been at work, and once more, as in the former triumphant days, was astonishingly accurate. On 2 May 1944 the Führer announced that the main Allied assault on his European fortress would be in Normandy. Further reinforcement of the appropriate sector would therefore be carried out.

Once again Hitler seemed to have had more strategic insight than all his professional military men put together. Whatever else we might say about his conduct of war, in this—on this occasion and many others—we must concede that his grasp was matchless. Von Rundstedt, perhaps the ablest of all the Wehrmacht's soldiers, the man who had spent his life studying strategic problems, whose 'soundness' was a watchword amongst the conservatives of the General Staff and the Nazi clique alike, got it all wrong. His original conviction that the main blow would be north of the Somme remained unshaken. Even the intuitive Rommel agreed that the Allied effort would be where von Rundstedt placed it and that the Normandy affair, of whose imminence he was equally certain, would be a side-show, a distraction. Yet Hitler compromised once more. He refused fully to back his intuition. Although Rommel, getting his priorities in the right order as so often before, tried to persuade von Rundstedt and Hitler to move one of the reserve panzer divisions, 12th SS, to the St Lô-Carentan area, opposite those beaches where the US divisions came ashore, he was not successful. The German strengthening of Normandy in general, while it made more difficult the Allied task of getting themselves firmly established ashore, did not produce a balance of power in which the Allied build-up would be outweighed by enemy dispositions. For Hitler, in spite of his conviction that Normandy was the place and in pursuit of his normal refusal to concede an inch of territory, was proposing to defend the whole of France, not just a part of it.* As a result he left the entire 15th Army, which contained no fewer than 15 divisions, north of the Seine doing nothing, while the Allies set about tightening their grip on the Normandy beachhead.

That they were able to do so emphasizes the difference in respective methods of command. Hitler nullified his intuition about Normandy by not backing it with appropriate reinforcement and by not allowing his subordinates the freedom to take advantage of it. His method of command, which robbed commanders on the spot of all initiative and all opportunity, completely neutralized the advantages which might have been obtained from his strategic grip. To insist that his own authority must be received, even as to details of execution, for a local counter-attack once the landings had taken place was to ensure either that the counter-attacks would never be launched or if they were that they would fail. It is hard to reconcile such contradictions.

For Montgomery it was perhaps fortunate that despite all Churchill's historical instinct and strategic enthusiasm and

---

* Quite apart from his original estimate that the Allies' main assault would be in the Pas de Calais, Hitler was anxious to protect this area, from which his V weapons would be launched.

despite also the Americans' understandable reluctance to play second fiddle to so arrogantly Celtic a propounder of tactical ideas, he was in the event left alone, within the limitations imposed by material and manpower, both to conceive a plan and to execute it. His exposition of what was going to happen did not fall short of his former performance in the North African desert.

Montgomery had been appointed land force commander of the US-Canadian-British troops for *Overlord*, and, knowing Rommel, knew too that his old antagonist would try to disrupt the landings by what he was so good at—the spoiling attack. 'He will do his best to Dunkirk us,' declared Montgomery in his Final Presentation of Plans on 15 May at which both the King and Churchill were present, 'not to fight the armoured battle on ground of his own choosing, but to avoid it altogether by preventing our tanks from landing by using his own tanks well forward. On D-Day he will try to force us from the beaches and secure Caen, Bayeux, Carentan.' At the same time Montgomery pointed out that Rommel would aim to contain what penetrations were made by occupying the tactically important ground commanding roads which led inland through the bocage. Therefore, he went on, the key to confounding Rommel was to get well inland, thrust deeply beyond the beaches, peg out claims to plenty of space, disrupt Rommel's plans and contain his reserves, while more strength was built up. 'Once we get control of the main enemy lateral Granville-Vire-Argentan-Falaise-Caen and have the area enclosed in it firmly in our possession, then we will have the lodgement area we want and can begin to expand.'

In his *History of Warfare* Montgomery explains that after obtaining this lodgement area—and it was many weeks after D-Day before he did—he would conduct the battle in such a way that the British would draw and hold the main German, particularly armoured, strength against them on the left flank, allowing the Americans to push forward, gain more ground and break out on the right, the western, flank. 'So, more or less, the battle developed.' Once again the master plan worked. The battle for Normandy had four main parts: the foothold was established, the race for build-up won, the dog-fight fought, and the break-out made.

Montgomery had insisted during his presentation on 15 May that the soldiers must be so possessed with offensive, fiery spirit and so imbued with confidence in the plan that nothing would stop them. Then they would succeed in getting ashore and staying there. An officer of the South Lancashire Regiment remembered getting up at 3 o'clock in the morning of 6 June, having breakfast at 4 o'clock and almost at once seeing a destroyer on the flank of his landing ship go down, sunk by a torpedo. 'I have very rarely met,' observed Napoleon at St Helena, 'with the two o'clock in the morning courage.' But as this member of Montgomery's great Army surveyed the ocean and saw it covered with Allied shipping his confidence was restored. He and his men got into their assault craft without trouble and in spite of a heavy swell began their run-in to the beach in company with the rest of the flotilla. The clouds of dust caused by naval bombardment which rose from the beaches so obscured them that he was unable to make out whether the point where they were about to land corresponded with the oblique photographs they had so often studied. They had studied the matter of underwater obstacles too, but on actually coming level with them they were surprised to find them so tall, so high out of the water, and as the boat crews weaved between the pickets and rails with mines on top of them, it seemed like 'groping through a grotesque petrified forest'. On the beaches themselves the noise was continuous— mortar fire, machine-guns, tanks and 88-mm guns. The battalion fought a series of small, yet desperate, actions mainly to over- come the various strongpoints and pillboxes which opposed them. Many officers were killed, including the Colonel who, in order that he could readily be recognized, carried a small flag of the battalion colours—too easy a target for snipers. Once the beaches had been cleared, the battalion was to rendezvous at Hermanville. First to get there was *Battalion HQ*, more con- ventionally later arrivals at the objective, and by H+4 hours the battalion despite its losses had dug in round the village, ready for the expected counter attack which in this case did not come.

For one of the parachute battalions inland, which indeed

had been there since landing during the night, the counter attacks had already been and gone. A captain of the 12th Parachute Battalion, in charge of a dozen men put out as a reconnaissance screen, recalled how quiet it all was in his immediate area at dawn on D-Day, with no enemy movement to be seen at all. Above, the Spitfires circled, and well behind him the rumble of battle told him about the struggle for the beaches. Yet just in front of the positions he and his men had taken up, concealed in slit trenches with camouflaged steel helmets and blackened faces, a farmer led his horse and cart. But by 1030 the enemy had found them. Infantry and SP guns appeared, the guns firing straight into their position, the infantry beginning to work round to their right flank. After failing to bring down the supporting fire he called for and seeing the enemy fire reduce his effective strength to three men, the captain chose discretion, evacuated his position and withdrew to the main battalion area. He then had the satisfaction of noting that the two enemy SP guns following up were quickly knocked out by his battalion's anti-tank guns, that the attacking infantry withdrew and that the battalion position held firm.

A week after D-Day, as the Allies were slowly strengthening their hold on the bridgehead, the commander of an artillery battery had had what he called a 'bloody day'. After hours of exhausting activity and thousands of shells fired, he was fixing up the night tasks and enjoying a glass of whisky with one of his Forward Observation Officers, sitting on the bonnet of his jeep, when they heard a *plop* and a whine. At this stage in the war such noises were not listened to with curiosity alone. Hurling themselves on the ground, the battery commander escaped unhurt, his FOO received a large piece of shrapnel in the leg; the whisky bottle, the two glasses, even the jeep itself were written off. At least, they reflected, it had not been an 88-mm whose shells arrived before you heard the plop.

Some days later it was clear not just that the foothold was truly established, but that the Allies were winning the battle of the build-up, for by 18 June Montgomery had 20 divisions ashore and opposing him were only 18 divisions, some so under strength that their fighting capacity was perhaps but three-quarters of this number. Hitler refused to acknowledge

the realities of the situation when on the day before he conferred with Rommel and von Rundstedt at Margival, in the
command post which had been specially constructed for the
Führer to supervise the invasion of England but four years
earlier. Speidel, Rommel's Chief of Staff, who was present,
reported that Hitler appeared 'worn and sleepless, playing ner-
vously with his spectacles and an array of coloured pencils
which he held between his fingers'. While Hitler sat on a stool,
the two Field-Marshals stood up and had to listen to a condemnation of their conduct of the defence. He could not yet see
that there was no question of throwing the invaders back into
the sea so that he could once more turn back to deal with the
Red Army. It was annihilation he wanted, and meanwhile every
foot of territory was to be contested while the V weapons
brought England to its senses.

When Rommel urged Hitler to end the war, he was sharply
told to look to his own front and leave the war's future course
to the Supreme Commander. Later that month both Rommel
and von Rundstedt renewed their efforts to persuade Hitler to
end the war. But facts and reason had no interest for Hitler
and certainly could not prevail with him to the extent of making
him change his mind. When the battle of the Odon removed
any chance the Germans might have had to split the Allied
forces by striking to Bayeux and von Rundstedt warned OKW
that the battle for Normandy was lost, Keitel was in despair.
'What shall we do?' he wailed. 'Make peace, you fools,' was
von Rundstedt's uncompromising answer. He was replaced by
von Kluge. Hitler could not admit that he was in the wrong;
rather it was that one more of the 'gentlemen who write "von"
in front of their names' had let him down. But not von Kluge
or any other soldier could alter the realities of the situation,
and von Kluge himself was obliged to concede a few weeks
later that 'in face of the enemy's complete command of the
air, there is no possibility of our finding a strategy which will
counterbalance its truly annihilating effect, unless we give up
the field of battle'. He added that in spite of his determination
to stand fast, as the Führer had ordered, the price to be paid
was the destruction of his armies and the dissolution of the
front.

Meanwhile Rommel had soldiered on until 17 July and was only stopped, a fitting end for such a man, by enemy action. His car was attacked by British aircraft; he was gravely injured and finished with Normandy for ever. Yet before he went he had made such dispositions that the progress of Operation *Goodwood*—Montgomery's great armoured attack to engage the German panzers and 'write them down' to the extent that they could no longer prevent a break-out—was seriously hindered. The broad plan for VIII Corps commanded by O'Connor—of Beda Fomm renown—and consisting of three armoured divisions was for it to advance, dominate the area Bourguebus-Vimont-Bretteville and destroy the enemy there. After the II Canadian Corps on their right had secured Caen, VIII Corps could 'crack about' as the situation demanded. During their attempt to dominate this area VIII Corps contested the battlefield with Sepp Dietrich's 1st Panzer Army and more particularly the old sparring partners from desert days of 7th Armoured Division (which was part of O'Connor's Corps)—21st Panzer Division. In it Colonel von Luck commanded a battle group.

He had left Paris by car very early on the morning of 18 July—the day *Goodwood* began—early, because even single vehicles moving by road could not escape attention from the RAF or USAF. He arrived just in time to make a real contribution to the battle. From the British point of view *Goodwood* started well. This was hardly surprising as the armoured divisions were supported by the heaviest and most concentrated bombing attacks that had yet been made. The leading armoured regiments of 11th Armoured Division met little proper resistance until they approached Cagny; and it was here between 8 and 9 o'clock in the morning that von Luck came into the picture. From the western corner of Cagny he was appalled to see some 50 to 60 British tanks which had crossed the Caen-Cagny road and were negotiating the Caen-Vimont railway embankment. Unable to get in touch with his battalions by radio, von Luck began to retire through Cagny when he suddenly came across a Flak battery whose guns were appropriately pointing skywards. He was at first unable to persuade the battery commander that first things came first and an imminent attack by tanks demanded more urgent attention than a chimerical attack by aircraft. Sweet reason getting him nowhere, von Luck drew a pistol and asked the Flak commander whether he would prefer to die now or be recommended for a coveted decoration. The battery commander chose the second, and redeployed his guns to meet the tank threat. Von Luck then organized piecemeal a most effective anti-tank defence of the whole sector, and by skilfully deploying his anti-aircraft guns, tanks and SP guns, making full use of fire and movement together with defilade positions supplied by the various villages, successfully held up the British until the Bourguebus Ridge was reinforced by the 1st SS Panzer Division. Von Luck recalled that his little groups 'operated very useful' and 'knocked out' many British tanks. By 19 July *Goodwood* had petered out, yet it had achieved its purpose of 'writing down' the German panzer strength, as Bradley's break-out was shortly to demonstrate. Next day, on 20 July 1944, while Hitler was struggling with perhaps the worst crisis which the Eastern front had presented him with, he was nearly assassinated.

Six months earlier Guderian had tried in vain to convince Hitler of the need to appoint a Generalissimo with supreme responsibility for the East, just as von Manstein had before him. Guderian had already had a go at Goebbels and Himmler on the same point, but however much they might agree with him, they did nothing. Circumstances being as they were— with Guderian having lost all confidence in the Führer's military direction (not that this stopped him continuing to serve in the hope that his own influence would save something from the wreck) and the Führer being unwilling to trust any individual or the Army as a whole with independent power—this being so, it was no surprise that things bumbled on as before. Jodl perhaps put his finger on the real point when he asked Guderian: 'Do you know of a better supreme commander than Adolf Hitler?' It would not have been easy to name one, yet in June and July 1944 when the war on two fronts was bringing home to Hitler problems he had not formerly encountered, he was exercising his supreme command about as badly as he could. To insist that all important tactical decisions should be referred to him at Berchtesgaden meant that on 6 June, when only immediate tactical response could be effective, he simply threw away any opportunity there might have been; as the days and weeks passed this same refusal to delegate simply made more certain than it already was both the bridgehead's inviolability and the ease of breaking out from it. It was not just that Hitler could not bring himself to trust his commanders in the field; it was that his will-power had become a substitute for everything else.

His orders for the defence of Cherbourg were perhaps worst of all. Sticking to his rules of not giving up any ground which in his view need not be given up, he required von Schlieben to defend Cherbourg on an indefensible line, completely dismissing the advantages of prepared perimeter defences. For a commander to demand great sacrifices of his troops when the tactical situation justifies it may be comprehended. But to give impossible orders for the sake of having them obeyed is insupportable.

In Italy the skilful and relentless generalship of Kesselring had enabled him to hold the Winter Line until May, but then he was obliged to withdraw and allow the Allies to enter Rome on 4 June. On the Eastern front things were far more serious. June saw the Red Army begin its summer offensive. The German Army's attempt to hold lines which were far too extended to defend properly and which Hitler would not agree to shorten led to an inevitable result. The front disintegrated. In July Minsk, Vilna, Pinsk, Grodno—all were taken. Even East Prussia was threatened. No wonder there were those in the Wehrmacht and outside it who once more plucked up the courage to get rid of the man whose disastrous military policies were heading Germany for total defeat.

But on 20 July von Stauffenberg's bomb at Rastenburg failed to kill the Führer. His escape showed Hitler at his most remarkable and most vile. Nothing seemed able to shake his conviction that he had been chosen to shape the world's destiny. That in failure, in defeat, utterly doomed, he still exercised the ability—and not through fear or tyranny alone—to control events and people speaks much for his unbreakable will-power, however diabolical it was. Such iron resolution must command, if not admiration, if not respect, at least awe. Yet how vindictive and how appallingly comprehensive was his revenge. In *The Nemesis of Power* John Wheeler-Bennett lists 160 of the victims—Canaris, von Hassell, von Witzleben, Beck and Rommel amongst them—and notes that his list is not complete, that many more were executed. The 160 included two field-marshals, 17 generals and more than 50 other officers. Those members of the Offizierkorps who did not know it already—and there could not have been many of them—thus had it brought home to them once and for all that the Führer was bad, mad and dangerous to know. Churchill might have talked often enough of shooting generals. Hitler did it. 'I'm beginning to doubt,' Hitler declared on the afternoon of 20 July, 'whether the German people are worthy of my great ideals. No one appreciates what I have done for them.'

Yet however unworthy of him the leaders of the Army might in his view have been, he could not in time of war do without them, particularly as the military situation was worse than it had ever been before. First things had nevertheless to come first, and what came first now was the final subservience of the Army to National Socialism. Guderian became Chief of the Army General Staff on 21 July and two days later issued an Order of the Day in which he pledged to the Führer and the German people 'the unity of the Generals, of the Officer Corps and of the men of the Army'. Worse was to come. The Nazi salute became compulsory, and every General Staff officer was required to declare himself a 'National Socialist officer-leader'. In spite of this capitulation Hitler held the Army in open distrust. Germany's military position was hopeless enough already. That the commanders on all fronts should be distrusted and despised by their Supreme Commander was hardly a factor calculated to improve it. Just as the 20 July plot showed that the General Staff knew Hitler had lost the war, so henceforth all military set-backs were classified by Hitler as acts of treachery.

The Führer's directives of July and August 1944 show that his battles for Europe were about to become one battle—for Germany; they are concerned with building defences to delay or frustrate the invasion of Germany. Subjects vary from the Alpine Approaches position to constructing a defensive line in the west, completing defences in the German Bight, placing the West Wall in a state of readiness, ordering new preparations in the south east, and so on. Their theme is a constant one. It was none too soon for the German fronts, east and west, were collapsing. By July the Russians broke through in Poland, cutting off the German Army Group North in the Baltic States, and were advancing unchecked in Rumania, although Guderian and Model did manage to stabilize the line in the central sector. Everywhere rigidity of defence had taken the place of blitzkrieg. Gone now was all Hitler's former talk of free operations and their superiority, of the degeneracy of frontal struggles, his guarantee that fronts would never again be petrified.

In France another battle was lost, another army murdered by his insane interference and refusal to allow the man on the spot, in this case von Kluge, to know best what was happening there. Blumentritt, von Kluge's Chief of Staff, made this comment on Hitler's plan, drawn up in *Rastenburg*, to counter-attack the American corridor through Avranches and Mortain:

> The plan came to us in the most minute detail. It set out the specific divisions that were to be used.... The sector in which the attack was to take place was specifically identified and the very roads and villages through which the forces were to advance were all included. All this planning had been done from large-scale maps and the advice of the generals in France was not asked for, nor was it encouraged.

This sort of direction was even worse than Napoleon sending absurdly out-of-date instructions to the Marshals in Spain, for at least in 1944 communications, both by radio and by air, were such that there was no need for not knowing the facts, no excuse for ignorance. When von Kluge's operation failed as it was bound to, Hitler put it down to the fancy that Kluge had not wished it to succeed. His self-delusion had no limits. Kluge was recalled. On his way back from the front he committed suicide having written a letter to Hitler, in which, while confessing his admiration for the Führer's greatness, iron will and conduct of the gigantic struggle, he pointed out that Providence might be greater than even his genius and urged him to be 'great enough to put an end to a hopeless struggle'. He was succeeded by Model. But Model could not stop Patton's bold drive to the east nor the liberation of Paris. He withdrew the remnants of the German Army in the west across the Seine, and reported to Hitler that the Normandy battles had cost Germany some 2,200 tanks and assault guns and the best part of 20 infantry divisions. So much for the Supreme Commander's conduct of war against 'the infatuated plutocrats of the West'. By September the war was being fought on the soil of Germany itself. The Red Army was approaching East Prussia; the British and Americans were nearing the Rhineland. Yet not only did Hitler not despair; the Wehrmacht, for the time being, held its various enemies at bay. The time had not yet come, Hitler decided, for a political decision. The time, in fact, was out of joint. Political decisions could not be sought at moments of military defeat, only when you were having successes. Tension between the Allies would be sure to grow, for all coalitions disintegrated sooner or later. 'Since the year 1941 it has been my task not to lose my nerve', and he would not lose it now. He would set it right. He lived only for the purpose of leading the fight for the battle could not be won without an iron will behind it.

> Under all circumstances we will continue this battle until, as Frederick the Great said, one of our damned enemies gets too tired to fight any more. We'll fight until we get a peace which secures the life of the German nation for the next fifty or hundred years and which, above all, does not besmirch our honour a second time, as happened in 1918.

So one more effort was demanded, and one more effort was made. Germany's strength was still formidable. Quite apart from the Wehrmacht, which on paper still totalled 10 million men, in October Hitler proclaimed a *levée-en-masse* to form a *Volkssturm*, a Home Guard, for the protection of the Reich. Speer's extraordinary organization kept armament production going, although there were shortages of petrol and oil. All in all the German Army in the west made a remarkable recovery, not unassisted by British and American disagreement as to what strategy—broad or narrow front—should now be pursued. Montgomery, who had handed over command of the land battle to Eisenhower on 1 September, was forcible on the question. The disadvantages of a broad front policy were at once manifest and manifold: logistically it could not be supported; nowhere would strength be sufficient to be decisive; an advance on a broad front would therefore peter out and allow the Germans to recover. 'To get decisive results,' he writes in his *History of Warfare*, they had to concentrate somewhere, 'left, centre, or right, whichever the supreme commander considered most suitable. It was as simple as that, and the British chiefs of staff supported my view. But the American generals did not agree. The Germans recovered.' Hitler was not the only supreme commander whose subordinates knew better than he did.

Even the gallant attempt to turn the northern flank at Arnhem failed. Von Rundstedt, back once more as Commander-in-Chief, West and Model between them managed to impose stalemate west of the Rhine. In Italy Kesselring held a new winter line north of Rimini-Florence-Pisa. On the Eastern front, East Prussia for the time being held firm. 'I am staying in Rastenburg,' Hitler insisted when Keitel tried to persuade him that a short holiday in Obersalzberg would put him right—it was August 1944. 'If I leave East Prussia, then East Prussia will fall. As long as I am here, it will be held.' Not until November did he return to Berlin. By then the Balkan front was in ruins. Rumania had capitulated; Bulgaria had been occupied by the Red Army; the British were in Athens; Belgrade was in the hands of Tito and the Russians; and the Wehrmacht was doing its best to stem the enemy's advance on the line of the Danube in Hungary. Vienna was not far away.

On 25 November 1944 Hitler issued an order on the exercise of command in units which had been isolated and left to their own resources:

The war will decide whether the German people shall continue to exist or perish. It demands selfless exertion from every individual. Situations which have seemed hopeless have been redeemed by the courage of soldiers contemptuous of death, by the steadfast perseverance of all ranks, and by inflexible, exalted leadership.

A commander is only fit to lead German troops if he daily shares, with all the powers of his mind, body, and soul, the demands which he must make upon his men. Energy, willingness to take decisions, firmness of character, unshakable faith, and hard, unconditional readiness for service, are the indispensable requirements for the struggle. He who does not possess them, or who no longer possesses them, cannot be a leader....

The Leader would abide by his own rules, would stick to his nihilistic philosophy. *Weltmacht oder Niedergang,* victory or death. Having stabilized the fronts, however inadequately, and ignoring the growing dangers in the east, he was planning—had been secretly planning since September 1944—to mount yet one more offensive, one more gigantic illustration of blitzkrieg, which would capture Antwerp, drive a wedge into Eisenhower's forces, trap the British Army, in short be 1940 all over again. However excellent the idea, in only one other respect did its setting resemble *Sichelschnitt.* The *Schwerpunkt* was once again to be in the Ardennes. Yet as so often before Hitler hopelessly overestimated his own strength, gave von Rundstedt tasks totally beyond his resources, and by insisting on assembling all the new divisions he could in the West, dangerously weakened the east. When Guderian protested, he was sharply rebuked:

> There's no need for you to try to teach me. I've been command-ing the German Army in the field for five years, and during that time I've had more practical experience than any 'gentleman' of the General Staff could ever hope to have. I've studied Clausewitz and Moltke and read all the Schlieffen papers. I'm more in the picture than you are.

In deciding to make such reckless use of the resources he had scraped together, Hitler was about to make the blunder to end all blunders and in flinging away the last ounce of offensive strength to ensure that the Reich itself could not be defended. No reason could move him. No appeal could prevail. The Allies would never be defeated by fighting defensively. Only an offensive would serve his purpose. The gambler was resolved to have one more throw.

11

The Gambler's Final Throw

What though the field be lost?
All is not lost; th'unconquerable will,
And study of revenge, immortal hate,
And courage never to submit or yield;
And what is else not to be overcome?
Milton

So oder so, one way or another—this was the last time that Hitler was to have a choice, but it was not really a proper choice at all. There were but two things to choose between—*rouge ou noir*, East or West. In any event the dividend would be dubious. At best defeat might be delayed; at worst it would be accelerated. Hitler, of course, did not see it in this light. To him the gamble was far more promising. He rejected all idea of the East for several reasons. What quick or dramatic decision could be gained there? Distances were too great, logistic resources to cope with such endless tracts were not to hand, objectives were indeterminate, the Red Army was inexhaustible. How different might prizes in the West be! To split the Allied armies, deny them a main port of entry, dismay them with the seemingly unbreakable power of the Wehrmacht, fasten upon the vulnerability of an Alliance between an empire in decline and a great democracy eager to usurp that empire's property and authority, to recapture the initiative at last, gain a little time and then turn on the full fury of new weapons—might not a gamble of this sort pay infinite odds? In one respect Hitler's choice was characteristic. He was prepared to risk all his winnings on one turn of pitch-and-toss. But if he lost, there would be no starting again at the beginning. It was all or nothing, victory or death.

However divided the Allies might have been as to the strategy to be adopted after the battle for Normandy had been so

30 Churchill, Roosevelt and Stalin at Yalta

31 Hitler decorating *Hitler Jugend* in Berlin, March 1945

32 Russian artillery on the outskirts of Berlin

33 Soviet troops in the ruins of Hitler's Chancellery

successfully concluded, on one thing they were agreed. The Germans would not, could not attempt any large-scale counter-offensive. On 7 December 1944 Eisenhower discussed the situation with his two senior commanders, Bradley and Montgomery, at Maastricht. All were disturbed by the German recovery, by the enemy's revived morale and obvious ability to fight a co-ordinated defensive battle, particularly while the bad weather, which robbed the Allied air forces of their power to influence affairs, persisted. Of major concern to them was the question of what use von Rundstedt would make of 6th SS Panzer Army, his principal strategic reserve in the west. Montgomery's Intelligence Chief, Williams, did not believe that von Rundstedt would risk throwing away the most effective means he had of countering future Allied advances. He anticipated no surprises.

What appears strange to us now that all the facts are known is that Allied intelligence experts still seemed to expect the Wehrmacht to be manipulated in accordance with the military requirements of any given situation. They had not somehow grasped, in spite of the many demonstrations given to them by Hitler, that this was not the way things were conducted. Had it been as they thought, there might have been no Stalingrad, no Tunisia, no Kursk, no Avranches. Perhaps the stalemate of autumn 1944 and the changeover from Hitler's rash handling of Normandy to von Rundstedt's more conventional behaviour once the Western front had been stabilized lulled them into a state of optimism quite at odds with the real position. General Bradley's chief intelligence officer had noted on 12 December that the Wehrmacht's breaking point might be reached at any moment. Even the circumspect Montgomery, who a year earlier had laid a bet with Eisenhower that the war with Germany would not be over by Christmas 1944, and was shortly to collect his winnings, wrote on 15 December that the enemy could not stage major offensive operations.

One thing, therefore, was certain; a German offensive would take the Allies by surprise—and so it did. Any idea that the Germans would behave in a rational military manner, was at once put to sleep by recognizing that it was Hitler who made the decisions, not von Rundstedt or any other soldier. Furthermore, that an attack in the Ardennes would be bound to enjoy

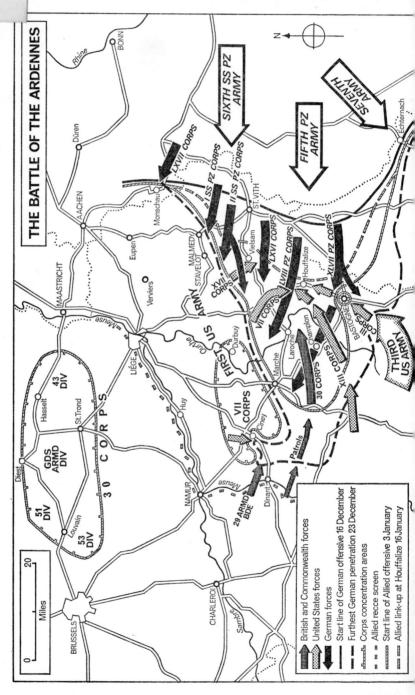

THE BATTLE OF THE ARDENNES

initial and partial success was more or less guaranteed by American weakness in the precise area chosen by the Führer for the last of his blitzkrieg *Schwerpunkte*. In the Ardennes Bradley had deployed only four divisions on a front of 75 miles. Considering that Hitler had assembled no fewer than 28 divisions for his offensive, there was little doubt that they would advance fast and far. The broad plan, imposed by the Supreme Commander on his generals whether they liked it or not, was that three armies would attack between Montschau and Echternach. In the north Sepp Dietrich's 6th SS Panzer Army was to deliver the main blow, crossing the Meuse at Huy and Andenne and then striking towards Antwerp; Manteuffel's 5th Panzer Army in the centre would advance through Namur and Dinant to Brussels; 7th Army under Brandenberger had the task of covering the southern flank.

It was fitting that for a final desperate failure the plan— endorsed in Hitler's hand *'Nicht abändern!'* 'Not to be altered' —was his own. Orders of battle, timing, artillery programmes, axes of advance, objectives, special forces using American equipment and uniforms—all were included down to the last detail. As in *Barbarossa*, three and a half years before, the offensive's design outran resources. The Führer's imagination, never cramped or idle when toying with his own brain-children, soared, and set his admittedly formidable, but by no means unlimited forces tasks and exploitations far beyond their capability. Three days after the start of the attack, Maastricht, where Eisenhower, Bradley and Montgomery had conferred, was to be taken and possible US moves from Aachen blocked; a week later forces from northern Holland would capture Breda and pin down the British; then as soon as possible after that and not later than D+15 a great pincer from the Saar and Colmar would reconquer Northern Alsace and push through what, by virtue of American switching of resources to counter the Ardennes thrust itself, would have become a greatly weakened part of the front. Such grandiose ideas may be compared with Napoleon's when after his astonishing whirlwind successes with a tiny army of 50,000 men he won mini-victory after mini-victory in February 1814 and was heard to cry after one of them, Champaubert: 'Another day like this and I shall be on the Vistula.' But the truth was that neither Napoleon in 1814 nor Hitler in 1944 had the cards to play a sustained hand. Once their bluff was called, there were no more cards and no more counters to play with.

When he received the plan von Rundstedt was flabbergasted. Hitler had not consulted him, and it was at once clear to the Field-Marshal that the forces available were quite inadequate for so ambitious a design. Knowing his master, however, he sent Model to argue the point. All Model's efforts to persuade Hitler to modify the plan to one which could be undertaken with some guarantee of achievement failed. He had written 'Nicht abändern' and had meant it. The plan was not to be altered. He was determined to have Antwerp and that was that. Von Rundstedt's subsequent comment was that had they reached the Meuse they should have gone down on their knees and thanked God. Reason with their Supreme Commander, Model and the other generals might. Convince him they could not. He was once again riding on a wave of confidence; once more he had been proved right and the General Staff wrong in such matters as holding firm in the West and creating a strong reserve—neither of which had the generals thought to be possible.

On 12 December at the Führer HQ near Frankfurt, Hitler harangued all the senior commanders who were to take part in the offensive four days later. Bayerlein, commanding Panzer Lehr division, reported that he looked broken and old, reading a long prepared speech with a shaking hand. For two hours he went on while the generals sat, watched over by SS men. Bayerlein was 'afraid' even to reach for his handkerchief lest one of the SS watchdogs should think he was going for a gun. Montgomery might harangue his generals too, and even forbid coughing, but he was not in the habit of talking for so long. Manteuffel recalled the Führer as 'a stooped figure with a pale and puffy face, hunched in his chair, his hands trembling, his left arm subject to a violent twitching.... When he walked he dragged one leg behind him.' If their Supreme Commander's appearance did little to inspire his subordinates, what he had to say could have done little more. The Grand Alliance against Germany was fraught with incongruities—capitalists hand in hand with Bolsheviks, imperialists in league with anti-imperialists, Russia and Britain so long antagonists in the Near and Middle East again at loggerheads over the Balkans and the Persian Gulf—the whole thing was ripe for disintegration. 'If we can now deliver a few more heavy blows, then at any moment this artificially bolstered common front may collapse with a mighty clap of thunder. ... Wars are finally decided by one side or the other recognizing that they cannot be won. We must allow no moment to pass without showing the enemy that, whatever he does, he can never reckon on a capitulation. Never! Never!' As we listen to this we are brought back 12 years and Hitler is discussing with Rauschning the tragical turn that German victories have taken in the past. How prophetic were his words, how accurately echoed by events. 'We shall not capitulate—no, never. We may be destroyed, but if we are, we shall drag a world with us—a world in flames.'

On 16 December the Ardennes offensive was launched. In spite of initial successes and advances, it was blocked and defeated. The heroic defence of Bastogne by McAuliffe and the US 101st Airborne Division—it was he who rejected von Lüttwitz's call for surrender with the famous 'Nuts!', surely the best of all Counterchecks quarrelsome; the grip established by Montgomery on the northern shoulders of the German penetration; the intervention of Patton's 3rd Army; the weather clearing on Christmas Eve allowing 5,000 Allied aircraft to fill the sky above the battlefield, swoop on the German columns and prevent supplies from reaching them—all these moves added up to the conclusion that by 27 December the German forces' momentum had been broken. The question now was whether they could be extricated. Hitler, not surprisingly, spurned his generals' advice which called for withdrawal. Yet there were doubly compelling grounds for doing so. Not only was there the danger that his armies committed in the Ardennes would be destroyed, but the situation in the East, as Guderian had come all the way from that front to tell him, was such that if troops were not transferred there soon, the coming Russian winter offensive could not be held. Hitler's reply was the very embodiment of his refusal to look hard facts in the face, of his locking his mind away in a world where only his own wishes had any reality at all. He dismissed Russian preparations as bluff. 'It's the greatest imposture since Genghis Khan. Who's responsible for producing all this rubbish?' No, there would be no transfer of troops to the East and no withdrawal from the West. Quite the contrary, there would be a renewal of the western offensive, both a new attempt to reach the Meuse and an attack into Northern Alsace.

His long-suffering commanders were again assembled on 28 December, and again put through the mill. Not ready for an attack? Of course they were not ready! 'Gentlemen, I have been in this business for eleven years and during those eleven years I have never heard anybody report that everything was completely ready.' Then—and could self-deception have gone further?—he compared the German position in the West with that of the Russian position two and three years earlier, able to take advantage of an enemy whose front was extended and whose offensive strength was dwindling. The question now was whether Germany had the will to remain in existence. Besides the Ardennes attacks had achieved great things, thrown the enemy off balance, upset all their offensive plans. Hitler was somehow moved to make a strange confession to the effect that the enemy 'has had to admit that there is no chance of the war being decided before August, perhaps not before the end of next year'. He was quick to deny the implications. There was no possibility of his envisaging, even remotely, the loss of the war. He had never learned to know the word 'capitulation'. He would fight on until at last the scales tipped in their favour. Then they would smash the Americans, destroy a complete half of the enemy's Western front. 'We shall yet master fate.'

Words, words, words.... To suit the action of them would have demanded forces on land and in the air which no longer existed. By mid-January, a month after it had begun, what remained of the forces he had committed to this last throw were back east of the start line. Losses had been fearful— 120,000 men, 600 tanks and guns, 1,600 aircraft, 6,000 vehicles. It was the last shot in the locker. Reserves, as Napoleon had shown at Marengo, Wellington and Blücher at Waterloo, Hitler himself in *Sichelschnitt* and Montgomery in every engagement he had conducted, were the key to winning battles and wars.

Now Hitler's reserves had gone.   Bryant 247

'I have always maintained,' wrote Arthur Briany as early as October 1944, 'that, once battle was joined in the West, it would be the cumulative effect of the struggle that would bring Hitler down.... Once the necessary build-up had been made behind the new Allied lines, the gruelling, wearing battle to waste and destroy the German Army was resumed. The great bleeding process which the Russians began in 1941 is now continuing. It is not only doing so along the five hundred mile front from Walcheren to the Swiss frontier, but in Italy from Ravenna to Pisa, in the Aegean and on the Greek mainland, in Yugoslavia, in Finland, and on the immense Russian front from the Baltic to the Danube. ... It is only a question of time before the aggressors must break.' Just so; but the time had not yet come and would not come until the Supreme Commander relinquished command and life alike, until Germany had been overrun and her armies taken, until, so to speak, there was *Kein Volk, kein Reich, kein Führer.*

It is just before this happens that we have illustrated for us the extraordinary grip over the German people that Hitler, even in the depths of adversity, still maintained. Speer's visit to the front on the Rhine in February 1945 (which we touched on earlier) when he sat unrecognized amongst a group of miners in a dug-out, proved to his amazement that the ordinary soldier and worker still believed in Hitler. 'They believed that he, and only he, both understood the working class from which he had risen, and the mystery of politics which had been concealed from the rest of the German race, and that he would therefore be able, as no one else, to work the miracle of their salvation from this forlorn predicament.' It was understandable that during his first triumphs from 1936 to 1940 and even 1941 the German people should look upon him as a genius, an almost superhuman ruler who found solutions to all problems no matter how intricate or profound, who struck down all enemies of the Reich no matter how numerous or powerfully armed. But when this same man, almost bereft of power, surrounded by military failure, his policies cracking in absolute ruin, and in any event no longer visible or audible to these same German people, still held them spellbound, we may perhaps give way to astonishment. When living in a world of his own, remote from the shattered cities, secreted in his various Führer headquarters, bunkered, wired in and SS-guarded from the country he ruled, with only an Alsatian bitch and his own henchmen for companions, he was able to prolong the struggle long beyond the time when its hopelessness was obvious to all and yet keep alive in his countrymen some spark of hope, then we may allow ourselves to agree that Hitler's will-power was extraordinary indeed. We may even discern some faint resemblance between the man and his great hero, Frederick the Great, for both had (though in what different ways and with what different results) 'given an example unrivalled in history of what capacity and resolution can effect against the greatest superiority of power, and the utmost spite of fortune.'

In January 1945 the Supreme Commander of the Wehrmacht had so disposed his armies that the most vulnerable front of all, both militarily and politically, the front in Poland and East Prussia, was in comparative terms the most weakly held, the one least likely to be capable of withstanding the knock it was about to receive. In the west were 76 divisions, in Italy 24, 10 were in Yugoslavia, 17 in Scandinavia—in short 127 divisions were deployed elsewhere than on the Eastern front; only a few more, 133, were in the East. In the same month of January 300 divisions and 25 tank armies of the Red Army were getting ready to end the war: in the north two groups of armies under Chernyakhovsky and Rokossovsky were to converge on East Prussia; Zhukov's and Koniev's groups in the centre would aim at Berlin and Upper Silesia; further south two more groups would clear Slovakia and take Budapest and Vienna; finally Petrov was to re-occupy the Northern Carpathians.

The Russians could afford to operate over such broad fronts, but the German divisions facing them were inadequate to do so. Yet they were in no sense concentrated to meet what was coming in the critical, central sector. Some 30 were cut off in the north, in Courland and Memel and a similar number were blocking the Russian advance in Hungary, so that only about 75 divisions were in the vital area, East Prussia and Poland, where the front was 600 miles wide. So inept had Hitler's handling of the war become that on this 600-mile front the

Russian forces likely to attack were twice as strong as those which the United States and Great Britain could bring to bear against a defensive strength comparable to that in the east. Such a curious juggling of resources, so distorted a reading of priorities, could not add up to military security. But Hitler was no longer concerned with military security. He was living in his own fancied world into which all facts had to be fitted. In the west the initiative would be maintained—even though it had been lost for ever; in the east there would be neither reinforcement nor withdrawal. 'I get an attack of the horrors,' he declared, 'whenever I hear that there must be a withdrawal somewhere or other in order to have room for manoeuvre. I've heard that sort of thing for the past two years and the results have always been appalling.'

Withdrawal or no withdrawal, on 12 January 1945 Stalin launched his greatest offensive of the war. For the central stroke in Poland and East Prussia he had collected 180 divisions with 4 tank armies each of which contained 1,200 tanks. Koniev's Army Group rapidly broke out of its bridgehead on the Upper Vistula, and the first of a series of disasters which engulfed the Eastern Front was under way. On 16 January Hitler moved to the Chancellory bunker in Berlin. From here he would conduct the last battles of all. Shortly before the Eastern front began to collapse Hitler had congratulated and thanked Guderian (who had been desperately trying to shore it up with any troops he could get his hands on from other theatres) for assembling such strong reserves there. Guderian's retort was that the Eastern front was like a house of cards—the exact phrase used by Warlimont about Tunisia in 1943—and that if it were broken anywhere it would collapse everywhere. Two weeks after starting their offensive the Russians were on German soil, in Silesia and Pomerania, whence Hitler's first blitzkrieg against Poland had been mounted.

Guderian, never one to despair, set to work in forming a new Army Group Vistula to stem the Russian advance. Its front would stretch from Poznan to Graudenz, and Guderian intended to give this Army Group all the reserves he was mustering from the West, including Sepp Dietrich's 6th SS Panzer Army. Hoping to be able to direct its operations himself, and it would have been impossible to find anyone better qualified or more likely to make more telling use of it, Guderian proposed von Weichs as a nominal Army Group Commander. Hitler, finally disillusioned with the professional soldiers, appointed— Himmler. Guderian was so appalled that in conversation with Ribbentrop on 26 January he suggested the two of them should go to the Führer and try 'to secure an armistice on at least one front'. At this Ribbentrop jibbed, but was himself aghast when Guderian asked how he would feel when the Russians were at the gates of Berlin in three or four weeks time. When Ribbentrop asked if he really thought this was possible, Guderian replied that it was not merely possible, but, because of Hitler's leadership, certain. The conversation was duly reported to Hitler who in Guderian's presence referred to it as treason. But the great Panzer Leader did not lack the courage of his convictions and flatly tried to argue the strategic issues with the Führer there and then. The Führer refused to discuss it.

As might have been expected Himmler was no more capable of stemming the Red Army than the professional soldiers were, and even when the Russians seized a bridgehead over the Oder and extended their leading columns to the point where Guderian saw a great opportunity to crush them, he was not permitted to take advantage of it. Hitler had despatched 6th SS Panzer Army—which might have done much under Guderian's hand —to relieve Budapest. The process of robbing Peter to pay Paul was almost at an end. When Speer sent Hitler a letter beginning 'The war is lost' and followed it in person in order to see Hitler alone and discuss it, his master refused to see him, adding with a wry humour, not common with such a breed of diabolical tyrants, that he could no longer bear seeing people alone because they always wanted to tell him something unpleasant.

During the first two weeks of February the disagreements between Guderian, still Chief of the Army General Staff, and the Supreme Commander of the Wehrmacht as to the war's conduct as a whole and the Eastern campaign in particular reached a crescendo during which the Führer's capacity for vituperation and stubborn inflexibility was displayed to full advantage. It was the old story—Guderian urging withdrawal,

Hitler refusing to give up an inch. Guderian would insist that he was not being obstinate; he was thinking of Germany. Hitler would shout back that his whole life had been one long struggle for Germany. What else had he been fighting for? At one point Guderian's adjutant was so alarmed by Hitler's shaking his fist at the Chief of the General Staff that he took hold of his master's tunic and pulled him back out of range.

It would not be long before Hitler's orders to his armies ceased to be obeyed, either because, as the various commands were separated from each other and communications were severed, the orders were not received, or because even if received they were not heeded. Before we reach the time when he was no longer able to exercise military command, two further illustrations, one written, one spoken, of his methods in this role he regarded as his own may be fitting. One of Hitler's last directives on the question of command itself showed how absolute and how fatal had become his grip on operations; it is worth reading in full.

I order as follows:
1 Commanders-in-Chief, Commanding Generals, and Divisional Commanders are personally responsible to me for reporting in good time:
(a) Every decision to carry out an operational movement.
(b) Every attack planned in Divisional strength and upwards which does not conform with the general directives laid down by the High Command.
(c) Every offensive action in quiet sectors of the front, over and above normal shock-troop activities, which is calculated to draw the enemy's attention to the sector.
(d) Every plan for disengaging or withdrawing forces.
(e) Every plan for surrendering a position, a local strong-point, or a fortress.
   They must ensure that I have time to intervene in this decision if I think fit, and that my counter-orders can reach the front line troops in time.
2 Commanders-in-Chief, Commanding Generals, and Divisional Commanders, the Chiefs of the General Staffs, and each individual officer of the General Staff, or officers employed on General Staffs, are responsible to me that every report made to me either directly, or through the normal channels, should contain nothing but the unvarnished truth. In future, I shall impose draconian

punishment on any attempt at concealment, whether deliberate or arising from carelessness or oversight.

3 I must point out that the maintenance of signals communications, particularly in heavy fighting and critical situations, is a prerequisite for the conduct of the battle. All officers commanding troops are responsible to me for ensuring that these communications both to higher headquarters, and to subordinate commanders, are not broken and for seeing that, by exhausting every means and engaging themselves personally, permanent communications in every case are ensured with the commanders above and below.

signed: ADOLF HITLER

With his own hand, therefore, and in a vain attempt to preserve control of the war's prosecution, the Supreme Commander made successful exercise of his command impossible. To this nadir of mistrust, vindictiveness, pedagogism and sheer impracticability had his directive brought the management of military matters. So much for the written word; now for the spoken. On 13 February Guderian attended one more Führer Conference in the Berlin Chancellory. Apart from Hitler, Keitel, Jodl and other normal members of the staff, were Himmler, still in command of Army Group Vistula, Sepp Dietrich and Wenck, whom Guderian had brought with him. The main issue was how and when the Army Group would conduct a counterattack from Arnswalde against Zhukov's extended right flank. Guderian rightly insisted that it should be done quickly before Russian reserves came up and be directed by Wenck, not Himmler. Hitler was arguing every point with Guderian and being in turn contradicted by Guderian.

> And so it went on for two hours. His fists raised, his cheeks flushed with rage, his whole body trembling, the man stood there in front of me, beside himself with fury and having lost all self-control. After each outburst of rage Hitler would stride up and down the carpet edge, then suddenly stop immediately before me and hurl his next accusation in my face. He was almost screaming, his eyes seemed about to pop out of his head and the veins stood out on his temples.

Military affairs conducted by conferences of this sort could hardly be expected to prosper. Even though Guderian gained his point—with his most charming smile Hitler told him that the General Staff had that day won a battle—it was, he writes, the last battle he was to win and it came too late. In the event, Krebs (not Wenck, who had been injured) commanded the counter-attack—last of all offensives mounted by the German Army in the war—which flawed by intrigue, lack of both men and material, and bad leadership, all three symptoms of the disease from which the Third Reich was about to die, petered out after a few days in failure.

The field was lost. All was not lost, however. The unconquerable will remained. Eleven years earlier Hitler had proclaimed that if Germany found herself at war with Russia, Britain and France and found she could not conquer them, half the world would be dragged into destruction. No one would triumph over Germany. There would be no surrender. The time to draw on that courage never to submit or yield was at hand. So was immortal hate and study of revenge. But Hitler, like Satan in *Paradise Lost*, vented his hatred and revenge on those about him. He gave orders for the destruction of Germany.

> If the war is to be lost [he told Speer] the nation will also perish. This fate is inevitable. There is no need to consider the basis even of a most primitive existence any longer. On the contrary, it is better to destroy even that, and to destroy it ourselves. The nation has proved itself weak, and the future belongs solely to the stronger eastern nation.

Having made it his business in the past to erase—*ausradieren* was a favourite and much-used word—other nations, he now made it his business to erase the German nation. That he was thwarted owes much to the courageous disobedience of Speer, who had so often told his master that the war was lost.

There had been those who were saying so as early as 1943. Soon even Hitler was to acknowledge defeat. Yet he would not submit or yield. If he himself was to be *ausradiert*, it would be by his own hand. Having indulged in slaughter on an unprecedented scale, for his last act he chose self-slaughter.

12

'The Greatest Strategic Genius of all Time...?'

I expect the relief of Berlin. What is Heinrici's Army doing?
Where is Wenck? What is happening to the Ninth Army?
When will Wenck and Ninth Army join us?
Wireless message from Hitler to Keitel, 28 April 1945

'All the world except one man knew that the game was up.
There was no money in France, and no industry, no commerce,
no army, no navy, no horses, no munitions, while advancing to
the Rhine and crossing it were Russia, Prussia, Bavaria, Saxony,
Austria, and Sweden, and England was already north of the
Pyrenees. But the greatest brain of the age, alone among men,
either could not or would not grasp the situation, and the
struggle went on.' It was thus that A. G. Macdonell summed
up Napoleon's predicament in 1814. In February 1945 while
the greatest strategical genius of all time was bellowing at
Guderian instructions about how best to use his reserves to
defend Germany, Churchill, Roosevelt and Stalin were deciding
at Yalta how the Reich was to be partitioned. The Allied leaders
may have argued about how much German territory should
be given to Poland, who was to govern Poland, and the amount
of German reparations; but on two things they were agreed—
unconditional surrender and maximum pressure to finish the
war quickly. The end came more suddenly than expected, and
their final military moves determined Europe's political future.

By February the Russians were threatening Vienna and even
Berlin; in March the American and British armies crossed the
Rhine, and the Red Army attacked at Küstrin, east of Berlin,
and in Hungary; in April Model's Army Group in the Ruhr was

surrounded, Alexander's armies broke into the Po valley, the Americans reached the Elbe, Königsberg fell to the Russians, then Vienna, and by breaking the Oder defences the road to Berlin was open to them; by the middle of the month no further effective German resistance was possible. But the Supreme Commander of the Wehrmacht had not yet abandoned hope. He had once more shuffled his subordinates. Kesselring replaced von Rundstedt in the west; Krebs relieved Guderian as Army Chief of Staff. The Führer himself however remained, as he had done for five and a half years, intimately concerned as Commander-in-Chief of the Wehrmacht and of the German Army with the war's direction. His difficulties arose by virtue of the fact that the German Army had been totally defeated in the field. What is more, he himself was cut off in Berlin; yet still he sent out orders and conducted futile conferences.

On 15 April Hitler issued his last two directives—one dealing with command arrangements made necessary by the cutting of communications. In an area where he was not present, a Commander-in-Chief appointed by him would take charge of military operations and command all forces on all fronts. If Hitler were cut off in the south, Doenitz would command in the north; if Hitler were in the north, Kesselring would take charge in the south. But still 'the unified control of operations by myself personally, as hitherto, will not be altered' and 'the activity of the Commander-in-Chief of a separated area will be initiated only on special orders from me'. Even when in reality he had no control over operations, Hitler clung to the illusion. The second directive was a defiant exhortation to his soldiers of the Eastern front:

For the last time our deadly enemies the Jewish Bolsheviks have launched their massive forces to the attack. Their aim is to reduce Germany to ruins and to exterminate our people. Many of you soldiers in the East already know the fate which threatens, above all, German women, girls and children. While the old men and children will be murdered, the women and girls will be reduced to barrack-room whores. The remainder will be marched off to Siberia.

We have foreseen this thrust, and since last January have done everything possible to construct a strong front. The enemy will

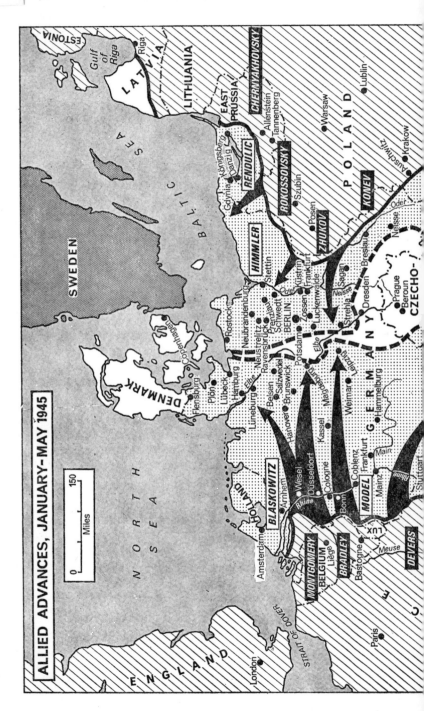

ALLIED ADVANCES, JANUARY–MAY 1945

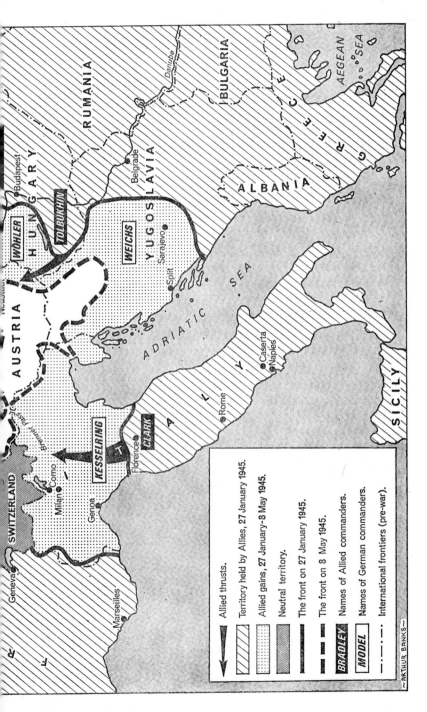

Allied thrusts.

Territory held by Allies, 27 January 1945.

Allied gains, 27 January–8 May 1945.

Neutral territory.

The front on 27 January 1945.

The front on 8 May 1945.

BRADLEY Names of Allied commanders.

MODEL Names of German commanders.

International frontiers (pre-war).

~ARTHUR BANKS~

be greeted by massive artillery fire. Gaps in our infantry have been made good by countless new units.... If every soldier on the Eastern front does his duty in the days and weeks which lie ahead, the last assault of Asia will crumple, just as the invasion by our enemies in the West will fail, in spite of everything.... At this moment, when Fate has removed from the earth the greatest war criminal of all time,* the turning-point of this war will be decided.

At this point in his career Hitler resembled the great Napoleon not only in his lust for devastation—for there was little to choose between the Führer's dragging a world in flames down with him and the Emperor's burying the world beneath the ruins of his throne—but also in his disposition of imaginary forces, his manipulation of great armies which no longer existed. The truth was that he had completely lost control of what was happening outside his immediate entourage. He had become *ein Feldherr ohne Truppe*, a War Lord without the means to wage war.

It did not at first stop him from making detailed plans to save Berlin, cling to his belief that the new weapons would by some miracle rescue him, or that there would be a last minute split in the Grand Alliance. The Alliance survived, the weapons were defeated and the last battle for Berlin was never fought. Nonetheless it was in Berlin that the Führer would stay, direct the city's defence and die there, shooting himself at the last moment. Yet as we have seen, after his conference on 22 April Hitler refused to continue with the direction of the war. When Keitel and Jodl protested that after leading and directing for so long, he could not suddenly expect his staff to lead and direct themselves, he replied that he had no orders to give. He pushed aside their offers to withdraw troops from the west and divert them eastwards to save Berlin from the Russians, would have nothing to do with the forces still intact in the south. He had decided on *Götterdämmerung*.

It was here that Hitler failed as a military commander in a way that he had never failed before. In abdicating responsibility

---

* Goebbels and Hitler exulted in the death of Roosevelt and saw in it a historical parallel with the Czarina's death which saved Frederick the Great. Their triumphant mood did not last long.

he betrayed his command. He had talked enough of a soldier's duty and of himself discharging his own duty merely as the first soldier of the Reich. Now, the first soldier, the Supreme Commander, Commander-in-Chief of the German Army, *der Oberste Feldherr, der Führer* abandoned leadership and duty alike. Even the pliant Keitel and Jodl could not understand it. They left the bunker on 22 April, Keitel to go to Wenck, Jodl to Krampnitz. Yet such was the almost incomprehensible magic of the man that even after this he was able to maintain his personal ascendancy in the Party and imbue others with hope in the military situation, hope which he himself had thrown away. We cannot forget the extraordinary impact Hitler had on Field-Marshal Ritter von Greim telephoning from the bunker on 27 April with promises of certain victory. It was no whistling to keep his spirits up. He really believed it. The Führer's presence had inspired him. And such was the habit of command that in spite of having given up his direction of the war, Hitler himself still made military plans, for after all perhaps as long as he remained in Berlin, Berlin would not fall. Professor Trevor-Roper's picture of Hitler's Last Days as a military commander is memorable indeed:

> Hitler had long been accustomed, from underground bunkers, to direct the operations of non-existent armies, to dictate their strategy and tactics, dispose their forces, calculate their gains, and then to denounce the treachery of their generals when the actual results failed to correspond with his private conclusions. So in these days he would expound the tactics whereby Wenck would relieve the city. Pacing up and down in the Bunker ... he would wave a road-map, fast decomposing with the sweat of his hands, and explain to any casual visitor the complicated military operations whereby they would all be saved. Sometimes he would shout orders, as if himself directing the defenders; sometimes he would spread the map on his table, and stooping over it, with trembling hands he would arrange and rearrange a set of buttons, as consolatory symbols of relieving armies.

But the truth was that Wenck's Army and Heinrici's and Busse's —all those referred to in Hitler's agitated signal to Keitel—were phantoms.

However fast remained Hitler's grip on those who were subjected to his presence in the bunker, two of his principal deputies, not being there, were slipping out of his coils. First Göring offered to take over the leadership in a wireless message from the Obersalzberg. 'A crass ultimatum,' was the Führer's shouted reaction. 'Nothing is spared me. No allegiances are kept, no honour lived up to, no disappointments that I have not had, no betrayals that I have not experienced—and now this above all else. Nothing remains. Every wrong has already been done me.' There was, however, one wrong still to come. During the evening of 28 April news was brought to him that Himmler —*Treuer Heinrich*—had conferred with Count Bernadotte of Sweden in order to negotiate peace. Apart from taking what revenge he could—Himmler's representative, Fegelein, in spite of being the husband of Eva Braun's sister, was shot—and dictating his will and political testament, Hitler now had but two things to do. After all the Russians were only a few streets away. He married Eva Braun on 29 April and next day committed suicide. Treason had done his worst: nor steel, nor poison, malice domestic, foreign levy, nothing, could touch him further.

Once the Supreme Commander was dead, it was not long before he became the repository for all the strategic errors, all the tactical blunderings of the German Army. A comment made on Halder's *Hitler als Feldherr* was that it gave the impression that if Hitler had not interfered, his generals would have won the war. How different is Alan Clark's assessment. 'No truly objective historian,' he writes, 'could refrain from admiring this man. His capacity for mastering detail, his sense of History, his retentive memory, his strategic vision—all these had flaws, but they were brilliant nonetheless.' We have seen where Hitler's talents lay and where they did not. He could plan a campaign brilliantly and say how a small-scale action should be conducted with a sure grasp of weapons and tactics. But when it came to handling army groups and their components in battle, he faltered. Military campaigns could be compared with political ones for intuition played a major role; low-level tactics too could be mastered by an amateur; but tactics on the grand scale with all the problems of movement, fire support, air co-operation, logistics and the interdependent operations of many formations, both enemy and friendly, requires years of training and practice which Hitler necessarily lacked. Particularly surprising—in view of his immediate understanding of the blitzkrieg potential of Panzer and Stuka and his declaration to Rauschning as early as 1932 that 'in the air we shall of course be supreme'—was his refusal to see that the Wehrmacht, no matter how determined its commanders, excellent its equipment, brilliant its tactics and devotedly brave its soldiers, simply could not prevail against an Allied air supremacy which was both absolute and omnipresent.

Estimates of what qualities make for great generalship are innumerable. Napoleon maintained that it was not cleverness you needed in war, but accuracy, simplicity and character. Hitler certainly did not lack strength of character, however demoniac, but he tried to subjugate accuracy to his own will; as for simplicity, he did seem able to reduce problems to simple terms —for example he believed that force would solve anything, but in its application he rejected simplicity and erected a complex system of control to which he and he alone held the key. If one of the marks of being a great captain is to try to dethrone the Czar and bring your country to ruin, then Charles XII, Napoleon and Hitler all qualify. Like Charles Hitler proved himself to be a better soldier than general; unlike Charles his real flair lay in politics and strategy. Amongst other qualities that have been named as indispensable to the successful exercise of command are imagination, eloquence, dedication, professional skill, humanity, political acumen, will-power and nerves of steel. It is curious to see how heavily Hitler scores in some of them and how wholly destitute he is elsewhere.

In spite of evidence to the contrary (one front-line officer who later served at OKW thought Hitler too soft, too concerned about the sufferings at the front and in bombed cities to visit them, and he was not one of the Führer's admirers), of humanity we must judge that he had nothing. He cared not a jot for the millions of lives expended in securing, broadening and maintaining his own power. Neither scruple nor loyalty nor any moral boundary could move him. And lacking humanity—for it is indispensable to the great commander, as perhaps Nelson showed more than any other—he could not see that the finest sort of military leadership was bound to evade him. Even Wellington, while we would never have expected him to say

'Kiss me, Picton', did feel for his soldiers and wept at the loss of his friends. It was quite in order for Frederick the Great to cry *'Ihr Racker, wollt ihr ewig leben?'*—'Rascals, would you live for ever?'—when his Guards hesitated at Kolin, for he was beside them exposed to the same dangers. But to condemn von Paulus' Army to death or captivity at Stalingrad from the safety of Führer HQ was to show that Hitler had no regard for what a commander should regard above all else—his own troops.

In the same way, Hitler's dedication, absolute though it was, was not to the German people or his soldiers or to a patriotic cause. It was simply to his own power. That he led so monastic a life at the various Führer headquarters was not because he wished to dedicate himself in this sense; it was that he wished to keep alive the myth of his own self-imagined world in which events were controlled by him. Each deterioration of the military position was met by reiteration that he would continue to pursue his aims with fanaticism, that nothing would wear him down. There was in short no doubting his dedication. It was just that it was misplaced.

As for professional skill, Hitler was of course self-educated. He had read widely—history, war, biographies of 'world-historical' figures, political and philosophical matters. His grasp of military and technical detail amazed all who came into touch with it. His memory was astonishing. But the education which mattered for a military commander—experience of command in the field at all levels—he totally lacked. It is thus an inescapable fact that while Hitler did have both an extraordinary grip of military detail and an unrivalled capacity for strategic generalization, nearly all decisions on the field of battle are dictated by considerations in the middle, and here Hitler was deficient. He could not be accused of deficiency in eloquence. He cast a spell on his audiences perhaps as no military leader before or since has ever done. He himself said of the orator that 'from the living emotion of his hearers the apt word which he needs will be suggested to him and in its turn this will go straight to the hearts of his hearers'. He is almost echoing de Tocqueville who talked of men bringing forward but a single idea—'somehow they lay it down on a rostrum like an inscription in capital letters, which everybody understands and in which each instantly recognizes his own particular thought'.

Hitler's political acumen, nerves of steel, infinite reserves of resolution and unshakable will need no iteration here; they have been in evidence throughout the telling of this story. So has been his imagination—in the sense of his gift for grasping how to exploit situations to his own advantage, whether by propaganda, political or military means, and how to put these means, all of which contained a core of violence, to extreme use. Extreme use meant war, and war meant reliance of a sort on the generals.

The evidence of Hitler's generals is varied, and is perhaps most revealing not during the battles of conquest when most of them were more or less convinced, but during the beginnings of defeat. Their views are coloured too by the positions from which they were formed—whether from Hitler's OKW making the plans or in the field carrying them out. 'I must testify,' declared Jodl to an audience of *Gauleiter* in November 1943, 'that he [Hitler] is the soul not only of the political but also of the military conduct of the war, and that the force of his will-power and the creative riches of his thought animate and hold together the whole of the Wehrmacht'. Of the few generals who would have agreed with all Jodl said—for about his will-power holding the machine together there was no doubt anywhere—Keitel was one. For Keitel the Führer could make no mistakes. At Nuremberg he testified that all professional soldiers admired Hitler's grasp of strategy and tactics; furthermore it was not Keitel, the life-long soldier, the Field-Marshal, who advised his Supreme Commander; it was exactly the other way round.

Commanders in the field saw things differently. When Rommel heard Hitler announce that if the German people were incapable of winning the war, they could rot, he commented: 'Sometimes you feel he's no longer quite normal.' Rommel had no illusions about Hitler's shortcomings as a strategist. Although dazzled by the successes of Poland and France, and fortunate enough not to serve on the Eastern front, he had been over-ruled too often in Africa and Normandy, had seen too many opportunities missed, too many mistakes made, to be in doubt. Yet until he became convinced that Hitler was out to destroy Germany, his loyalty did not waver. Guderian's loyalty never wavered at all, but it was to the Army and to Germany that this loyalty was directed. Yet he was associated with Hitler from the very beginning until almost the end. Guderian judged Hitler's will-power to be his most outstanding quality. By it 'he compelled men to follow him'. His principal failing as Supreme Commander—and the criticism is fitting from so brilliant an exponent of blitzkrieg—was in Guderian's opinion that he did not match the boldness of his strategic vision with a comparable boldness in its execution. If he had planned more carefully and then acted with more single-minded speed, results might have been different. But when Guderian points out that Hitler turned upside down Moltke's recipe to weigh the considerations first, then take the risks, he forgets Hitler's whole concept of blitzkrieg, which was that by taking huge risks and backing them with huge force, considerations would take care of themselves. It worked in France; then when Britain's defiance made clear that only a very different strategy involving long preparations could wrest decision from stalemate there, the same formula was applied to Russia. There his strategy, 'lacking in consistency and subject to continual vacillation in its execution', crashed in ruins. He was 'a man lacking wisdom and moderation ... going in solitary haste from success to success and then pressing on from failure to failure, his head full of stupendous plans, clinging ever more frantically to the last vanishing prospects of victory ... with a fanatic's intensity he grasped at every straw which he imagined might save himself and his work from destruction. His entire and very great will-power was devoted to this one idea which was now all that preoccupied him—never to give in, never to surrender.'

Another soldier, who equalled Guderian as a Panzer Leader, was von Manstein. He too points out that intuition no matter how inspired was no substitute for military ability based on experience. He thus regards Hitler's lack of judgment as his most serious deficiency, a lack which caused him 'to fritter away Germany's strength by taking on several objectives simultaneously' and which, because he could not bring himself to dispense with or put at risk less important fronts, prevented his staking everything on the decisive objective. Von Manstein finds that Hitler's strategy fell down because he did not ensure the destruction of the enemy's armed forces first, and deal with territorial and economic gains second. As for handling armies in the field, he rightly emphasizes Hitler's refusal to base his plans on a proper appreciation of all the proper factors, most notably his disregard for enemy resources and likely reactions. While recognizing the value of will-power, von Manstein justly concludes that Hitler allowed his early successes both to distort his estimate of what the will by itself could achieve and so to exaggerate his own military ability that he could not see that sometimes two minds can be better than one. 'To him the acceptance of advice from a jointly responsible Chief of Staff would not have meant supplementing his own will but submitting it to that of another.' In the same vein von Manstein recalls that what impressed him most when discussing operational matters with Hitler was 'the incredible tenacity with which he would defend his point of view'. In sum, the defects of Germany's military leadership were partially those which sprang from the Supreme Commander's character and partially those inherent in 'an impossible organization of the Supreme Command'. Yet for all his condemnation of Hitler's meddling in detail, absurd insistence on 'holding on at all costs' and mistrust of his subordinates, one is left with the impression that von Manstein found a lot to admire in the Führer's resolution and his extraordinary knack of inspiring confidence in others even when all facts seemed to point the other way.

Not so Halder; his short book, *Hitler als Feldherr*, is little more than one unmitigated condemnation of the Führer's military faculty. While he concedes that Hitler by virtue of his overpowering will dominated the political and military leadership of the war, was in fact 'the dynamo of the war effort', he maintains that failure to balance political aims against the limitations of what the Wehrmacht could do is enough in itself to dismiss any idea of Hitler's being called a great military leader. If this is to be rule for gauging greatness, if those great commanders whose ambition outran resources—Alexander and Napoleon among them—if ultimately to fail is a mark of smallness, then who shall escape calumny? In Hitler's case there were special reasons for his overestimating his capabilities. His whole career had shown him that nearly all problems could be resolved by force; indeed the threat of it alone was often enough. A mere three battalions had cowed the Western Powers in 1936's reoccupation of the Rhineland; provided the use of military force went hand in hand with sound political calculation, its effect could be wholly out of proportion to its extent. Only when Hitler ceased to weigh these political considerations accurately, did he begin to rely on will-power and force by themselves, even though they were palpably insufficient to subdue the force and will which were set in opposition.

Again, Halder writes that Hitler was incapable of inspiring his executive commanders and staffs with confidence in his guidance. Of course there were individuals and there were times when this was altogether true. But as we have seen there were many others—both persons and occasions—when just the contrary was the case. The evidence of Rommel, Guderian, von Manstein, Speer, to say nothing of Keitel, Jodl and many lesser figures is emphatically unanimous that he seemed able by the power of his personality and the ascendancy which he obtained over them to inspire confidence in those around him even when the situation appeared hopeless. What is true is that whereas in the earlier years of the war, he conducted his military conferences with moderate restraint, seeking opinion, feeling his way, success bred both confidence in his own strategic genius and contempt for others, worst of all contempt for fact.

Furthermore when Halder maintains that a great war leader is one who can quickly understand the promise of new weapons and devise new methods of employing them and that he looked in vain for such an ability in Hitler, he weakens his case by ignoring the facts that it was Hitler who grasped the potential of blitzkrieg, Panzer and Stuka, and who against the General Staff's advice created a powerful enough force of them to win a series of lightning campaigns. Later, it is true, he refused to recognize the restrictions of operating in the face of Allied air superiority, but this was at a time when he refused to acknowledge any unpalatable truth. Where Halder is right, of course, is in his contention that Hitler was not a general—his *forte* was not the handling of armies in the field. He was far too impulsive, too impatient, too inclined to chop and change, to overestimate to a ludicrous degree the capacity of his forces, to take no account of enemy opposition or logistic restraints; having once pronounced that making war was a matter of intellect, tenacity and nerves of iron, he jettisoned the intellect and relied on tenacity alone. In his constant interference in detailed operations from the outset of *Barbarossa*, we see Hitler at his worst. Yet we cannot forget that in December 1941 it was his insistence on standing firm which saved the German Army from disintegration.

Once the war reached the stage of defensive strategy, he was unable to cut his losses, unable to concentrate except for brief and disastrous counter-attacks, unable to accept that space had become an enemy, unable to divorce the details of a campaign from its management as a whole. The truth was that he had given himself too much to do. No man could be Supreme Commander of the Wehrmacht and Commander-in-Chief of the Army; no man could direct in detail campaigns as numerous and widespread as he attempted to do; the very command structure he had created—in order to concentrate the power of decision in his own hands—led inevitably to his being required to work in a methodical way, the reverse of the intuitive field in which he had excelled; worse, by insisting that he retained control of low-level tactical operations, he made it certain that he had neither the facts on which to make a sound decision nor the time to make any decision quickly enough for it to be effective.

When we look at actual operations we see that Hitler's strategic errors were matched by tactical ones. During the supremely successful *Sichelschnitt* we have noted that Hitler stuck to his principal aim of destroying the French Army; the tactical blunder in this campaign was not that he stopped the panzers before Dunkirk, but that he did not insist on their continuing to advance; the strategic mistakes which followed were first not gambling his entire strength in an effort to knock out England by a direct blow, and second in not seeing that the Mediterranean was a decisive theatre which deserved more than mere defensive moves. *Barbarossa*, on the other hand, was hampered from the start by not having one single clear purpose and concentrating all available forces to achieve it. In Russia this pattern was to be repeated again and again until Hitler had so

dissipated the Wehrmacht and committed himself to the reten-
tion of so much territory that except for fleeting occasions like
Kursk and the Ardennes, he forfeited the initiative for ever. In
defence his policy of no withdrawal was strategically sterile and
tactically suicidal. The Supreme Commander threw away a pearl
richer than all his tribe—mobility. Resistance to the last drop
of blood was no substitute for the whirlwind tactics of blitzkrieg.

In spite of the General Staff's reluctance to mount another
Russian offensive in 1942, it is worth recalling Halder's response
at the time to Hitler's confident assertion that the Russian was
finished—'it looks uncommonly like it'. Yet before long the
greatest victory in world history had become—Stalingrad!
Thereafter when Hitler gave his Army Groups tasks totally
beyond their capability, and they failed, his comment would be
that 'the Army Group can very well do it; only they will not' or
that von Kluge's operations failed because von Kluge did not
want them to succeed. Hitler's inability to mould events beyond
his control is caught by his own 'Even I cannot get the Field-
Marshals to obey me!' 'This demoniac man,' is Halder's final
conclusion, 'was no soldier leader in the German sense. And
above all he was not a great General.'

Alan Bullock, whose study of the man (although not like
Halder's at first hand) is incomparably more scholarly, impartial,
detailed and profound, arrives at a different judgment. He
points out that in 1940 Hitler had achieved in a matter of four
weeks what the Kaiser and the Imperial German Army had
failed to achieve in four years; that he alone had insisted on
the French Army's rottenness and the certainty of rapid successes in the West; that he had seized on von Manstein's plan
and Guderian's tactics and forced their adoption against powerful professional fears and doubts; that he had built the
Wehrmacht which made victory possible. 'If Hitler, therefore,
is justly to be made responsible for the later disasters of the
German Army, he is entitled to the major share of the credit for
the victories of 1940; the German generals cannot have it both
ways.' But, Bullock goes on, it was this very victory, the most
startling of German arms, which was his undoing, for having
ignored the professional soldiers' advice once and triumphed,

he never allowed himself to be influenced by them against his
inclination again. His greater grasp of political matters had never
been in question; now there was no doubt either about his
superior judgment in strategy and tactics. We might almost
observe that the General Staff had only themselves to blame,
for had they supported Hitler's strategic and tactical ideas more
enthusiastically during the years of conquest, they might have
been able to influence him more easily during the years of
resistance; ironically enough it was while Hitler was creating
the image of his own infallibility that his strategic gambles
came off, and it was once he began, despite much evidence to
the contrary, wholly to believe in himself that he and the
Wehrmacht started to falter.

Professor Trevor-Roper's view is that Hitler's military talents
were by no means contemptible. He emphasizes the width of
Hitler's knowledge, his mastery of detail, and points once more
to the results he achieved against the professionals' advice. He
observes too that the Führer's operational plans merit at least
an acknowledgement that they were controversial. He refrains
from commenting on those critics who pooh-pooh Hitler's
strategic successes because his ideas were liberally executed by
soldiers and at the same time dismiss his tactical successes
because they led to strategic set-backs. But it might not be
unfair to comment for him here that the critics once again
cannot have it both ways. While Hitler was winning he displayed
the same puzzling combination of brilliant discernment at one
moment and crass stupidity at the next, both in the tactical and
strategic fields, as he did when he was losing. As war lord he
defies a rival.

It is impossible to pronounce sensibly on Hitler's execution
of command without touching again on the machinery and
methods he used. In adapting OKW to be an instrument of
political and military control over the Army General Staff at
OKH and by declaring certain theatres of operations to be
peculiarly his, Hitler concentrated suzerainty over the Wehrmacht—both as to policy and operations—in his own hands.
Moreover, by making himself both Supreme Commander of the
Armed Forces and Commander-in-Chief of the Army, he
strengthened his hold over the entire field of military activity

on land in a fashion which for continuity and intimacy had no precedent. Still further to be remembered is that his principal subordinates in OKW—Keitel, who believed that it was impossible for the Führer to be mistaken about anything, and Jodl, who whatever his doubts was indefatigable in turning Hitler's requirements into operational orders—were such that no system of checks and balances was imposed on the Supreme Commander's strategic and tactical decisions. He arbitrated absolutely as to what military policies were necessary and how they were to be pursued. We must never forget that it was not a one-sided affair. Hitler had never enjoyed the confidence, loyalty nor whole-hearted support of either the General Staff or his subordinate commanders. From the very outset he was handicapped; he had to overcome the opposition both of the enemy's army and his own. Hence his devised system of Supreme Command.

This single-handed and unrepresentative leadership made it impossible for the General Staff to challenge Hitler's infallibility whilst his success continued. Even when his fallibility was obvious to all, attempts to remove him from the scene failed, and since their failure was capped by a comprehensive revenge which removed instead the main sources of opposition, direction from Führer HQ went on. Yet although Hitler, unlike Churchill, Roosevelt and even Stalin, did personally direct the operations of armies in the field, by cutting himself off from the soldiers in the front line and by refusing to take account either of the military facts which confronted him or the military advice which was proffered, he directed in a way that a sleep-walker might have done. He had once claimed to go the way that Providence dictated with the assurance of a sleep-walker, and this might be done with assurance while he was still firmly in possession of the initiative. Once others held it, his movements and directions were uncertain and remote.

As power began to slip from his hands, Hitler's coarseness, barbarity, distrust and hatred grew even stronger. Yet his political astuteness did not desert him. Alan Bullock reminds us of the prophetic picture which Hitler gave the sinister Bormann on 2 April 1945:

With the defeat of the Reich and pending the emergence of the Asiatic, the African, and perhaps the South American nationalisms, there will remain in the world only two Great Powers capable of confronting each other—the United States and Soviet Russia. The laws of both history and geography will compel these two powers to a trial of strength, either military or in the fields of economics and ideology. These same laws make it inevitable that both Powers should become enemies of Europe. And it is equally certain that both these Powers will sooner or later find it desirable to seek the support of the sole surviving great nation in Europe, the German people.

'Those who dismiss Hitler's political gifts as negligible,' concludes Bullock, 'may well be asked how many in the spring of 1945, with the war not yet over, saw the future so clearly.' The Führer's *Vorhersehung* did not forsake him even at the end.

It is perhaps with this re-emergence of Hitler's mastery of political matters that we may reach some conclusions as to his standing as a military commander. Military policy and political aims are indivisible. Together they add up to strategy. But during the course of a major war, first one, then the other is predominant. At one point political considerations call with an urgency which cannot be denied for military operations whose practicability is wholly secondary. Thus Churchill's insistence on succouring Greece in 1941 led those military forces engaged into untenable positions, and yet in the end paid unsought and unforeseeable dividends; Roosevelt decided—against the advice of all his military commanders—to effect a landing in North Africa in 1942, in response partially to Churchill's persistence, more to his pledge to Stalin that US forces would engage the Germans somewhere on land in that year; Hitler's leaving 50 divisions cut off in the Baltic States in 1944 was dictated by his view of the grave political effects that withdrawal would have on Sweden and their supply of iron ore.

At other times military factors take charge, and however pressing the political arguments for a particular course of action might be, they are not permitted to modify the timing or nature of a military enterprise. Thus *Overlord*, no matter how desirable 1943 might have been politically, could not be mounted until 1944; Montgomery and Alexander were able to overrule Churchill as to the timing of the Alamein battle because of military considerations alone; Hitler's decision to wipe out—*ausradieren*—opposition in the Balkans in 1941 was actuated primarily by the military need to secure his southern flank before the great *Barbarossa* adventure, no matter what the political consequences might be; Eisenhower's command arrangements which gave Montgomery the task of handling the Ardennes bulge's northern flank was intensely unpopular politically, but militarily was palpably right.

In all these cases, in all these decisions, a sense of balance between the respective claims of political and military considerations was obviously required. Yet as the war advanced Hitler's assessment of the need for balance deteriorated to the point where it no longer existed. His military judgment was almost always inclined to be coloured and controlled by political calculations, and while his political calculations were still made from a position of power in the sense of holding the initiative, they were supremely successful. Hence his appreciation of the true state of the French Army and the French nation led to triumphant success. What is more, in this case his political assessment was reinforced by a military plan whose boldness and shock tactics were at one with his overall conviction that after a few set-backs, France would crumble. When therefore naked will-power had taken the place of *Fingerspitzengefühl*— Hitler's uncanny finger-tip feeling as to what should be done and when—and when military strength was quite inadequate for will-power to be translated into the numbers necessary to take on his enemy's, all balance of this sort disappeared and with it all hope of victory.

One of the most curious aspects of Hitler's leadership is that although he always intended to make war sooner or later —and Speer's *Erinnerungen* seem to clear up this point, so implacably contested by A. J. P. Taylor, once and for all—he did not properly prepare for it, neither in the strategic armoury he provided himself with nor in the measures taken to mobilize Germany's resources. He missed altogether one of the supreme lessons of history—that sea power is indispensable to prolonged international conflict on the grand scale. He believed that by blitzkrieg alone he could subdue Europe and come to terms with England. At the height of his conquests he allowed himself to take on England, the United States and Russia, and yet neglected to arrange either that the entire resources of the Reich were committed to a total war effort, or that whilst the balance of strength was in his favour he struck down the one enemy whose defeat might have ended the war in his favour—Great Britain, or that the sea and air power, without which he could not hope to challenge the Anglo-Saxon nations, was sufficient to do so. He missed one opportunity in the Mediterranean and another one in the Atlantic. Yet of all his strategic blunders, surely the greatest was that of attacking Russia. It was Russian space, Russian soldiers and Russian doggedness that bled the Wehrmacht white and made possible, together with the invincible air and sea power which by then they commanded, the Allies' descent on *Festung Europa* from the west.

That Hitler's strategy during the battles of resistance, when he consistently refused to yield space in good time, was self-defeating is readily comprehensible. That even during the battles of conquest, when the initiative was wholly his and the successes achieved were staggering, his strategy faltered by not seizing upon decisive objectives is only explained when we remember that success breeds over-confidence. As we have observed, his fundamental error lay in his inability to see the war as a global entity, to adapt his strategy to exploit his enemies' vulnerability while there was still time, for once Britain had recovered from the battle of France and her Mediterranean losses, once the United States had recovered from Pearl Harbor and once Russia had recovered from the blows of 1941 and 1942, the war's pace and direction was necessarily dictated by them. In short, even with all the cards in his hand, Hitler could not quite bring the thing off. He tried to do too much with too little, and in spite of being a gambler was unwilling to stake all on a winning number.

We may conclude therefore that Hitler emphatically was not 'the greatest strategical genius of all time'. If any figure of the Second World War were to be a candidate for so unlikely a title and if the qualification for election were that of finishing the war in a position which satisfied most strategic requirements, it would certainly be Stalin, who was wise enough to eliminate his General Staff before the war started and lucky enough to command almost unlimited resources of men and material once it did. Strategically Hitler waged his war in the simplest terms. Security in the West in order to concentrate in the East; security in the East in order to concentrate in the West—a formula to be repeated year in, year out, and by its repetition, or put another way, by lack of final decision either in the East or the West, doomed.

Equally to be rejected is the suggestion that Hitler was a 'facile amateur'. Of all military leaders in this century who have embarked on a programme of expansion, he is perhaps the one who achieved the most astonishing successes in the shortest time—witness the sum of his conquests between 1938 and 1942—and his is the Army, which, the most crushing defeats notwithstanding, gave the most remarkable demonstration of resolution and skill.

Guderian said of him that he knew more about active service than the majority of his military advisers, but the truth was that he surrounded himself with sycophants who avoided the front line, and once the military tide turned against him, he avoided the front line himself. In choosing or taking a course of action, he was constantly finding good reasons for supporting a policy already decided on rather than examining all the factors involved and so arriving at a good policy. There was far too much reliance on intuition and will-power, not enough on reasoned military calculation, too much over-estimation of his own strength, too little recognition of enemy capability. It was no good shouting 'The Russian is dead' when he so palpably was not. The world did hold its breath when *Barbarossa* began, but not for long.

Hitler then may not have been a great strategist even though he thought of himself as one. But in conceiving of himself as a great man, 'he was,' Trevor-Roper writes, 'surely not mistaken; for it is absurd to suggest that one who made such a stir in the world was of ordinary stature. The Germans accepted him as the Messiah for whom they were waiting, and in the hours of his apparent success they sacrificed their political institutions to him; for they believed not in them, but the man.' William Shirer calls him 'a person of undoubted, if evil, genius . . . of a demonic personality, a granite will, uncanny instincts, a cold ruthlessness, a remarkable intellect and—until towards the end, when, drunk with power and success, he overreached himself —an amazing capacity to size up people and situations.' The word 'genius' constantly recurs in the judgment of others. When at Nuremberg Schacht was asked for his true opinion of Hitler, he replied that he was a man of 'diabolical genius'. He added that Hitler may have started with fine ideas, but became infected with the poison he himself instilled in the masses. Halder detected the diabolical, but not the genius. There was, of course, one other man who was in no doubt about Hitler's historical greatness—the Führer himself. 'At long intervals in human history it may occasionally happen that the practical politician and the political philosopher are one.... Such a man does not labour to satisfy the demands that are obvious to every philistine; he reaches out towards ends that are comprehensible only to the few.' So he made war on a cosmic scale and with a recklessness that consumed everything, even himself.

Professor Trevor-Roper's answer to his question—'why the Nazis so nearly won the war'—is not really an answer at all, in that he suggests it was not the Nazis, but German industry and the German Army, fostered, as he concedes, by Nazi dictatorship, which nearly won it; further it was the extremes to which this dictatorship went which lost it. This reasoning is perilously close to that of the German generals who wanted to have it both ways. Perhaps a better question is—how was it that Hitler so nearly won the war? The answer then may become— partly because of German industry and the German Army and partly because of Hitler himself; that Hitler lost it we need not doubt. In other words Hitler's creation and exploitation of German industry and arms were what made possible so many victories and got him so close to *Weltmacht*; German resistance and Hitler's will-power were what made *Niedergang* so slow and painful a process. A reviewer of Speer's *Erinnerungen* marvelled that it took us so long to defeat Hitler; it may be doubted whether many of those who found themselves actually arguing the toss with the Wehrmacht would agree with him. So long did Hitler call the tune over the bulk of Europe and so long did it take to wrest his grip loose that his formula came to be not World Power or Ruin, but World Power and Ruin, *Weltmacht und Niedergang*, not one or the other, but both.

Hitler certainly repudiates the determinist view of history. Whatever Tolstoy might say about Charles IX's only thinking that he had decreed the Night of St Bartholomew or Napoleon's only fancying he had brought about the war of 1812, and however much Carlyle might refute such argument with his contention that the history of the world is but the biography of great men, of one thing we can be sure. The Second World War was Hitler's war. When after the war Speer asked himself whether Hitler was an inevitable product of the years which followed the First World War, Versailles and the Revolution, he was prepared to admit that here was fertile soil for such a product, but that they could not fully explain 'the whole demonic figure of the man.... For Hitler was one of those inexplicable historical phenomena which emerges at rare intervals among mankind. His person determined the fate of the nation. He alone placed it, and kept it, upon the path which has led it to this dreadful ending. The nation was spellbound by him as a people has rarely been in the whole of history.'

Motive, means, opportunity—as we have seen Hitler needed all three for the murder of Europe. He knew how to sense, seize and manipulate, yet not when to forgo, opportunity; he could create and use, but not husband, means; his motives were wholly evil. What had it all led to—Hitler's military command? The defeat and destruction of Germany—he, who had so often threatened, promised and then seen to it that other countries and other armies would be smashed and wiped out—*ausradiert*— had arranged that same fate for his own country and his own armies. He at least did not capitulate, but nor, in spite of his country's destruction, did he drag a world in flames down with him. Even though his death was quickly followed by capitulation, there was, as he had promised there would not be, no stab in the back, but rather several stabs to the heart. The Wehrmacht's honour in the field was not besmirched, but the honour of the nation was. 'A thousand years will pass' [the predicted era of the Third Reich itself] said Frank, Governor-General of Poland, 'and the guilt of Germany will not be erased.' As Johnson had pointed out, only by the diminution of all other virtues could a nation's martial character prevail.

At 10 o'clock on the evening of 29 April the Supreme Commander of the Wehrmacht held his final military conference. He had been holding military conferences, day in, day out, for years, and if there is but one among many military lessons which we may draw from that endless series of a War Lord's listening to situation reports and giving his orders as a result of, or despite, them, it is that in a war from which so much human error had been eliminated by technological advances alone, human error was nonetheless still the principal factor in determining the war's outcome. At this conference General Weidling, Berlin Commandant, described the ever-deteriorating situation and gave it as his opinion that the Russians would reach the Chancellory three days from that time at the latest. The defensive troops should therefore seek to break out at once. In accordance with the pattern that had gone before Hitler pronounced against this course of action, and there the matter rested. One other participant of the conference was Colonel von Below, and to this long standing member of his entourage Hitler entrusted a postscript to his testament. It was, as Professor Trevor-Roper records, Hitler's valediction to the Wehrmacht and does its Supreme Commander little credit:

> The people and the Armed Forces have given their all in this long and hard struggle. The sacrifice has been enormous. But my trust has been misused by many people. Disloyalty and betrayal have undermined resistance throughout the war. It was therefore not granted to me to lead the people to victory. The Army General Staff cannot be compared with the General Staff of the First World War. Its achievements were far behind those of the fighting front.

Out of thy own mouth will I judge thee! Hitler had himself manipulated the General Staff, and as a final judgment we may perhaps draw on his own comparison to conclude that Hitler's achievements as Supreme Commander in the Second World War were inferior to his achievements as an ordinary soldier in the First.

Yet it was as a great military commander, as a man of historical greatness, that Hitler saw himself. He would have been gratified while acknowledging it as no more than his right to have seen his name coupled with that of Alexander the Great.

'He was clearly paranoiac,' wrote Cyril Connolly of the latter, 'with a Hitlerian gift of involving whole nations in his destiny, through their willing acceptance of his self-styled divinity. He heads all lists of conquerors.' But Hitler's name would not be far below. Was he perhaps last of the German conquerors? If so, if he helped to persuade his self-adopted country to renounce for ever the use of force as a means of national policy, then he may in spite of everything have done the state some service. This service will not compensate for his tyrannical exercise of power, the vicious acts of revenge, the blood lust which seemed insatiable, the nihilism as an end in itself. One of his subordinate commanders, von Brauchitsch, may perhaps be allowed the last word in contemplating the Führer's evil genius: 'Hitler was the fate of Germany and this fate could not be stayed.'

Bibliography

Anders, Gen. Wladyslaw, *Hitler's Defeat in Russia*, Chicago, 1953.

Baldwin, Hanson W., *Battles Lost and Won*, London, 1967.

Barnett, Correlli, *The Swordbearers*, London, 1963.

Berlin, Sir Isaiah, *Mr Churchill in 1940*, London, 1949.

Bryant, Sir Arthur, *The Turn of the Tide*, Vols. I and II, London, 1957 and 1959; *The Lion and The Unicorn*, London, 1969.

Bullock, Alan, *Hitler, A Study in Tyranny*, Revised edition, London, 1962.

Carsten, F. L., *The Reichswehr and Politics*, Oxford, 1966.

Churchill, Winston S., *The Second World War*, London, 1949–1954.

Ciano, Galeazzo, *Ciano's Diaries, 1939–1943*, London, 1947.

Clark, Alan, *Barbarossa*, London, 1965.

Clausewitz, Gen. Carl von, *On War*, London, 1949.

Collier, Basil, *A Short History of the Second World War*, London, 1967.

Derry, T. K., *The Campaign in Norway*, London, 1952.

Ellis, Major L. F., *The War in France and Flanders*, London, 1953; *Victory in the West*, Vols. I and II, London, 1962 and 1968.

Essame, H., *The Battle for Germany*, London, 1969.

Faerber, Hanns Adam, *Der Zweite Weltkrieg im Bild*, Baden, 1961.

Fest, Joachim C., *The Face of the Third Reich*, London, 1970.

Fleming, Peter, *Invasion 1940*, London, 1957.

Florentin, Eddy, *The Battle of the Falaise Gap*, London, 1965.

Fothergill, Brian, *Sir William Hamilton; Envoy Extraordinary*, London.

Fuller, Maj. Gen. J. F. C., *The Second World War*, London, 1947.

de Gaulle, Gen. Charles, *War Memoirs*, Vol. I *The Call to Honour 1940–1942*, London, 1955; Vol. II *Unity 1942–1944*, London, 1959.

Gilbert, Felix, Ed., *Hitler Directs his War*, Oxford, 1950.

The Goebbels Diaries, 1924–1943, London, 1949.

Guderian, Gen. Heinz, *Achtung-Panzer!*, Stuttgart 1937; *Panzer Leader*, London, 1952.

Halder, Franz, *Kriegstagebuch*, Stuttgart, 1962–1964; *Hitler as War Lord*, London, 1950.

Hitler, Adolf, *Mein Kampf*, London, 1939; *The Speeches of Adolf Hitler, 1922–39*, Ed. Norman H. Baynes, 2 vols., Oxford, 1942; *Hitler's Table Talk, 1941–44*, London, 1953; *The Testament of Adolf Hitler: The Hitler-Bormann Documents, February–April 1945*, London, 1961; *Hitler's War Directives 1939–1945*, Ed. H. R. Trevor-Roper, London, 1964.

Hofer, Walther, Ed., *Der Nationalsozialismus Dokumente 1933–45*, Frankfurt, 1957.

Horne, Alistair, *To Lose a Battle*, London, 1968.

Howard, Michael, *The Theory and Practice of War*, London, 1965; *The Mediterranean Strategy in the Second World War*, London, 1968.

Jackson, Maj. Gen. W. E. F., *The Battle for Italy*, London, 1967.

Jacobsen, H. A. and Rohwer, J. Ed., *Decisive Battles of World War II: The German View*, London, 1965.

Kietel, Field-Marshal Wilhelm, *The Memoirs of Field-Marshall Keitel*, London, 1965.

Keitel, Field-Marshal Wilhelm, *The Memoirs of Field-Marshal Keitel*,

Liddell Hart, Captain Sir Basil, *The Other Side of the Hill*, 3rd edition, London, 1951; *The Tanks*, 2 vols., London, 1959; *Memoirs*, 2 vols., London, 1965 and 1968; Ed. *The Rommel Papers*, London, 1953.

Macdonell, A. G., *Napoleon and his Marshals*, London, 1934.

Majdalany, Fred, *The Monastery*, London, 1945; *Cassino, Portrait of a Battle*, London, 1957; *The Fall of Fortress Europe*, New York, 1968.

Manstein, Field-Marshal Erich von, *Lost Victories*, London, 1958.

Mellenthin, Maj. Gen. F. W. von, *Panzer Battles 1939–1945*, London, 1955.

Montgomery, Field Marshal the Viscount of Alamein, *Memoirs*, London, 1958; *A History of Warfare*, London, 1968.

Moorehead, Alan, *Eclipse*, London, 1945.

Nicolson, Harold, *Diaries and Letters 1945–62* (ed. Nigel Nicolson), London, 1968.

O'Neill, Robert J., *The German Army and the Nazi Party, 1933–1939*, London, 1966.

Petrie, Sir Charles, *When Britain Saved Europe*, London, 1941.

Playfair, Maj. Gen. I. S. O., *The Mediterranean and the Middle East*, 4 vols., London, 1954–1966.

Rauschning, Hermann, *Hitler Speaks*, London, 1939.

Rommel, Field-Marshal Erwin, *The Rommel Papers*, Ed. B. H. Liddell Hart, London, 1953.

Rosinski, Herbert, *The German Army*, London, 1966.

Sammis, Edward R., *Last Stand at Stalingrad*, New York, 1966.

Scott Daniell, David, *4th Hussar*, Aldershot, 1959.

Shirer, William L., *Berlin Diary, 1934–1941*, London, 1941; *The Rise and Fall of the Third Reich*, London, 1960.

Shulman, Milton, *Defeat in the West*, London, 1949.

Spears, Maj. Gen. E. L., *Assignment to Catastrophe*, 2 vols., London, 1954.

Speer, Albert, *Erinnerungen*, Berlin, 1969.

Speidel, Gen. Hans, *We Defended Normandy*, London, 1951.

Taylor, A. J. P., *Origins of the Second World War*, London, 1961; *English History 1914–1945*, Oxford, 1965.

The Times, 2 May, 1945, Hitler's Obituary.

Toland, John, *The Last 100 Days*, London, 1966.

Trevelyan, Raleigh, *The Fortress*, London, 1956.

Trevor-Roper, H. R., *The Last Days of Hitler*, London, 1947; Ed. *Hitler's War Directives 1939–1945*, London, 1964; *Admiral Canaris*, London, 1968.

Vercors, *Put Out The Light (Le Silence de la Mer)*, London, 1944; *The Battle of Silence*, London, 1968.

Warlimont, Gen. Walter, *Inside Hitler's Headquarters 1939–1945*, London, 1964.

Westphal, Siegfried, *et. al.*, *The Fatal Decisions; Six Decisive Battles of the Second World War*, London, 1956.

Wheeler-Bennett, Sir John, *The Nemesis of Power. The German Army in Politics, 1918–1945*, London, 1953.

Wilmot, Chester, *The Struggle for Europe*, London, 1952.

Index

Reichswehr, *see* Germany, Armed Forces
Rhine, 206, 215, 222
Rhineland, 50, 57-9, 205, 234
Ribbentrop, Joachim von, 65, 84, 180, 218
Richard III, 84
Rimini, 206
Röhm, Ernst, 26, 28, 32, 42, 43, 47
Röhm purge, 26, 43, 50
Rokossovsky, Marshal Constantin, 216
Rome, 85, 127, 178-9, 183, 185, 202
Romeo, 164
Rommel, Field-Marshal Erwin, 17, 106-7, 109, 124, 127-9, 142, 155-6, 160, 162, 189-92, 195-6, 199, 200, 203, 231
Roosevelt, Franklin D., President of the United States of America, 51, 128, 142, 156-8, 165, 169, 178, 222, 226n, 238-9
Rostov, 138, 141
Rot, Operation, 61
Round-Up, Operation, 157
Royal Air Force, 104, 112, 114, 121, 126, 156, 166, 183, 200
Royal Navy, 104, 112, 118, 121, 126, 127
Ruhr, 27, 29, 94, 222
Rumania, 59, 119, 122, 124, 130, 153, 193, 204, 206
Rundstedt, Field - Marshal Karl Rudolph Gert von, 100-2, 109, 111, 136, 138, 141, 145, 186, 188-95, 199, 206-9, 212, 223
Russia, 41, 55, 57, 62, 65, 73-4, 79, 80, 82, 83, 92, 95, 115-23, 128, 130, 132-50, 157, 159-63, 170, 173-7, 179, 188, 213, 221-2, 232, 235, 239, 241
Russian Army, *see* Red Army

Saar, 49, 50, 211
SA (Sturm Abteilung) 27-32, 42-3, 46-7, 51
Sadowa, 143
St Lo, 195
St Quentin, 108
St Vincent, Earl, 112
Salerno, 178-9
Salzburg, 69, 153, 180
Sammis, Edward, 160
Santayana, George, 13, 20
Saxony, 222
Scandinavia, 105, 216
Schacht, Dr Hjalmar, 60, 65, 67, 243
Schellenberg, Walter, 186
Schlabrendorff, Fabian von, 175
Schleicher, Gen. Kurt von, Reich Chancellor, 24-6, 32-4, 43, 51

Schlieffen, 51, 207
Schlieffen Plan, 99, 207
Schmidt, Paul, H's interpreter, 59
Schuschnigg, Kurt von, Chancellor of the Austrian Republic, 66-8
Schweyer, Franz, 27
Sea Lion, Operation, 114, 116
Secret weapons, 186, 195n, 199
Sedan, 101-2
Seeckt, Gen. Hans von, 13, 24, 26-7, 29-31, 36-8, 44, 51, 80, 82, 87, 92
Seine, 194-5, 205
Sevastopol, 138
Seyss-Inquart, Arthur, 67-9
Shirer, William L., 16, 58, qu 242-3
Siberia, 223
Sichelschnitt, Operation, 97-116, 136, 207, 214, 235
Sicily, 113, 122, 166, 169, 171, 177, 186
Siegfried Line, 59
Silesia, 88, 216, 217
Singapore, 148
Sledgehammer, Operation, 157
Slovakia, 88, 90, 216
Smigly-Rydz, Marshal Edward, 88
Smith, Sir Sydney, 118
Smolensk, 136-9, 175, 182
Smuts, Field-Marshal Rt. Hon. Jan, 130
Social Democratic Party, 21, 31
Somme, 101, 108, 195
Soviet-German Pact, 82-5
Soviet Union, *see* Russia
Spain, 61, 118, 120, 159, 204
Sparta, 126
Speer, Albert, 17, 52-3, 146, 152-3, 174, 205, 215, 218, 221, 234, 240, 243, qu 244
Speidel, Gen. Hans, 199
S.S. (Schutz Staffeln) 15, 32, 47, 98, 143, 212, 216
Stalin, Josef, 83, 91, 122, 137, 152, 158, 159, 160, 180, 185, 217, 222, 238, 241
Stalingrad, battle of, 122, 130, 152-4, 159-65, 172-3, 175, 193, 209, 230, 236
Stauffenberg, Col. Claus Schenk, Graf von, 202
Steiner, Obergruppenführer, 14
Stevenson, Robert Louis, 130
Strasser, Gregor, 43
Stresemann, Gustav, German Chancellor and Foreign Minister, 29
Student, Gen., 127
Stuka, 45, 61, 90-1, 98, 106, 109-10, 121, 127, 136, 149, 168, 188, 229, 234
Sudetenland, 72-8
Suez Canal, 115, 118, 127-9, 149, 155-6